The Vaughan family wish to dedicate this book to the officers and men of the Royal Warwickshire Regiment

SOME DESPERATE GLORY

The World War I diary of a
British officer, 1917
EDWIN CAMPION VAUGHAN

with an Introduction by Robert Cowley

A Touchstone Book
Published by Simon & Schuster Inc.
New York · London · Toronto · Sydney · Tokyo

Touchstone

Simon & Schuster Building
Rockefeller Center
1230 Avenue of the Americas
New York, New York 10020

First Touchstone Edition, 1989
Published by arrangement with Henry Holt and Co., Inc.
TOUCHSTONE and colophon are registered trademarks
of Simon & Schuster Inc.
Manufactured in the United States of America

10 9 8 7 6 5 4 3 2 1 Pbk.

Library of Congress Cataloging in Publication data
Vaughan, Edwin Campion, 1897–1931.
Some desperate glory.

(A Touchstone book)
Reprint. Originally published: New York : Holt, 1988.
1. Vaughan, Edwin Campion, 1897–1931. 2. World War,
1914–1918—Personal narratives, British. 3. World War, 1914–
1918—Campaigns—Western. 4. Soldiers—Great Britain—
Biography. 5. Great Britain. Army—Biography.
I. Title.
D640.V434 1989   940.4'31   88-32746
ISBN 0-671-67904-X Pbk.

If you could hear, at every jolt, the blood
Come gargling from the froth-corrupted lungs,
Obscene as cancer, bitter as the cud
Of vile, incurable sores on innocent tongues—
My friend, you would not tell with such high zest
To children ardent for some desperate glory,
The old Lie: Dulce et decorum est
Pro patria mori.

Wilfred Owen
From *Dulce Et Decorum Est*

INTRODUCTION
by
Robert Cowley

The publishing history of the Great War diary of Edwin Campion Vaughan is an editor's dream come true. The manuscript arrives, unsolicited, at the offices of Leo Cooper, the respected London publisher of military books, and is plucked out of a slush pile. (Occasionally—very occasionally—books are still discovered that way.) The quality and authenticity of the diary are recognized immediately. In 1981, fifty years after the author's death, it appears as a book, with the title *Some Desperate Glory*—a phrase taken from Wilfred Owen's poem, "Dulce et Decorum Est." Reviewers compare it to such accepted classics of the First World War as Robert Graves's *Goodbye to All That*, the poems of Owen, and Siegfried Sassoon's *Memoirs of an Infantry Officer.* Before long, *Some Desperate Glory* becomes something of a classic in its own right.

Vaughan's diary records eight months in the life of a British Second Lieutenant in 1917, ending in the killing fields of Passchendaele. Just as a first-hand account of what combat is like, and how men react to its unimaginable stresses, the book has few equals. But it has noteworthy qualities beyond that. The most memorable journals read like novels—as if, in the act of setting down the day-to-day events of their lives, the authors come to view themselves as part of a story. The diary of Edwin Vaughan is no exception. We see him changing before our eyes. Those eight months of entries present a young man growing not just older and wiser, but old before his time. But diaries are not novels, of course, and it is their very rawness, their presumed lack of premeditation, their sense of what it is like to live at a certain moment, that can make them special. Vaughan may lack the literary touch of a Graves or a Sassoon; but then, he had little time for the niceties of reflection. Even so, some of his sentences and his quick descriptions can be very good indeed: "The misty darkness seemed pregnant with emnity." Not bad for a beginner.

Though the British authorities officially forbade the keeping of journals, out of fear that they would fall into enemy hands, it was a regulation mostly honored in the breach. The several thousand Great War diaries in the Imperial War Museum in London are testimony to that.* For an historian of the period, few thrills are greater than the experience of sitting under the dome, where the IWM library is housed, and untying one of those prim red boxes—to find inside notebooks that some soldier in the trenches actually filled with his tight scribbling.

Vaughan himself mentions his own diary only once, but it is one of the most vivid moments of the book. There is a direct hit on a cellar which serves as an officer's dugout, and men are flung "in all directions and into darkness." Vaughan is stunned, obviously knocked a little silly. "It felt quite pleasant to be dead. There was such utter quiet and peacefulness. Just a light singing in my ears, restful blackness around me, and a sense of absolute freedom and abandon . . ." He stands up, and encounters, "with a slight disappointment," a brick wall. Now comes the mention of the diary: "During the few seconds when I had believed myself dead, I had closed my notebook, snapped round the elastic and returned the pencil to its socket."

"I had expected that on leaving for France I would be overcome by grief, for I knew that I would not see my home again for many, many months—and possibly not again. But when the moment came the excitement of the venture into the dreamed of but unrealized land of war, eclipsed the sorrow of parting." So on January 4, 1917, in the great train sheds of Waterloo Station, begins the diary of Edwin Campion Vaughan. Those opening lines would do credit to the sort of Victorian novels that were all but a birthright of an educated

*Devotees of the ironic often point to the fact that the Imperial War Museum was, in its original incarnation, Bedlam.

Englishman. Vaughan was just a month past his nineteenth
birthday when he set off for the Western Front, a war so close
that its worst eruptions could be heard in London. He was a
freshly minted subaltern in the Royal Warwickshire Regiment,
who not long before had been a student in a Jesuit preparatory
school. Brought up in the Midlands, Vaughan was one of nine
children; his father, a Roman Catholic and an Irishman, was a
customs and excise officer. Though there is no evidence that
he had known them, Vaughan had trained in the same camp,
and at the same time, as two of the most notable literary casualties of the war, the poets Wilfred Owen and Edward Thomas.
He himself arrived at the front with a copy of Palgrave's
Golden Treasury in his pack.

You have the impression of a young man who could be over-
bearingly cocky, and frankly disdainful of companions he
never would have chosen under normal circumstances. That
would count against him, as would his ill-concealed nervousness. In his diary, Vaughan does little to hide his bewilderment
and fear—"windy" was the slang word, and it is one that as-
sumes an awesome prominence in these pages. Officers and
gentlemen were not supposed to show that they had the "wind
up." Memoirs written years after the end of the war tend rarely
to mention terror, as if it was not a subject fit for literary examination; in the privacy of diaries, men admitted to it
constantly.

> *Happy are men who yet before they are killed*
> *Can let their veins run cold*

wrote Owen, whose poems have the immediacy of journal entries (or of his own letters home), and who had himself been
accused of cowardice under fire. No wonder Vaughan kept his
notebook secured with a rubber band.

Vaughan's fellow officers obviously looked down on him, not
only because of his inexperience but because he had a perfect
knack for doing the wrong thing. Vaughan would survive long
enough to become a fine leader—after some initial discomfort,

he seems to have enjoyed a close relationship with his men—but not before he had received a couple of brutal tongue-lashings from his superiors. He was even threatened with being sent back to England in disgrace.

Vaughan could not have arrived at the front at a worse time. The Warwicks had just been through what quite possibly had been history's worst bloodletting—the four-and-a-half-month-long Battle of the Somme. A figure widely accepted today is 600,000 casualties *for each side*. Not only was morale at a low ebb, but the winter of 1916–1917 was one of the coldest in memory. The Warwicks had just taken over trenches to the south of the Somme River that had recently been held by the French, and it was here that Vaughan first served. Those trenches were of the traditional sort—as traditional, that is, as two years could make them. They were labyrinthian; they had scarcely budged one way or the other in all that time; and they were also reasonably continuous. I say "reasonably," because the unbroken line of legend, stretching 470 miles from the North Sea to the Swiss border, never existed. (In the river fens near Biaches, for example, where Vaughan spent February and part of March, you could find one of the largest gaps of all—three miles wide.) If you took the total length of all the trenches in Belgium and northern France at that time, you would come up with a figure that strains belief: the equivalent, approximately, of one-and-one-half times the circumference of the earth. The average width of the dead ground between the trenches—No Man's Land—was a couple of hundred yards, though in places the lines almost touched. Vaughan's first tour was in one of those. The lines are so close that the Warwicks are once hit by their own artillery, with horrifying results that he is assigned to clean up. Another time, he finds himself dashing across a sunken road raked by a machine gun not twenty yards away—and in a nearby outpost he can hear German voices. Later, after the line has moved on, he returns to the same spot as a sightseer, and discovers that he had been standing against the wall of a cellar in which enemy soldiers had been living.

The Western Front was about to go through drastic altera-
tions, and Vaughan's diary gives a telling picture of the evolv-
ing nature of the war. The Somme had proved, as a Captain
von Hentig put it, "the muddy grave of the German field
army." The Germans were now desperately short of man-
power. In what can either be taken as a tactical masterstroke or
an admission of defeat, they retreated by as much as thirty
miles to new defensive positions, the so-called Hindenburg
Line. By doing so, they conserved thirteen or fourteen divi-
sions. They left a desert in their wake, a kind of vast glacis,
blowing mine craters in road and rail junctions, levelling
towns, poisoning wells, cutting down apple orchards, and setting booby traps. One of Vaughan's friends dies when an explosive charge blows off his legs; Vaughan himself can't sleep
for fear of time bombs. While passing through the burning
town of Peronne, he spots on a wall of the Hotel de Ville "an
enormous blue notice board" with the foot-high words: "Do
not be angry, only be surprised."

Vaughan misjudged the ominous significance of that sign.
"With Jerry retiring," he writes, "it was obvious the war was
ended." The war had not. The Allied infantry had become so
accustomed to the trench stalemate, and so unsettled by their
first taste of open warfare since 1914, that they let the enemy
slip clean away. But do not look to Vaughan for historical con-
text. You hear nothing in these pages of the great events of that
spring of 1917: The Battle of Arras, the first Russian Revolu-
tion, the French mutinies, or the entry of the United States
into the War. His horizon rarely extends beyond his own battalion. But within those limits we see a brief universe taking
shape.

The war settled down for a time. The new lines in those empty
downlands of northern France were as much as a thousand
yards apart, and were a series of isolated strong points rather
than a more or less unbroken trench system. It was still a
molelike existence, however, and you might find a certain
whimsical symbolism in Vaughan's entry for May 31: "I was

disturbed for a long time by a mole which at intervals kicked earth down on my face as he burrowed into the roof. I kept frightening him away but he always returned, until he thought I had had enough, then smiling eerily he went over to Ewing and gave him a dose. I fell asleep to the music of Ewing's broad cursing . . ."

The fatigue, monotony, and unwonted isolation of those months seemed oddly liberating. The Western Front had become as much a state of mind as a physical and historical presence, a separate nation almost. As one officer remarks to Vaughan, "This is the only country where a bloke can feel at ease." By day, men play Indian in the high grass and don gas masks, making animal noises. By night, they explore No Man's Land, denying it to the enemy. They listen apprehensively to the distant thunder of an artillery barrage. "I tried to imagine," Vaughan writes, "how I would behave if I ever were engaged in an attack, and the thought made me tremble all over, so that I was forced to go into the dugout and dispel the images with a whisky."

Death's unpleasant reminders are never far off. A raiding party goes out into No Man's Land. One of the officers is a boy named Cooper. "Poor little Cooper was a bundle of nerves and very frightened. This was his first taste of fire of any sort." The raid succeeds. Prisoners are brought back. There is only one serious casualty. It is Cooper:

> A large chunk of shell had entered his back and he was only half conscious . . . As the stretcher bearer raised him, we grasped his hand and Hammond said, "Cheerio, Cooper, I'll see you in Blighty again." "No, Laurie," came the faint voice, "I shan't see Blighty again." And he was right, poor little chap. He died on the stretcher.

As Vaughan remarks elsewhere, "One of the most pathetic features of the war is this continual forming of real friendships which last a week or two, or even months, and are suddenly shattered for ever by death or division."

In this book, remember, almost everyone will be swept away.

We now come to the sinister climax of *Some Desperate Glory:* that holocaust in the mud of Flanders known as the Third Ypres, or Passchendaele, after the village where the great Allied Offensive of 1917 would eventually stall. Vaughan fought in a sub-battle of that campaign, which the British *Official History* labels "The Battle of Langemarck." It was launched on on August 16th, and lasted until the end of the month, by which time British troops had lurched forward a mirey thousand-odd yards. Vaughan witnessed almost all of this little epitome of World War I, and though he came through it physically unscathed, there were other wounds that plainly never healed.

The Ypres Salient was a place where inconclusive fighting had been going on for three years, and beyond several hundred thousand dead, the two sides had precious little to show for their enormous efforts. The worst was to come. Vaughan must have suspected that when, on August 11th, he writes of dismounting from a bike to watch lorry after lorry throb by, each filled with silent, dispirited men heading to the front: "I had a vision of the dead armies stealing back to the battlefields to help us in our next push." Even his companion feels "the eerie influence, for when the long column had passed, he mounted and we rode home without a word."

At Ypres, the Germans had replaced the old trench lines with a system of defense in depth organized around a loose but interlocking chain of pillboxes. They were supported by heavy concentrations of artillery; machine-gun crews roamed the intervening craterfields. Many of the pillboxes were located in agricultural ruins, and the British often called them "farms." They were built of ferro-concrete—the materials being specially imported from the Rhine—reinforced by iron rods. The front walls and roofs were several feet thick, and could withstand all but the heaviest shells. Gunners fired through loopholes. (There were entrances but no loopholes in back: in case of capture, the Germans did not want the pillboxes to be used against them.) Nowhere on the Western Front did you find a greater concentration of pillboxes—they still squat amid the fields of Ypres with ancient menace, today used mainly to store fodder or agricultural implements, or to house swine. You will read much about those pillboxes in the closing pages of *Some Desperate Glory.*

Passchendaele, though, will always be remembered for one thing: mud. No sooner had the offensive started than it was swamped in a hurricane, and the rains continued with few letups for the rest of August. "We found the conditions which prevailed even worse than the reports had led us to believe," the historian of the First Buckinghamshire Battalion wrote, with tight-lipped understatement. In his dispatches, the British commander, Sir Douglas Haig, described how "the low-lying, clayey soil, torn by shells and sodden with rain, turned into a succession of vast muddy pools, the valleys of the choked and overflowing streams were speedily transformed into long stretches of bog, impassable except by a few well-defined tracks, which became marks for the enemy artillery. To leave those tracks was to risk death by drowning."

For all the preternatural wetness of the month, the morass was, as much as anything, manmade. The British bombardment had created its own worst obstacle. There is a terrifying moment recorded in Vaughan's diary when he is almost swallowed up himself while trying to flounder forward to some gunpits:

> I paused for a moment in a shell-hole; in a few seconds I felt myself sinking, and struggle as I might I was sucked down until I was firmly gripped round the waist and still being dragged in. The leg of a corpse was sticking out of the side, and frantically I grabbed it; it wrenched off, and casting it down I pulled in a couple of rifles and yelled to the troops in the gunpit to throw me more. Laying them flat I wriggled over them and dropped half dead, into the wrecked gun position.

Vaughan's diary is filled with such moments, and in the last pages of *Some Desperate Glory,* they are practically nonstop. There are miraculous passages through curtains of shellfire.

(Artillery was the great killer of World War I, accounting for some seventy percent of all deaths.) His friends drop away, and alone in a shellhole, he breaks into tears. "I was a company commander now, but of what company?" He leads an attack on a notorious pillbox called Springfield Farm, and captures it. He sends back German prisoners, and looks on as they are mowed down by their own machine guns. (The British were not the only ones to kill their own by mistake—if it was a mistake, for it may have been a deliberate message to those who thought to give up.) He comforts a dying German officer—there are touching communions here between enemies. As the rain continues to fall and the shellfire diminishes, "a more terrible sound now reached my ears." It is the most memorable passage of a memorable book:

> From the darkness on all sides came the groans and wails of wounded men; faint, long, sobbing moans of agony, and despairing shrieks. It was too horribly obvious that dozens of men with serious wounds must have crawled for safety into new shell-holes, and now the water was rising about them and, powerless to move, they were slowly drowning. . . . And we could do nothing to help them; Dunham was crying quietly beside me, and all the men were affected by the piteous cries.

Vaughan prepares for the inevitable counterattack, and waits for the end. Help comes, unexpectedly; someone else will die. (The Germans would soon retake Springfield Farm, and the British would retake it from them.) Vaughan somehow manages to get back to camp: only fifteen of his original ninety men, he learns the next morning, have survived. "I returned to my tent to write out my casualty report; but instead I sat on the floor and drank whisky after whisky as I gazed into a black and empty future."

Wasn't it Joyce who said that history is a nightmare from which we are trying to awaken? Edwin Vaughan was apparently never able to put the nightmare of the war behind him.

He did go on to distinguish himself. In October 1917 he was promoted to Captain; he served on the Italian Front, returned to France, and was awarded the Military Cross for capturing a bridge across the Sambre Canal on November 4, 1918. (It was the day that Wilfred Owen was killed, trying to cross the same canal.)

Of Vaughan's subsequent life we have only the bland facts. He married and had four children. He had trouble adjusting to civilian life, and in 1922 reenlisted, eventually qualifying as a pilot in the Royal Air Force. (Vaughan seems to have had an aptitude for risk.) He made Flight Lieutenant in 1928 but bad health forced him to retire. In 1931, Vaughan died in a hospital as the result of a doctor's error in the administering of a drug: He was injected with cocaine instead of novocaine. In going through his effects, one of Vaughan's brothers hid the diary away in a cupboard, and there it remained, unexamined, for more than forty years. He was apparently afraid that Edwin Vaughan's children would think that their father had been a drunk. No one reading these pages would deny that Vaughan and his fellow officers—all except those who were "TT" (tea-total)—consumed liberal quantities of whisky. But he was hardly an alcoholic. Whisky (or rum for the men) was simply the one tranquillizer available.

As far as we know, Vaughan never wrote anything else, not even more of his diary. But we do at least have *Some Desperate Glory,* and it is an unpremeditated triumph, a small masterpiece of extemporaneous prose. Vaughan's account is a testament to the kind of superhuman endurance that most of us think ourselves incapable of. That was a quality which, in war, might save your soul but not your life. Death's lottery may have passed Edwin Vaughan by, but the fact remains: he was prepared to be chosen. Archibald MacLeish, who served in the war (and whose brother died in it), spoke of the conflict in terms of "a lack of real purpose, only a presence of accidental mechanical purpose." The aristocratic few were as likely to be obliterated as the Cockney dockworkers from the East End. If, in an indifferent universe, we could not control our destiny, we could at least be responsible for our dignity. But it was dignity purchased at a terrible price. I think of the lines by John Peale Bishop:

> *And because we had courage;*
> *because there was courage and youth*
> *ready to be wasted; because we endured*
> *and were prepared for all the endurance;*
> *we thought something must come of it . . .*

Something did not.

A NOTE ON LANGUAGE

You will occasionally come upon slang expressions that may seem puzzling, especially to modern American readers. *Blighty* was, of course, England, and a *Blighty one* was a wound serious enough to get a man sent home—presumably, though, not to die. *Miking* was an English school boy's equivalent of playing hooky. To *take down a pip* was to drop one grade in rank—a person would have a pip, or stripe, removed. But the phrase was also used in the sense of taking down a peg. *Pontoon* is ordinarily a card game, twenty-one; but to the men in Vaughan's regiment, it was a stew with ingredients of uncertain origin. A *thin red hero* refers to the famous "thin red line": when Vaughan sets down the phrase, he is thinking of himself as a genuine fighting man, which he certainly wasn't yet.

Some military expressions, too, may need explanation. A *parados* was the back wall of a trench (the parapet being the front one). A *valise* was an officer's carry-all—which could sometimes be unrolled to make a sleeping bag. Vaughan owned one of the latter. *Dixies* were elongated galvanized iron buckets that held food, tea, or water. Unpolluted drinking water was a scarce commodity on the Western Front, and those who ventured to drink out of shellholes, which often contained not just rainwater but poison gas, bodies, and other human waste, did so at their peril.

In the event, I have chosen not to weigh down Vaughan's narrative with an apparatus of footnotes: the story speaks for itself.

—R. C.

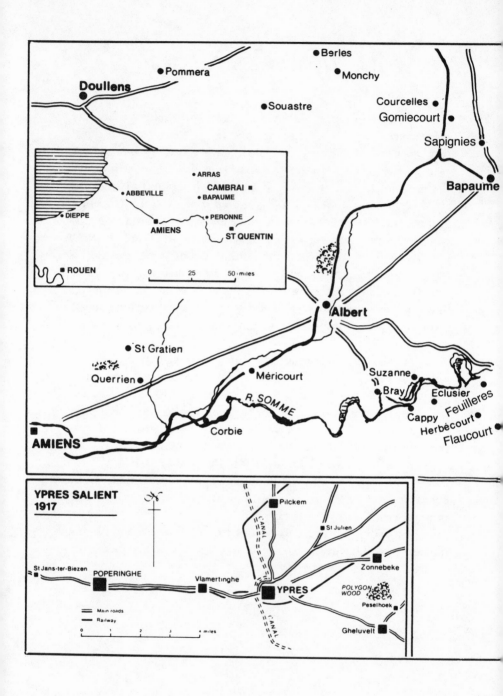

Berles

Pommera

Doullens

Monchy

Souastre

Courcelles
Gomiecourt

Sapignies

Bapaume

• ARRAS
CAMBRAI ■
• ABBEVILLE   • **BAPAUME**
• DIEPPE   • PERONNE
AMIENS   ■ **ST QUENTIN**

■ **ROUEN**

0   25   50 miles

Albert

St Gratien

Méricourt

Suzanne
Bray   Eclusier

Querrien

R. SOMME   Feuilleres
Cappy
Herbécourt
Flaucourt

Corbie

AMIENS

**YPRES SALIENT
1917**

Pilckem

CANAL

St Julien

St Jans-ter-Biezen

POPERINGHE

Vlamertinghe

YPRES

Zonnebeke

POLYGON
WOOD

Peselhoek

CANAL

Gheluvelt

——— Main roads
——— Railway

0   1   2   3   4 miles

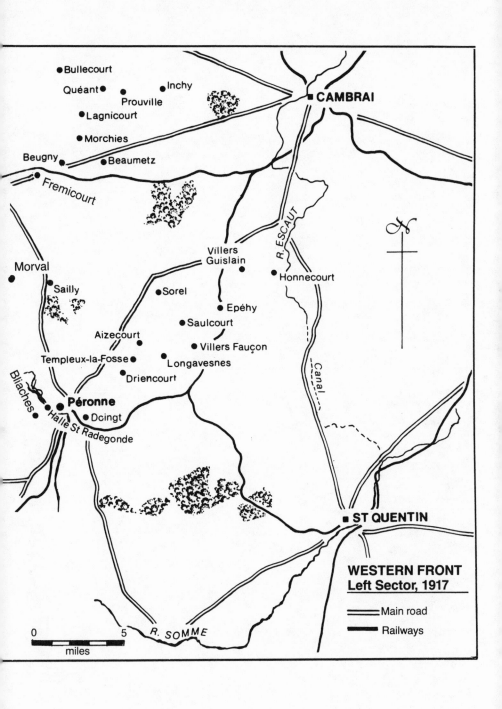

Bullecourt

Quéant · Inchy

Prouville

Lagnicourt

Morchies

Beugny · Beaumetz

Fremicourt

CAMBRAI

R. ESCAUT

Villers
Guislain

Honnecourt

Morval

Sailly

Sorel

Epéhy

Saulcourt

Aizecourt

Villers Fauçon

Templeux-la-Fosse

Longavesnes

Driencourt

Bliaches

Péronne

Dcingt

Halle St Radegonde

Canal

N

ST QUENTIN

WESTERN FRONT
Left Sector, 1917

Main road
Railways

0   5

miles

R. SOMME

SOME DESPERATE GLORY

THE DIARY OF
EDWIN CAMPION VAUGHAN

January 4 I had expected that on leaving for France I would be overcome by grief, for I knew that I would not see my home again for many, many months—and possibly not again. But when the moment came the excitement of the venture into the dreamed of but unrealized land of war, eclipsed the sorrow of parting, and I know now how much harder it is for those who lose us, than for us who go.

It was an incredible moment—long dreamed of—when the train steamed slowly out of Waterloo, a long triple row of happy, excited faces protruding from carriage windows, passing those which bravely tried to smile back at us—we were wrapped in the sense of adventure to come, they could look forward only to loneliness. We took a last long look at the sea of faces and waving handkerchiefs—and we had left.

When we had swept round the bend, away from the crowded platform, ringing with farewell cheers, I sank back into the cushions, and tried to realize that, at last, I was actually on my way to France, to war and excitement—to death or glory, or both. Some of my fellow-passengers had obviously been 'out' before, and now they settled down to their 'Tatlers' and 'Bystanders' with no outward sign of perturbation or interest in the situation; but as we raced through bushy parks and grazing fields my mind was filled with a confusion of Boer War and other martial pictures, behind which loomed vaguely the strained brave faces I had last seen, so that with all the excitement of my brain, I felt a horrible aching at my heart, and I was forced to bury myself in my magazines to avoid being foolish.

At Southampton the train drew up on the quay, beside the trooper, but learning that we did not sail until 7 p.m. I went into town with another fellow and had lunch.

We embarked at 4 p.m. and having with great skill evaded the lynx-eyed red-hat who was allotting duties, I managed to snuggle down in the hold, with no weight on my mind but the fear of sickness—and a much less formidable fear of submarines.

The crossing was very rough indeed: the hold was soon uninhabitable, and as I could find no one I knew who was not sick, I went up on deck and stood alone in the bows, thoroughly enjoying the pitching of the tub (which, by the way, will live for ever in the minds of half the British Army—the trooper *Caesarea*). Far ahead in the darkness I could see the tail light of our leading destroyer, darting from side to side, forging ahead and then waiting, and as it grew light the whole of the escort became visible, sweeping off in all directions and then returning to us. They lent a wonderful sense of power and security, and I stood watching them until we were close on to the French coast, when I went down to breakfast, soaked to the skin with spray and feeling very fit.

January 5 As I had done the journey down the Seine before I was not quite so thrilled this time, but it did our hearts good to see the French villagers, soldiers and nuns running down to the river bank, waving and cheering. Everybody on board was now quite happy and we sang and cheered all the way down until at dusk we ran into Rouen.

Here the 2,000 of us turned out onto the quay, and were taken in hand by a corporal of the Embarkation Staff, who sorted and arranged us, dumped our kit in various sections and finally told us off to different camps of the Infantry Base Depot. We then attached ourselves to various bodies of troops and as night fell, marched off through the town. A crowd of kiddies ran beside us begging for 'bulee and biscuits' all the way to the camp, where they were chased off by the Military Police.

I was told off to No 29 IBD. The mess is pretty good and people all quite nice to me. I am billeted in a tiny hut with a boy called Crawford, who was in the 20th Londons and knew Leslie Keating and Bunny Owen. He is a silly kid but very friendly and anxious to make me comfortable. Being pretty fagged I turned in immediately after mess. Already the glory of war seems to have faded somewhat, now that we are under control, and duty and routine are toning the great adventure down into commonplace.

January 6 The days here are spent in training and lectures—chiefly intended to inculcate the offensive spirit. At 8 a.m. we parade and march past numerous sentries to the 'Bull Ring'—a large dreary expanse used by Napoleon as a parade ground. I have already learnt the art of, and spotted the opportunities for, 'miking' and today I attended only one lecture—which put the wind up me thoroughly being a graphic account of a mine eruption in which the narrator had been blown up. I went through the gas chamber to see what it was like, but the rest of the day I spent in a secret nook deep in the forest with a brother-miker.

This evening I went to benediction in the cathedral and on leaving was presented with a little medal by a nun. This I have attached to a ring on my braces where there is an ever-increasing bunch presented from various people.

January 7 Sunday. Very tiring day. Had hoped to have a long sleep and attend late mass. But at 7 a.m. we were aroused by the Officers' Call and ordered to parade at 8 o'clock in fighting order. We were served out with ammunition and marched to the Bull Ring where were assembled about 8,000 troops, including cavalry and colonials. All officers were called up and the following scheme expounded:

Nine Australian Tommies, who were in hospital under arrest, prior to going to clink for various offences, had escaped some days previously and were roaming the district committing outrages of a serious nature. Several murders were attributed to them, and our instructions were to take them dead or alive. We were quickly organized into platoons and companies and the whole depot distributed round the sides of a square of 25 miles.

At one o'clock we all commenced to advance, the idea being to sweep every inch of ground and meet in the centre. Any suspicious looking person was to be arrested or shot if he resisted. We advanced solidly for about four miles, and then the animal spirits of the New Army took control. Officers, Australians and discipline were fogotten in a mad rabbit hunt with fixed bayonets, and hundreds of men broke loose: yelling and shouting they dashed into the bracken on all sides.

All control was lost and as soon as we were able to get the fellows together again, we marched back, the search being abandoned. I didn't see the general, but judging from the faces of his staff, he is at this moment in a violent fit. We are expecting a few remarks tomorrow!

January 8 We were today summoned to the Orderly Room for allotment to our regiments. Acting on advice, I claimed to belong to the 1/8th Warwicks; I lied heartily about it but when asked to produce proof, I had to admit that I had not been with them before. However, I pleaded so piteously that they admitted that there was *one* vacancy at that unit and that they would give it to me on condition that I did the paying out of the whole depot on pay parade. To this I gladly agreed and so spent the afternoon and evening handing over French notes to several hundreds of troops. I am quite glad to have done this as I was not previously acquainted with the active service system of paying out.

January 9 Miniature battle today: quite a good effort too! There are two opposing trench systems representing the Boche and English lines. We were the 'English' and were subjected to a raid carried out by the instructors. Having formed up in our lines with sentries posted, we were warned by whistle that the raid was about to commence. We had just time to get into shelter when a whirring and thumping told us that the 'artillery' barrage had commenced.

Dozens of bombs in the shape of jam tins were hurled from

catapults and rifles and crashed into the trenches with loud
explosions. (There was no make-believe about it, they were
real explosions of sufficient strength to lay out any unlucky
recipient.) After a few minutes, and before we had time to get
back to our positions, the instructors were amongst us, with
bombs made of detonators wrapped in clay. These exploded
but could do no harm. Of course we were hopelessly licked
but it was an interesting and instructive show.

Went to see the padre tonight and learnt that Father
Prevost is in a neighbouring camp. Am going to see him
tomorrow.

January 10 Went to see Father Prevost tonight. He
seemed awfully pleased to see me, and produced, with great
glee, a box of sweets sent him by Miss Hewitt. We sat and
talked and smoked and chewed for a long time, swapping
news of Ilford and its inhabitants. He is very much bolder
than he was and has had some interesting experiences. He
was home on leave last November.

January 11–12 Simply awaiting orders now. I go down to
Rouen nearly every day and mix with people. It's awfully
interesting to pick up with people and talk with them for an
hour or so. I have met French and Belgian officers and
soldiers, English girls and French actresses and *demi-
mondaines*, padres and police, and talked and drunk in the
cosmopolitan atmosphere of the French cafés.

Nobody seems to worry about the war and so far I have not
heard one word of war news since I landed. It seems to be the
last topic of conversation. However, from the manner in
which we are allowed to do exactly as we please, we can guess
that the time for our departure is drawing near.

January 13 Cut parade today and walked about the forest
in pouring rain trying to realize that in a few days we would be
up the line. Very hard to imagine it, for no one seems to worry

and 'going up' is treated like going into mess or on parade.

Had dinner at the Brasserie de l'Opera with Crawford. As I was going out of the swing doors a fresh-cheeked officer of the Gloucesters bumped into me. In great confusion he murmured 'Pardon, M'sieur', to which I replied 'All Right Cobbo! I can talk a bit of English.' Gathering from his air of bewilderment and Christmas-tree equipment that he had just arrived from England, I asked him if he came from the 4th Battalion and if he knew my brother Frank. He told me that he had come across *with* Frank and that they were meeting on the Grand Pont at 9.30.

Needless to say I attended the rendezvous and we greeted each other with mutual pleasure. We travelled back together in a rattling taxi, and at the camp separated to our several depots, arranging to meet at mass tomorrow.

January 14 Sunday. Went to mass this morning. Frank did not turn up, but sent a message to say that he was on duty and would call to see me tomorrow evening. He may call, but he will not see me for the afternoon has been spent in drawing steel helmets, gas helmets and iron ration, and tomorrow is the day when—at last—I move up to the front.

January 15 Said goodbye to everyone this afternoon, and went down to the station, to start my long-anticipated journey to the front. As I drove down in the rattling, bone-shaking old taxi, I tried hard to convince myself that the moment I had lived for had arrived and that I was now a real Service man. But this was difficult: there was no band playing, no regiment bearing the old colours into the fray, only little *me*, sitting behind an unwashed, unshaven driver, finding my way alone because I had been told to.

As the semi-official truck-train jerked out of Rouen, it began to snow hard, and the bare truck wherein I, the only passenger on the train, sat on my rolled up valise, was soon full of whirling snow. It was quite dark and the icy wind simply cut through me from one open door to the other.

Slowly we rolled on into the night; the snow continued until every part of my body was numb and senseless. Sometimes a black patch marked a town; rarely there was a light. For the most part there was nothing but the dim grey open country and the ever-whirling snow.

At 11 p.m. we reached Roman Camp, and as the train was not going any further I was turned out onto a wooden platform. There was a tiny shelter in which I saw the flicker of a fire, and entering I found three Tommies, of whom two were asleep and the third was dozing over a brazier. I learnt from the latter that there was a supply train going on at 1 a.m. and as I could not squeeze into their shelter, I walked about in the snow, or huddled against the open paling until that time. The cold was intense, and in addition I was wet through, beastly hungry and over the boots in snow.

January 16 At about 1.30 a.m. the train turned up, and I got into the guard's van. There was no guard but I had company in the form of a trooper of the 8th Hussars who addressed no word to me, but lay down in the straw rolled up in his greatcoat. Very slowly we bumped and jogged along, and the cold became even more intense. The Hussar was whimpering and crying aloud and one or two rats were whisking about, squealing and fighting in the straw in one corner. I found a bit of candle and tried to read, but it was continually blown out and so I was driven to tramp up and down and throw myself against the sides until morning when we drew up at the railhead—a place called Sénapont.

It was now 6 a.m. and dumping my kit on the station I made enquiries, learning that a train of lorries was leaving for Divisional HQ at 7.30. I walked briskly about the still-sleeping village and gradually got a little warmth into my system. At 6.45 I found a tiny café just opened, and here I obtained some omelettes and coffee, after which I sat by the fire and smoked until life assumed a rosier hue. The sun rose, the lorries hooted and with ears strained for the whistle of the first bullet I climbed up and took my seat beside a driver who annoyed me by regarding this journey up the line as a matter of no especial importance.

As we drove out of Sénapont on to the main road, I began to question the driver about the line, picturing the Battalion in the midst of fire and smoke. He told me about the locality in which they were stationed, and I, with my eyes prepared to meet a scene of wire entanglements, shell bursts and trenches, was confused by his references to the estaminets the men frequented, the girls they met, and the cushy time they were having. Finally I discovered that we were just outside Abbeville and many many miles from the line! It was a drastic disillusionment and I did not know whether to be annoyed or relieved.

I was set down in the square at Hallencourt and reported to Divisional HQ. I was told that my Battalion mess cart was going back during the afternoon to Arraines-sur-Somme, where my unit was billeted. The young subaltern who showed me its position on the map, pointed out the mess cart, and I went across to two NCOs standing by it. One was a sturdy little sergeant major, the other a company quarter-master sergeant. Both saluted, and having eyed me up and down, and taken thorough stock of me, proceeded to smoke and lounge about whilst I questioned them. My sense of discipline received a severe shock but I hesitated to choke them off, as they appeared to be behaving in a manner usual to them.

At 2 p.m. I took my seat by the driver with the two warrant officers cramped in behind me. We pulled up before the Hôtel du Commerce in Arraines-sur-Somme, a tiny café-pub, used as the Battalion mess. On entering I found only one occupant—a major with a weak face and no chin who treated me as an acquaintance whom he knew very well but did not like. He told that everybody else was at a football match and would be back shortly—then I ceased to exist for him. His name I have since learnt is Willy Whitehouse and he is quite impossible. The Colonel simply declines to allow him to have anything to do with the Battalion and he just loafs all day whilst awaiting his transfer back to England.

At four o'clock the officers crowded in, and I reported immediately to the adjutant, a young Captain Harper, who evinced not the slightest interest in me, and asked no questions. I then met Berry, who I knew in England, a very loud fellow that I much disliked. I have chummed up with a fellow called Hawkins, attached from the 25th London Cyclists. He is an awfully decent boy and had told me lots about everybody. There is no one here that I know—except Berry; Sullivan, who was my chum in England, is on leave.

After mess we went into a little sitting room holding a small stove and a piano; here people played cards, sang and drank until 10.30—mess closing time. During the evening the CO came across and spoke a few words to me. He told me I was posted to D Company and added (quite unnecessarily I thought) that I would have to take down a pip. I did not see enough of him to decide whether I liked him or not, but everyone else adores him.

Halfway through the evening, the figure of a female appeared: a coarse stout figure in a filthy black torn skirt, black woollen bodice and red shoes through which black, much-darned stocking toes protruded. Her face was covered thickly with powder intended to hide a mass of purple pimples, and her right hand being septic was bound up and thrust into the front of her bodice. She tripped in with girlish mien and mincing steps, whilst 'Un Peu d'Amour' was crawling out of the tin piano and perceiving a newcomer she skittishly approached and sang 'I loff you' with evil-smelling breath and horrid leer into my face.

This is Madame, the keeper of the hotel—a vile hag. To assist her she starves two little girls—Madeleine and Andréa Allard. They are nice little sisters very very poor and hard worked. I have already exchanged hearts with them.

I am sleeping here in the hotel, as there are no more billets in the village. My room is quite clean and comfortable, but the wall is very thin and until midnight I was disturbed by the noise of two of our batmen wrestling and fighting in the next room.

January 17 Paraded at 9 a.m. and met my new Company Commander—Lieutenant Hatwell—whom I dislike and despise. He is very small and quite inefficient, though full of bounce and bluff. I knew him very slightly in England. We are the only officers in the Company, which consists of badly trained, undisciplined, slovenly men under indifferent NCOs. Our musketry and PT was carried out on a bleak snow-covered hillside, where we were thoroughly chilled. The men took no interest in the work, and no attempt was made to instil smartness or keenness.

There was no work during the afternoon and I took a long solitary walk around the neighbouring villages. These are very scattered and between them the roads stretch across flat plains coated in white broken here and there by tiny copses or isolated houses. Away from the villages, and even in them, I rarely saw a human being. It quite impressed me on these bare windswept roads, to come across the rough wayside cross, or calvary: behind the figure of Christ radiated metal stars, in the forked points of which the villagers are wont to insert their petitions for the prayers of passers by.

In the evening I censored letters for the first time. I found it very interesting but my pile took me rather a long time. The other fellows have a knack, which I have not yet acquired, of glancing over a page and spotting censorable matter without reading a line. Later on I improved my French by a long talk with Madeleine.

January 18 Two new arrivals—officers attached from the 7th Worcesters—today joined our company. Their names are Watkins and Thomas and my first impression of them was quite favourable. Paid out the Company during the evening and later issued the rum to the troops; tasted it myself for the first time and again the impression was favourable.

I sat up late in the mess with Berry and a man called Anstey. The latter should be an extremely nice fellow and has a remarkably handsome head, but both his character and his appearance are thoroughly spoiled by drink. We helped ourselves, from time to time, from a saucepan of rum punch on the stove, and Anstey got very drunk. He quarreled violently with Madame, who, dreading a raid by the gendarmes, was trying to get him to bed.

I am getting to know the fellows a little better now, but still do not like them very much. I am very disappointed with the Battalion, which in England had always been spoken of as the last word in fighting efficiency.

January 19 Parade as usual during morning. This afternoon we attended a concert given by one of Lena Ashwell's Parties. I only heard the first song then returned to the hotel to talk with Madeleine who is in bed unwell.

The concert artistes came in to dinner and a very loud evening ensued, which included unnecessarily indecent songs and recitations. A comic interlude was provided when screams of laughter interrupted a recitation which was not nearly as amusing as it purported to be. The humorist was highly gratified until he discovered that the merriment was caused by a fellow sitting hopelessly drunk behind him, making maudlin love to a bass-broom. One of the more reputable items was a sword-dance performed by two officers attached from the Royal Scots—Ewing and 'the wee' Guthrie—both of 'A' Company.

January 20 There was a football match at Sorel today: the mess was riding over *en bloc*, and although I had never been on a horse before, I did not like to refuse. So a horse appeared at the appointed time, and asked for me. Whilst the other fellows mounted, two or three grooms hoisted me into my saddle. I was just thinking how awfully high I was, when I felt myself bumped up and down at an alarming rate.

There followed half an hour of agony whilst Fat Dolly lumbered after the other horses, with me clinging to the saddle and swaying from side to side. I was a very unhappy spectator of the match, and do not even know whether we won or lost. After it was over I waited until all the other riders had left, and then, climbing up, I allowed Dolly to amble along at a slow walk. In the first ten minutes all the foot travellers had left us far behind, and finally we arrived, after an hour and a half, at the transport lines (Dolly insisted on this). Thence with a bursting head I walked home and went straight to bed. Was awake all night with sledge-hammers beating my brain.

January 21 Sunday. Went to mass in the little village church and was amused by the quaint decorations and customs. After mass I went into Hawkins' billet; he has there a dear little fifteen-year-old girl who plays the piano and flirts most delightfully. I had a nice afternoon and tea with them. Sullivan has returned and I was heartily glad to see his red old head and cheery smile again.

January 22 We learn that in a few days we are moving up, and have commenced our preparations for the journey. On leaving here we will cease to live in a battalion mess, and I have been appointed to the office of Company Mess Caterer—I am quite at sea with regard to my task. The girls are awfully upset at the idea of our departure, and a dozen times I have had to repeat my promise to write to them from the line. 'If you not write! Oh, zen I shall have such *fear*!'

January 23 Was sent to Hallencourt today to draw cash for payment of the troops. Went on a pushbike; Watkins started to accompany me but got a puncture and had to return. I found it beastly cold crossing the open plains and very difficult to cycle with 18,000 francs in the pockets of my British warm. The evening was spent in laying stocks of tinned meat, fruit, biscuits, whisky and wines, purchases from the local épicerie and the canteen.

January 24 Said a tearful goodbye to the kiddies at an early hour and went down to the billet to get the troops ready

and billets cleaned up. Marched down to the siding (just out
of the village) and entrained at about 1 p.m. There was no
excitement or interest in our destination—it was just a
'move'.

As soon as we got into the train, we opened the mess boxes
and had lunch, then alternately we ragged each other and
played cards. We were in a very primitive type of carriage—a
long open affair, with half-way backs, no cushions, the floor
covered in straw and dirt, and nearly all the windows broken.
The troops were in cattle trucks.

After a time I noticed that the train was rolling through a
broad band of barbed wire entanglements, and on enquiry
learnt that they were part of the outer defences of Amiens. All
this time I had been singing gaily, despite the remonstrances
of the bridge party, and now one of them—Johnny Teague, a
jolly cherub-faced youngster and Captain commanding 'B'
Company—as he scanned his hand with slightly squinting
eyes, said casually. 'You know Hatwell, Vaughan's much too
full of beans. Send him out on patrol for a few nights—that'll
quieten him down.'

That was all he said, but the realization that we were on the
point of reaching the line rushed upon me, and at once my
imagination began to run riot. I stopped singing and yielded
myself up to the influences of the approaching darkness and
dead quiet outside, the dim guttering candles, the broken
windows and general air of disorder.

And out of the tangle and confusion of my thoughts and
apprehensions, the fact gradually came uppermost in my
mind that all the empty-headed fellows who had been
laughing, joking and drinking ever since I had known them,
were real soldiers, who after many months in the line were
now returning without the slightest sign of perturbation or
nervousness. And I began to look around me with a greater
interest and more tolerant criticism.

It now became quite dark and in a few hours we pulled up
at a black deserted station and tumbled out onto the siding of
Méricourt. In a very few minutes our mess boxes were

stacked and we were trudging down the road from the station through the snow and slush.

Everything was quite black around us, and I was furious when an army lorry dashed past without any lights, sending us hurtling to the side. I said something to Watkins about his being reported for not having lights. He said consolingly, 'Never mind, I expect a Bobby will get him,' and there was something pitying about his tone that made me suspect he was pulling my leg—how, I did not know.

As we left the tiny village, the moon shone out, and I gazed curiously at the last house, which presented a very shattered appearance. About a mile further on we turned off the road on to a muddy track which brought us to a small group of hutments.

Here the men were put into long wooden huts, quite empty and holding no furniture or fitments of any kind; most of the windows were broken too, and in the bitter cold the men lay down on the floor, each rolled in his one blanket, and tried to sleep. We were shown into our quarters—consisting of a hut of the same kind but boarded off into cubicles. They were just as cold and cheerless as the men's, and I was at an absolute loss as to what to do to make things more comfy when Hatwell, who had just whisked in and out, reappeared with three servants. These latter just glanced round and were gone—and so was Hatwell. Watkins and Thomas now drew on their gloves saying 'Come on! Let's go and scrounge,' and out we went into the snow. We struck off towards the railway, searching every bit of the ground and later returned to the cubicle bearing one old steel helmet, one empty oil drum, one brick, one large bully-beef tin and a quantity of small sticks and twigs.

The servants had already been back and there was quite a dump of wood (wet of course) and one dry ration box resting beside our mess boxes. Hatwell appeared, too, bearing an enormous lump of coal, and with the aid of a bayonet he converted our oil drum into a most respectable brazier. Soon there was a cheerful blaze, the mess boxes were open and we sat round on our valises drinking whisky. It was early morning when, the servants having scrounged more fuel and laid out our blankets, we turned in, pleased with the comfort of our new quarters.

January 25   We got all the troops out at 10 a.m. and had the snow cleared from all the paths between the huts; and after lunch we walked a few hundred yards across to some big ice ponds on the frozen marshes. Here we played a fierce game of ice hockey against the officers of the 7th Battalion—using walking sticks as clubs. Lieutenant Ekins of 'B' Company (attached from the Essex Regiment) came an awful cropper, sailing through the air and landing on the back of his head. He was carried away, and the game continued, our enormous Irish doctor wreaking great destruction with a huge blackthorn.

After dinner, as we sat smoking round the brazier, we heard three blasts of a whistle—the signal for enemy aircraft. We ran out and saw quite clearly a zeppelin passing high overhead, but there was no firing of any kind.

January 26   A spell of PT this morning left the troops very fed up, so Watkins and I took them for a short march, in the course of which we turned them loose on the ice to amuse themselves. They became quite childish then, and marched back in a much happier mood.

In the afternoon, Watkins, Thomas and I walked to the neighbouring village of Suzanne, where we bought some chocolate and bottles of fruit at an exorbitant price from a pretty French girl. On our return to camp we learnt that we are due to move out tomorrow.

January 27   Paraded and marched off at 11 a.m. We had only a very short distance to go, for we soon reached the river at Eclusier where we were to camp, and where I had my first view of a shelled village. As we crossed the bridge on to the main road, before us we saw the church. There was an enormous hole through the roof, the doors were gone and the interior was heaped with bricks and debris. Turning to the right up the main road we marched for half a mile, and then following a track down to the river we reached the camp.

This was a string of huts, of wood and tarpaulin, laid at length upon the top of the canal bank. The French troops had just vacated them and they were so filthy that we had to take out and burn all the straw bedding before we could enter. After a short foray, we got a fire going and had tea. This was a very cheerful meal; the air seems charged with electricity, and everyone betrays unconsciously an alertness and excitement induced by our proximity to the scene of activities. Laughter and conversation are more spontaneous and ingenuous, and the troops are already treating us with a friendliness withheld whilst we were down the line.

I was astounded this evening on rifle inspection to see Corporal Wood, in charge of a platoon, report 'all correct' to Sergeant Bell, with a cigarette in his hand and his rifle slung. I took Bell sharply to task about it, and told him never to allow such a breach of discipline again. He raised his eyebrows in blank amazement and replied, 'Why, Sir! It's always done up here.' I wanted to say 'Well it won't be if I'm on parade,' but it would have been subversive of Hatwell's authority so I had to let it pass. I have a black mark against both Wood and Bell; they are very shabby and slovenly and far too familiar with the men. The Sergeant Major—Chalk—is on leave.

Issued rum at night, and stayed nearly an hour talking to the troops who were in great form. I am beginning to like them much more than I did at first.

January 28 Sunday. No parade. Spent an hour or so with the lads who were busy cleaning up the huts and their equipment, and then went down to a small bivouac occupied by our quartermaster sergeant—CQMS Corfield. This is a most soapy customer, who oozes servility when addressed by an officer. I was trying to induce him to part with a

waterproof sheet; I got it in the end, but it was a most
unpleasant half-hour's spadework.

We all turned out onto the canal in the afternoon and had a
cheery time sliding and playing the fool. The CO was one of
the cheeriest of the crowd; I think he is a thorough sport, and
like him immensely.

I hear that the Battalion is taking over a section of the line
on February 2nd, and that our Company will be in reserve.

January 29 I am getting slight windup! Last night the
guns sounded very near, and after the candles were blown
out, the sky through the windows was continually lit up by
their flashes. As we lay watching them from our valises,
Watkins hoped that they would not shell us out of the camp,
adding dryly that he knew from experience how unpleasant it
was at night. Until then, I had hardly realized that we were in
the danger zone, but now my imagination got to work, and in
a quiet panic I waited for the first destructive crash that
would send us running out into a hail of shrapnel. And
through my head there was running the air of a catchy but
extremely vulgar song. I tried to drive it away, thinking how
terrible it would be to be killed humming such a song, but
always it returned—Ta-rumty-tiddity-tum-ti-tum . . . until I
fell asleep and they didn't shell us out at all.

January 30 The cubicle in which the servants live is
separated from ours by five others; and to overcome the
indignity of having to yell several times for them before they
replied, I decided this morning to fix up a patent bell. To this
end I got our coil of wire and fastening one end in the
servants' room I tied to it a milk tin holding a few stones, then
bringing the coil over the partition I commenced to play it
out along the corridor. Of course I got it tangled and as I
stopped to unravel it, Martin, the mess cook, came along and
burst into an immoderate fit of laughter. 'Oo-hoo-hoo! Look
at Mr Vaughan! Hi. Dunham! Come and look!'

Now I knew that Martin needed a strong hand so I said

firmly, 'Martin! Go inside *at once*; close that door and don't come out again until I ring the bell.' Unfortunately, as I said this, I let slip my handful of wire, the coils of which sprang in all directions; I was hopelessly entangled around the legs and, crimson with rage, had to submit to being extricated by the grinning Martin, in front of the crowd of servants and officers evoked by his 'oo-hoo hoo-ing'. That's typical of Martin and I'll teach him one day!

Walked down to Cappy to buy stores, and whilst there had a look at the church, which is only slightly damaged. An English notice announces mass each Sunday. I went also into a large deserted house on the outskirts of the town; all the furniture has been removed, but I amused myself with Thomas for an hour rummaging amongst the piles of pictures, books and papers which were left in great piles on the floors.

There was more sliding in the evening and continuous gunfire in the distance.

January 31   Hung about camp and played cards nearly all day. Hatwell has now a useful but discreditable practice of ordering all defaulters down to the mess to collect and chop wood for our fire. If the Sergeant Major reports that there are no defaulters, he holds a surprise rifle inspection and 'crimes' enough men for having dirty rifles to carry on. He continues to grate on my nerves; he is a fairly good sort in his way, and certainly has a very keen sense of humour, but he is quite incompetent, very selfish and full of bluff. In a very weak moment three weeks ago, I lent him 80 francs; I regret it now, as I learn on all hands that I am not likely to see it back.

February 1   An electrically-charged atmosphere! Everyone working galvanically, sorting, writing and burning letters, discarding kit; inspections of iron rations and PH gas-respirators. I am quite befogged with regard to our programme. We have received no news or instructions from Hatwell and if we ask any questions he tells us to go to hell.

Sullivan and I had a long talk, starting with reminiscences of days on Salisbury Plain and ending with religion. This latter topic was always our standby for earnest argument, he being a very sincere C of E and one of the rare few whom I have met who can speak calmly on the RC faith.

February 2 Although the morning was spent in final packing, I did not feel at all excited; I think it was the long waiting that calmed me down, for we did not parade until 5 p.m., when we marched off in fighting order, along the road by the canal bank. Although the whole Battalion will nominally be 'in the line', our Company will not actually be in the trenches. One company, during each tour, is to remain in a village behind, and will nightly carry up rations to the firing line.

This evening we were engaged in carrying rations and tools and helping to pull the Lewis gun carts. It was a very lonely road along which we marched, rising in a gradual slope until we reached the crest of the ridge. Here we had to wait until dusk before we could cross. Around us where we were halted stretched a large dump of wire, stakes, pickets, sandbags, mine timber and all the materials used in trench warfare.

After about half an hour of sitting in the snow, and when we were thoroughly chilled, we were able to continue and at 7 o'clock we passed over the ridge and turned off the road onto a narrow track to the right. Ploughing through the snow, we came to the head of a trench, where we halted. It was now quite dark except for the dim light thrown up by the snow. We were not, of course, allowed to smoke and we stood freezing in the wind that blew steadily on to our flank from the icy darkness.

Hatwell had vanished, and for a long time we stood motionless, not having the faintest idea where we were or what to do. Ignorant as I was of trench warfare, I was sure that this was all wrong, for if he had been killed or wounded, we would have been of no use, and our duties would never have been fulfilled.

At last I saw the leading troops climbing down into the trench, and being in charge of the first platoon I ran along and jumped down beside Hatwell as he strode along towards the line. In reply to my questions he told me grudgingly and angrily that it was three kilometres to the support trench—as a matter of fact it was much more.

We had not gone very far before we were met by a small party of French Tommies, who flattened up against the side of the trench. It was far too narrow for us to pass them but it was a long time before they could be induced to climb out on top, and then they only did so with much frightened gibbering and mutterings about 'la mort' and 'mitrailleuses'. After a little further progress, the message was passed up from behind to 'Step short in front'. This I passed on to Hatwell but he merely swore heartily and passed back 'Step out!' Later came the shout 'Lost touch in rear. Sir!' Again he did not wait, but ordering me to stand in an alcove to hasten them up, he continued to stride along.

Obediently I wormed into a hole where the side had fallen in, and cursed the stragglers—poor devils who were staggering under boxes of ammunition or cases of rations. At last the caterpillar ended, and it was some considerable time before the remainder came up. I gave instructions to the leading man to step out quickly and then when they had all passed brought up the rear with Watkins.

As was to be expected, we wandered on, up and down dead-end trenches and saps until at last we came to a trench junction where Hatwell stood half crying and half mad with cold and rage. He cursed and shouted, pushing men in different directions and finally sending Watkins and myself one each way, with no instructions other than to 'follow the men'.

I followed mine very cleverly until we were stopped by a French sentry who in horrified whispers and with many dramatic gestures indicating swordplay and death, warned us that we were on top of 'les allemands!' So we simply turned round and walked back.

I may say I had not the vaguest notion where we were or what had happened. I was without any orders or information and I was too utterly lost in bewilderment at my first night in the trenches. It was so eerie and dull, no lights, no shots or shells, no raids or mines—just darkness, duckboards and rations.

Somehow we were back in the communication trench, and then back on the road. The loads the men had carried were in evidence no more, but where they dropped them I have no idea. As we marched back, I learnt from one of the men that we were not to go back to Eclusier—our billets were now to be in Cappy. This did not surprise me, as by this time I was used to being in complete ignorance of our plans. And he was right, for on arrival we found that our kits were awaiting us, and the rest of the Company were already settled down in their billets.

I joined Watkins and Thomas in a little house allotted to us, and after a plate of excellent hot pontoon which Martin had prepared during our absence, I issued rum to the troops, then to myself, and turned in—still marvelling at the ridiculous attempt at warfare I had just witnessed.

February 3   Like the idle rich I had my 'bed in breakfast' and then rose at 11 a.m. feeling the thrill of a real 'thin red hero'. On comparing notes with the others, I found that I was the only one who had been at all at a loss the night before. We spent the afternoon sitting around the huge open fireplace in the kitchen which is also our dining room. There is only one other room, in which Watkins, Thomas and I sleep. Hatwell is living with 'B' Company—Johnny Teague being his particular pal. There was a tremendous roar and clatter at one time which filled me with a sudden fear that the Boche were upon us. We all rushed out and found the mess servants standing among the ruins of the next house which they had pulled down bodily while cutting out rafters for firewood.

At 6 p.m. Thomas and I set out with the Company to carry the rations up to the line. This time we went straight up the road leading through Herbécourt. We had passed through the village and were descending the further slope, where all was dead quiet and peaceful, so that as I walked beside Thomas I had no qualms of fear, when he said in a low voice, 'If they start shelling, we will have to split up. You take the front two platoons onto the fields on the right and I will take the remainder onto the left.'

At that, my teeth started to chatter, and I had to stop talking, for my voice trembled so. I don't think I was really frightened physically, but there was a curious dread of the unknown and an excitement of the imagination. As we marched down the exposed lonely road to the communication trench, I heard in the far distance a curious musical moan which with a gradually changing key came nearer and nearer until, immediately overhead, it made a noise like an emptying drain and then died away. I asked Tommy what that was and he replied 'Oh! Just one for the back areas.' 'One what?' 'Shell, of course!' So I had heard my first shell, and it was quite pretty.

When we reached the commy-trench, Tommy pointed out that as all the troops knew the way, and were going in different directions, it would be useless for us to follow any group of two or three men. So we sent them off with their rations and then started to explore the ground around the trench head. The night was very much lighter, and for quite a distance we could see the undulating snow-covered ground, broken here and there by shell-holes, mounds and wire entanglements.

At first I was afraid to leave the vicinity of the trench lest any danger should catch me in the open, but after a while I grew more venturesome and went across with Johnny to a belt of broken wire around which the snow was uneven, with scattered rubbish. Here we found the grave of a Frenchman, with the equipment lying beside it, from which I collected the rapier-bayonet as a souvenir. Then we played about in the snow, exploring dumps and shell-holes and graves until an hour later when the troops returned and we marched back.

February 4   Sunday. It was Watkins' time to go up the line tonight, and when he had gone, Tommy and I sat by the fire smoking and talking. When he had been away about an hour, we heard a terrific rumble and growling in the distance. Obviously there was some trouble and after many conjectures and apprehensions, we were relieved when Watkins blew in and explained what had happened.

He had been leading the Company across the open road in front of Herbécourt, when a burst of enemy gunfire swept the road. The Company scattered and lay in shell-holes while shells and shrapnel rained about them. Along the front line they saw a terrific barrage falling and faintly distinguished the rattle of machine guns. After a while the shelling suddenly ceased and they went forward with their rations, to find the trenches wrecked but now peaceful. The enemy—the 4th Prussian Guard—had attacked three times, penetrating our lines on the third attempt, chiefly on the sector held by the 6th Warwicks. We had had some casualties, but he did not know how many.

This story seriously disturbed my rest: it brought danger so close to me. I lay awake for hours, thinking that *I* might have been in the line during that barrage and attack, or I might have been in Watkins' place. Then how would I have acquitted myself? I saw horrible pictures of myself lying dead in a shattered trench, or helplessly bleeding to death in a shell-hole, with no power to call for help. And not less terrible I saw myself on the road, panic-stricken and unable to go forward with the rations. Devoutly I wished that the war would be over before our turn came to go into the line.

February 5–6   As this was to be the Battalion's last night in the line, we did not have to take up any rations. Twelve men were, however, needed for some purpose and these Hatwell sent off under an NCO. An hour later, however, he considered that an officer should have gone, so I was instructed to take a pushbike, catch them up, and report with them to Battalion HQ in the trenches.

I started off in great fear, fully expecting a repetition of last night's barrage. The cold was terrible, and I had no gloves; I was wearing a pair of mittens and I moved my fingers as much as I could but my thumbs and first fingers were frozen to the handlebars which felt like white-hot metal. As I left Herbécourt and cycled out in to the open plain, I came to the place where the shelling had taken place. On every side gaped great black holes, and the snow around was blackened with debris, or yellow with explosive.

Very shortly I sniffed a curious, sweet, choking smell, and falling from my bicycle, I dragged out my gas-mask with numb fingers and pulled it over my head. Remounting, I continued pedalling down the deserted road, past ugly shattered tree stumps and graves, the clammy mask freezing to my face, and the glasses fogged so that time after time I rode into shell-holes or on to the edge of the road.

I sped on, almost mad with panic, passing no one on the way except two limbers, whose masked drivers were urging their teams into a stumbling trot, until, at last, I felt that my head and heart were bursting, and falling off my bike on to the side of the road I dragged off my helmet and took great gulps of air, not caring whether it were gas-laden or not.

As a matter of fact the air was now quite clear, and being close to the trench, I left my bike and walked along to it. Sitting on the duckboards I had a ten minutes' rest before I attacked the final kilometre to HQ. I was astounded and chagrined to find in the dugout a strange crowd of officers, who told me that my Battalion had been relieved some time before. They offered me a drink, after which there was nothing for me to do but to return.

This was such an anticlimax and I was so annoyed that I walked back to my bike and then cycled home in an unhurried and serene fashion, not giving another thought to the possibilities of shelling. The wind had to a large extent dispersed the gas, so that I only had to wear my mask for a few minutes, and when I reached my billet I was quite calm and only worried by my hands which were now really frost-bitten.

Everybody was in bed except Martin and Dunham (stout fellows) who had sat up for me with a hot meal. This went very well, and so did a peg of hot rum—and then bed.

February 7 I was very surprised this morning when Hatwell told us that we were to move up the line at dusk. I gathered that we would not be in the front trench but would be in support to the 7th Warwicks. The march up was uneventful and when we arrived at the trench head, Hatwell told us to wait and then vanished. For three-quarters of an hour we stood in the snow, lashed by an icy wind, until the troops became truculent and muttered very insubordinate remarks about all the officers, and particularly Hatwell.

At last I heard Hatty's voice calling from the trench, 'Vaughan! Vaughan! Come here, damn you!' I ran along to him and he dragged me down. 'Take 13 and 14 platoons at once to Brigade HQ and say you are for Désirée. Go *on*! Don't hang about!' I demurred a bit. 'Aren't there any further instructions?' '*No*, blast you! Get a move on.' 'Well, where is Brigade HQ?' 'In Stettin Trench. Go and find it.'

So I set off with the two platoons and, after much enquiring and wandering about, found Stettin Trench and halted before a blanket-covered dugout entrance. Descending about 30 steps, I found myself in a large dugout wherein sat a fair and curly-headed staff lieutenant, reading a novel. He took no notice of me until I spoke and then he just glanced up and told me to report to his sergeant. In a small room adjoining I found this character, and told him, as instructed, that I was 'for Désirée'; this did not thrill him, but he went into the other room, whence he returned after a few minutes and resumed his writing.

After ten minutes of patient waiting, I began to get cross, and stamped back in to the presence of the officer who, sensing my wrath, laid down his book and languidly raised his eyebrows. I told him vehemently, 1) That my men had marched a long way and were tired, 2) That it was damned cold outside, 3) That he had kept them waiting nearly half an hour, 4) That there was a war on, and 5) That I was entitled to more courtesy than he had shown me.

During my speech another staff officer came in, and having listened quietly, suggested that we should be sent up to relieve two platoons of the Ox and Bucks on the canal bank. Turning on him I shouted that we were the reserve company and had to report to 'Désirée', but he calmly told me that there was no room there as he had already put some troops therein.

At last he got on the phone to the Brigade HQ in rear. 'Oh I say, there's a fellow here from the Eighth, he says he's got two platoons or something. Doesn't know what to do, or where to go, or who he is or anything. Can you give them anything to do?'

After listening for a while he said cheerio and turned to me with an authoritative manner. 'I'll give you a guide, and you can spend the night carrying barbed wire from the trench-head up to the line.'

'No! I will not,' I replied. 'I am the reserve company to the Seventh Battalion, and am for "Désirée".'

As I was repeating my piece, the sergeant came in with a message which the Brigade Major had left and which he had overlooked until now. It was an order to Powell (my inter-viewer) to give us a guide, when we arrived, to show us some shelters behind Désirée Trench, where we were to remain as support for the 7th Battalion.

I was quite peeved when this message was read out, and I pointed out that my men were still tired, the war was still on, that it was now more damned cold than ever, all because of their inefficiency. Powell gave me a guide and said he would report me to the Brigadier. I said I'd see him in hell, and left. My poor frozen troops were led across the open to some shell-holes roughly covered with tarpaulin and corrugated iron, where they crammed in and went to sleep rolled in their greatcoats, while Dunham and I crept into the lousy straw of a tiny shelter and also slept.

February 8   This was a bright, clear day, but we could not stir out as our shell-holes are under observation of the enemy. So I sat at the entrance watching aeroplanes fighting overhead, and talked to Dunham. He is an oldish and rather dirty-looking fellow, with a long drooping moustache. As a servant he is absolutely useless, and was allotted to me by Hatwell because he would not spare a smart man from the Company. Before he joined up he was a lithographer in Dorset; he is quite well spoken and very religious, and although he makes me angry at times, he is very willing and I quite like him.

We had only one meal during the day, and that of bread and bully, but we made tea three times with water from our bottles. At night we worked, carrying wire up to the line. Everything was perfectly quiet and peaceful all day.

February 9   Day spent in the same way as yesterday. We had no food or water, but Dunham got a large chunk of ice out of a shell-hole behind us, so we had some milkless tea. I was a little dubious about using shell-hole water, but it was perfectly white and I should think any germs would be frozen.

I was rather cheered when a runner arrived during the afternoon with instructions for us to return to Eclusier when night fell. On arrival we found the rest of the Battalion already installed in our original billets. When a hot meal was put before me, I attacked it like a wolf, realizing for the first time how hungry I was.

February 10–13   We passed the next few days in a very slack manner, doing no work but occasionally holding an inspection of rifles or gas helmets. It must be getting gradually warmer, for, whilst drawing water a fellow went through the ice, and everywhere it is beginning to crack up. Thomas, after a couple of days in bed, has gone to the hospital with rheumatic fever.

February 14   Taking over the front line. Moved at dusk up the old Herbécourt road, which is now much softer; the snow is mostly melted and slushy but the ground underneath is still frozen. I knew the way up to Battalion HQ, of course, but from there on was new to me. It was a long and winding trench, which rather bewildered me, for the scattered sentry posts seemed to face in all directions. After a short time, the guide warned me in a whisper that we must now go quietly as we were close to the line. Then the trench got narrower and shallower until it was only knee deep, and we ran into a broken wall of a house. The trench recommenced at the corner of the building, and here was the entrance to the cellar used as the sergeant majors' dugout. Here we dropped Sergeant Bell to take over his duties, and we carried on down another 30 yards of deep narrow trench where I tore a great rent in my British warm. We hit the front-line trench at right angles, and almost opposite was another cellar into which Hatwell had disappeared in a moment.

I hardly noticed the troops melting away into different directions, but suddenly found myself quite alone outside the cellar. For a quarter of an hour I sat up against the side of the trench, soaking in the atmosphere. It was quite dark and damp, around my feet the mud was six inches deep, and above me I could see only the faint outline of the parapet all jagged and broken with bricks and stumps and over it the dim silhouette of loose wire. Occasionally a huge rat would scamper past, or a couple of men would stagger by, swearing gently at their load of sandbags or stakes. All was deathly quiet except for the low voices in the dugout or the faint click of a bayonet against a steel hat.

Soon, in twos and threes, men began to dribble back down the way we had come, and then a sturdy sergeant major lifted the blanket of the dugout and reported in a deep confident voice, 'Relief complete. Sir!' He went steadily off, hoisting his rifle-sling higher on his shoulder and was lost in the darkness. A few minutes later I descended the cellar steps to find a couple of officers finishing their drinks and putting out their cigarettes before they too said goodbye to the line for a while.

When they had gone, we sat down and took a peg of whisky each, taking stock of our surroundings. The dugout was merely the cellar of a house which had been knocked down over it. At one end a sleeping platform covered with straw was raised a foot above the ground. Our table was immediately in front of the entrance steps down which a stream of mud was slowly trickling.

The wall nearest the enemy had been hit by a shell and was stuffed up with sandbags. Beside the door a shaft had been dug, and in a small space, 20 feet down, I saw a candle burning and two signallers, one of whom, with the receivers strapped to his head, was reading a magazine; the other was preparing for sleep. Our table has been of good mahogany, but now is thickly coated with dirt and candle grease. One leg is broken and is supported on a champagne bottle.

The first four hours of duty was to be taken by Watkins, the second by me, and the third by Hatwell. When Sergeant Bell, with a dirty bandage round his neck, lifted the blanket and looked in, Watkins rose and prepared to go. I got up too, as I wanted to see the procedure. There are two blankets over the steps, one having to be lowered before the second is raised, to prevent the light showing, and also as a protection against gas. Passing out of the candle light, we stood still for a moment to get our eyes accustomed to the darkness.

The night was perfectly quiet, and we picked our squelchy way after Bell along the trench to the right. After ten or twelve yards we turned to the right, ducking under a trench board, and came to the first post. Here, with his head above the parapet, stood Private Newey, perfectly motionless. He answered our whispered questions without turning his head, and we stood beside him for a few moments peering into the darkness. Nothing could be seen or heard and we stepped down and talked to Corporal Bobby Wood who was in charge of the post. He showed us his shelter, a bare hole scooped out of the side of the trench; his six men were in a tiny shelter on one side.

Leaving them to their watch we passed on to the Lewis gun

post some dozen yards away. Here Corporal McKay, who was smoking his little pipe upside down, greeted us very cheerily and seemed quite happy. His gun was pushed forward down a little sap, along which we crept quietly to where the gunners were lying face downwards under a belt of wire, with their eyes glued on the faint outline of the ground in front. We could not talk so we returned to the trench.

The remainder of the line was very irregular and the posts seemed to be firing in different directions. At the end of our sector on the left, a communication trench ran back to the rear, and a little way down was a nice big shelter in which Sergeant Allsop and one or two men of 14 platoon were sleeping.

Close to our third post were two trees, one of which, stripped and shattered by a shell, was still standing; the other was cut in half and hung down across the trench like an arch. Under this ran a shallow trench which was a short cut back to our HQ. This trench we took, walking in the open for nearly 50 yards, which I thought a highly dangerous proceeding.

We very quickly struck the main trench almost at HQ and here I left them, re-entering the dugout to find Hatwell asleep and the servants gone. Helping myself to a large whisky and a chunk of bread and bully, I stared at Hatwell's muddy boots, and thought of what I had seen.

When we had been out of the line, I had despised these officers and NCOs and criticized the men, but now I realized that I was the most useless object in the Company. Immediately on entry, they had quietly melted away and taken up their duties, already keenly alert and capable, and here was I, still confused, wondering and fearful.

I drank several whiskies and dozed for an hour or two, but my brain was still active and my imagination running riot. After working myself into an acute state of nerves, I dropped off to sleep, but was almost immediately wakened by Watkins, who told me it was time for me to go on duty.

I waited for a few minutes, then, as my sergeant did not arrive, I went out alone in to the trench, where the eerie

influences of the night descended upon me. It was deathly
still, the mud, the smell of earth, the ragged sandbags, the
gruesome litter numbed my brain; a cold fear chilled my
spine and set my teeth chattering. I stood shaking and gazing
horrified into the darkness, thinking: 'this is *war*! and I am in
the firing line!' Then in a panic I set off down the trench.
Reaching the first corner I drew back sharply and my heart
stood still, for under the trenchboard bridge I saw a dark
form pressed against the side of the trench.

In horror I glued my eyes upon it; the light was growing
stronger, and it was quite distinct. And now I thought I saw
a stealthy movement. Drawing my revolver and with just my
head round the bend, I challenged it in a low voice. There
was no reply, and again I muttered 'Who goes there?' Still
silence, and with my gun well forward I advanced and
prodded—an old greatcoat hung on the trench side.

My relief at this anticlimax cheered me somewhat. Nevertheless, I hurried down that part of the trench to the first
post, where I stood beside Corporal Wood until Sergeant
Allsop arrived, apologizing for being late. For what seemed
an eternity we walked up and down the trench, until with
great relief I saw that it was 4 a.m. and I was able to go in and
wake Hatwell. After one or two more whiskies I turned in
and fell asleep in a moment.

February 15 At about 8 a.m. Hatwell woke me by shouting excitedly into the dugout. At first I was greatly alarmed
but seeing Dunham and Martin quietly preparing breakfast,
I took no notice until he came in and worried me to go out in
to the trench. When he got me out he waved his arm towards
the distance, beyond the Boche lines. 'Now isn't that beautiful? How can you lie hogging it on such a morning!'

I cursed him heartily. It was indeed a very nice morning,
but he had not called me out because he wanted me to see it—
it was because he was jealous of my being asleep while he was
on duty. As I turned to re-enter the dugout, he said 'There's
a job for you tonight,' and he pointed out a cluster of corpses

three or four yards behind the parados.

Lying flat on their backs, with marble faces rigid and calm, their khaki lightly covered with frost, some with no wound visible, some with blood clotted on their clothes, one with a perfectly black face, they lay at attention staring up into the heavens. This was my first sight of dead men and I was surprised that it did not upset me. Only the one with the black face has stayed with me. The thick, slightly curled lips, fleshy acquiline nose, cap-comforter pulled well down over his head and the big glassy eyes have become stamped on my brain.

Re-entering the dugout we sat down to breakfast, and with the bright sunlight streaming through the doorway, heartily did we enjoy the hot sausage and bacon that Martin laid before us. To me at least, the blue sky and bright air came as a wonderful relief after the never-ending night.

After breakfast I again went outside, and looking along the trench, could see in the distance a small town almost hidden amongst the trees, with the sun gleaming on the red roofs and stray patches of snow. This was the ancient town of Péronne, in the hands of the Germans.

It was now my turn for duty again, but during the day it is not necessary for us to remain in the line, as many of the posts are withdrawn and movement is not encouraged. As I mooned idly along, I picked up a tin hat, lying on the parapet. Turning it over I found the inside all gluey with blood, a small hole in one side showing where the bullet had entered. The coat which had frightened me last night had obviously been taken from a casualty, for the arm and side were ripped open and it was drenched with blood.

As I moved on, I found that this portion of trench ran towards the Boche, and seemed to be open to their view. I therefore crouched nearly double, and hurried along to the first post. In this posture I turned the corner and ran into Corporal Sissaman standing erect with rifle slung. He could not restrain his laughter, and blushingly I confessed that I was ignorant of the position and doubtful of the wisdom of

walking erect. Being assured that it was quite safe, I continued my tour of the line, walking freely. On reaching the
left post, I returned by the short cut, climbing out of the
trench over a huge rock which had blocked the junction of the
'switch'.

As I jumped into the trench by HQ, Hatwell cursed
Martin for a double-dyed idiot: he was preparing our lunch,
and from the brazier a steady column of smoke was pouring
above the parapet. Martin was not a bit disturbed, and told
Hatty that the sooner he went in and had his lunch, the
sooner the fire could be put out. So in we went and an
excellent lunch of fried steak was presented. As we ate it, we
revelled in the golden sunshine and blue sky and listened to
the cheerful and caustic banter passing between Martin,
Dunham and Davies who sat in the trench eating their own
food.

We were just finishing, when Martin gave a yell of warning
and threw himself on his face; in a moment the trench wall
opposite blew up, filling the dugout with dirt and fumes.
Two or three more explosions followed and the servants
came tumbling in, choking with dust and laughter. There
was quiet for a few seconds, then with a thud a great
grey-blue shell landed on the parados, rolled over, and lay
still.

Hatwell at once wrote the word 'Minnies' on a message
pad, speared it with a fork and chucked it down the shaft to
the signallers. These shells were 42-inch 'Minnenwerfers',
very destructive projectiles fired from a trench mortar; their
effect is so devastating and demoralizing that whenever they
are used we inform our artillery who plaster the enemy lines
heavily in retaliation. The idea is that their infantry will
know that every time the mortars are used, *they* will catch out
for it, so the weapon is most unpopular and its use is
becoming rarer.

For the remainder of the afternoon, our guns kept up a
continual plastering of the enemy support trenches. We were
left in peace and only one incident marked the next trip I took

into the open. I had decided to walk round the line, and started by traversing the short cut across the open. I had walked fairly leisurely along the shallow trench and was climbing over the fallen rock, when my foot slipped and I fell into the front line. Even as I fell, there was a crack and a chip of rock flew off. A sniper must have had me spotted all the time, and my slip was an act of Providence, though the sniper must have patted himself on the back for securing another victim. Obviously I must not use the short cut again in daylight.

When my tour of duty came round, I drew one or two men from the posts and went out to bury the bodies. It was very dark and we had to feel about to find them. When we tried to dig, we found the ground so hard that we could not get a pick into it. According to orders, also, we tried to take off their boots and equipment, but it was not very pleasant pulling frozen corpses about, so we decided that the country could afford to pay for that equipment, and we ended by covering them with old blankets, and piling the corners with stones, until the ground should be soft enough to bury them.

February 16 This morning, carrying out a few improvements to our dugout, we started to level up the ground under our table which is very rickety. The earth was spongy, and we started digging with entrenching tools, but we struck an old blue tunic, and when we gave it a tug, the resistance—and an unpleasant smell—warned us that we had a guest, so we apologized and patted the earth back. As we replaced the table, a message was brought up by a signaller that I was to report to HQ at 6 p.m. to proceed on a course.

So at 5 o'clock I filled my pack and set off with Dunham. The Battalion HQ dugout, being about 30 steps down, was very fuggy—no ventilation except the staircase which was screened by three blankets, a charcoal brazier glowing like a furnace, and 12 human beings living there. I stayed only long enough to get my papers and have a drink, but even then my head was throbbing when I climbed out with Thatcher of 'C'

Company, who is also going on the course—a refresher course in all subjects at the 48th Divisional School near Amiens.

When we reached the Herbécourt road, it seemed weeks since we had last seen it and, familiarity having bred contempt, we walked slowly, occasionally resting and watching the ration parties trudging by. At 9 p.m. we reached Cappy and took up our abode in an empty house whither our servants brought our kit from the Battalion dump. After a small meal of bully, we turned in. It must have been about midnight when I woke with violent pains in my tummy. I suffered agonies which grew worse and worse until I was hardly conscious. I groaned and rolled about until Thatcher thought—as I did— that I was going to die. Then at about 3 a.m. I was violently sick and the pain subdued. I think it must have been due to bad food or water. In any case I was quite fit in the morning.

February 17   We reported in the space outside the church, where were assembled two officers and servants from each battalion in the Division. We climbed into lorries and drove through Bray, Corbie, and Querrien to St Gratien, where the school is established in the grounds of a château. The mess is in the castle and we sleep in Nissen huts in the wooded park.

February 18   Sunday. Attended mass in the church of a tiny village which has obviously supported itself by catering for the château. After lunch Thatcher and I had a pleasant walk through the village and out into the country which is very charming. The snow has gone and the hillsides are delightfully green and fresh, dotted here and there with small copses and red-roofed isolated farms.

February 19–March 9   The course we are attending is typical of many which are continually running at similar places in the back areas. Its object is to keep officers in touch with those subjects of training which are necessarily neglected when in the line, particularly squad drill, company drill, musketry training and physical training. It may be refreshing for those who have been in the line for a long time, but being fresh from England, I find it very boring.

On Saturdays and Sundays we are able to get into Amiens where we have most enjoyable times. We revel in hot baths and delightful meals and occasionally a little flirtation. I have made friends with a dear little girl in a jewellery and gramophone shop in the arcade; we often call in and hear a few records, taking her a little gift of sweets. Once I met Bunn of the Gloucesters who told me that Frank was stationed close by and often came into the town, but I never ran across him.

I paid many visits to the Cathedral, which is very beautiful and dignified. We have also explored every part of the town and had meals or drinks in every hotel and café. Each Friday night we have a concert in the big salon of the château. I have sung at these, but was not a success.

A rumour was circulated, towards the end of the second week, that our line was about to advance, and on Friday, March 2nd we were warned to be prepared to join our units on Sunday. This attack did not, however, materialize and we completed the full three weeks of the course.

March 10   Departed in the lorry at 11 a.m. and bribed the driver to have a breakdown in Corbie where we had an excellent lunch in an excellenter club kept by two most excellentest little French girls. Then we proceeded to Cappy where we were dumped outside the church. Leaving our servants sitting on our kit, we walked on to Eclusier, where we were told our transport was stationed while the Battalion was in the line.

In an old billet on the canal bank we found the quartermaster, Harding, the French interpreter Talon, and Captain Billy Kentish whom I knew in England, and who has been in hospital for a few days with a metal chip in his eye. We despatched the mess cart for our kit and were just sitting down to tea, when we heard the sound of 'Archies' overhead.

Running out we saw the pink bursts surrounding a Boche aeroplane which was heading straight for a kite balloon hovering above us. He made one circle, one dive and then sped back to his lines. A wreath of smoke appeared and then the balloon burst into flames. We saw the two observers climb out of the basket and drop; their parachutes opened and very slowly they commenced to descend. But there was no wind to carry them away and after a few agonizing seconds the balloon collapsed and falling directly upon them bore them to the ground in its flaming folds, a few hundred yards from our hut.

One of the men, covered in flames and blinded, crawled out and collapsed; the other could not be reached, but his part soon burnt out, leaving him alive. He died, unconscious, at 7 p.m. The other is still alive. Almost simultaneously with ours, four other balloons in the distance came down in flames.

I learn that Hatwell is on leave in England, and that Anstey has taken over our Company, which is holding the front line just on the right of the dugout which I had been in during my last tour.

March 11   Sunday. Thatcher and I sorted out our trench kit during the morning, and at 3 p.m. started with our servants to walk up to the line. As we left Eclusier we saw a Boche plane making for the balloon which had ascended in place of the one burnt yesterday. But as soon as he approached, a circle of anti-aircraft fire was opened around the 'obso' and although he dived down, he did not fire it. The observers, however, were not taking any chances; they jumped out and with their parachutes floated away before a strong wind towards the line. As we reached Herbécourt we met them returning very red in the face, in an RFC tender which had followed them.

On reaching Herbécourt, we called in at the Divisional soup kitchen. These soup kitchens are established on one of the main roads whenever the Division is in the line. The idea is that any troops who are returning from the trenches tired, cold and hungry, can call in and have a can of mysterious broth which, if of doubtful composition, is at least hot and revivifying.

Here we learnt that the general opinion was that the Boche was shortly going to retire, and for that reason was destroying our balloons so that we could not observe his movements. We were also warned that there had been heavy shelling in front of the village and were advised to wait a bit. At this moment, there were four loud crashes further along the road, and a cloud of yellow and red dust marked the object of Jerry's hate—a new battery of 60-pound guns.

However, we decided to push on; and fortune favoured the bold, for with our approach the shelling stopped. It was really asking for trouble to walk down the road in the open, and as we were halfway down the ridge, a battery spoke in the distance. A salvo of shells crashed about us and we ducked into shell-holes, hoping this was but a casual burst. But more and more followed so we ran across the open field to the right as hard as we could go.

We jumped into an isolated bit of trench, where an RE Colonel joined us. He told us he was passing our Battalion HQ and offered to show us the way. So together we walked across the shell-pitted fields until we came to a battery of 18–pounders. Beside it was our HQ where we arrived just in time to join the CO and Adjutant at tea. Whilst we were eating, the pioneer sergeant brought in some crosses which he had made for the men whom I had covered with blankets and who were now buried. And when I went on to the front line, Dunham carried them along.

In an old cellar I found Watkins and an older fellow, attached from the 25th Londons, and chatted to them until 'Stand-to'. Stand-to is the name given to the period of one hour during which every soldier in the front line is on the alert. It takes place twice a day—the hour before sunrise and the hour after sunset. During these eerie periods of twilight, when normally all living things are just awaking or settling down for the night, the air is full of strange noises, the light is dim and deceptive and all things are most favourable for an attack. As a precaution, therefore, every officer and man gets into fighting order and for a solid hour remains at his post on the parapet with rifle loaded and bayonet fixed, until either day had broken or darkness descended and the order to 'Stand-down' is passed along.

Watkins was on duty first from 6 p.m. and I relieved him at 10 p.m. Sergeant Hughes was my NCO and I went out into the trench as he arrived. The rain has set in now, and all snow has long since disappeared. The trench sides are falling in, and the mud is up to our waists. It is impossible to walk through it and the only way to progress is to bury our arms in the sloppy mud of the trench sides and drag ourselves along.

We have still one post on the left of our dugout and this we visited; then, as I had not been round the trench on the right, I let Hughes take the lead, and dragged myself after him for about ten yards where he stopped and whispered to me that we were going straight on along the support trench but that on our left was a trench leading forward to post No 5, by which we would return.

The rain was pouring down and we were already soaked through. As we loosened ourselves in the mud, to continue our round, there was a faint 'pop' in the distance like a blank cartridge, followed by a rapid whistle and the sharp crack and flash of a bomb bursting about five yards away. Even as we ducked, there was another 'pop' and another bomb burst in the same place.

As we crouched low in the mud, they continued to fall about us, and Hughes whispered that they were *grenaten-werfers*—called by us 'blue pigeons' or 'pineapples'. He said that the sound of our squelching through the mud was perfectly audible in Jerry's line, and he would follow us with these bombs until we reached our right post, when he would open with a machine gun.

In no wise cheered by this prediction, I told him to push

on, and we continued to drag one leg after the other very, very slowly through the rain and darkness, ducking every few seconds as a singing, blinding crash flung 50 red-hot fragments about us. For about a hundred yards we proceeded thus and then we had to climb over an old iron pump which had fallen across the trench. While I was getting over, my tin hat fell on to it with a nerve-shattering clang and as I stooped to retrieve it, an angry burst of machine gun fire swept over our heads whilst a perfect hurricane of bombs fell about us. Several of them fell within two yards of us, but owing to the mud we were unhurt, one dud actually falling between us, and a few inches from where our faces were pressed into the side of the trench.

Another 50 yards, pursued in terror and with many prostrations, brought us to a voice, low and trembling, which commanded us to halt. It was Corporal Johnson who told me that his post was a few yards further on. In order to reach it, we had to cross an open sunken road, along which a German machine gun was trained almost at point-blank range. I waited while Hughes went across it at top speed; he had hardly set a foot on it when there was a violent crackling and spitting as bullets swept past us from a machine gun 30 yards away. With my heart in my mouth I waited until the burst ceased and then rushed across as fast as my casing of mud would allow me. As I reached the shelter of the trench on the other side the first rattle of bullets swept past.

The poor lads on this post were 'windy'. The long night of rain and darkness, the incessant bursting of 'pineapples' and bursts of gunfire, added to the loneliness, the strain of watching, the enforced silence and the nearness of the Germans, had played havoc with their nerves. I stopped for some time and tried to cheer them up in whispers before I moved forward up the short trench to the post in front.

Here we were right on top of the Boche and could move only by inches and breathe remarks. As I crouched beside the sentries I could quite distinctly hear the German sentries talking in low voices and an occasional burst of flame showed that the machine gun was only about a dozen yards in front. We were now obliged to recross the road, and much closer to the gun, but the road surface was so much harder that we were able to rush across together before he could switch his fire on us. So we reached the third post.

March 12 This post was a perfectly circular hole around which the six men lay in a little ring, the sentries peering over the top, the remainder huddled together chattering with cold and nerves. Corporal Bennett was in command, and he appeared to have thorough windup. When I had spoken a few words to them and was moving in down the trench, he came after me and asked if he could be relieved as he had lost his nerve. He was shaking with fear and I felt very sorry for him, but knowing that he would have to stick it, and that if I showed any clemency the rot would spread, I told him he was to return to his post at once, and set an example to his men instead of creeping away to ask to be allowed to run away from danger. This steadied him up, and he lost his nervous trembling. Pulling himself together he apologized in a firm voice, saying that he could not understand why he had cracked up then, as he had been in much hotter places without turning a hair. I told him not to worry and went on to No 4 post.

The rain had now ceased, and it was growing much lighter. The trench here, where Corporals McKay and Sissaman had post Nos 4 and 5, was much deeper and the men were fairly well sheltered. A German machine gun was, however, trained across this section, and incessantly sent mud flying over us as we plodded along. After passing the fifth post, the trench bent sharply back and grew very shallow. We crawled in the mud on our hands and knees under a coil of French 'concertina' which had dropped in from the wire entanglement above.

We were now back in the control trench outside our cellar. Our 300-yard tour of duty had taken $3\frac{1}{2}$ hours and now I just had time to re-visit No 6 post, when my time was up. I took

Hughes with me into the dugout and poured out a stiff tot of rum for each of us; then, sitting by the huge glowing brazier I commenced removing with a stick the two inches of slimy mud that encased me from the waist down and from shoulders to wrists.

After a few minutes Sergeant Bell looked in and I woke Holmes who shuffled out into the night; Sergeant Hughes finished his rum and went out too, leaving me alone with the fire and the rum. My revolver was choked with mud and I had to clean it before I could turn in, and this I did, sitting on one chair with my feet on another and the glowing brazier beneath my legs caking the mud upon me.

Finally, slightly loosening my equipment, and laying my tin hat and open gas helmet one on either side of my head, soaked and shivering outside, but glowing with rum inside, I fell asleep, to the sound of thuds and explosions outside and the rustle of magazine pages from the signallers down the shaft.

I was only able to sleep for about four hours as I had to be out for Stand-to at 6 a.m. However it was a beautiful morning, and as we cannot move about in daylight we do not have to do any duty during the day. Going into the cellar after Stand-down, I found Holmes making out a casualty report. When we had reached No 3 post, he had found Corporal Bennett dead, with three men; the other three men of the post were wounded. A few minutes after I had left them, a bomb had fallen amongst them. I told Holmes about Bennett's nervousness and sudden return to fatalism and we agreed that he must have had a premonition.

We were very quiet during the day; Jerry left us severely alone, although his aeroplanes were over all day. During the afternoon a message came through that we would be relieved tomorrow by the 7th Battalion. The night too was very much quieter although another bomb fell in No 3 post killing one and wounding two. The machine gun was farther back and less active. During my tour I buried the four casualties of last night, in shell-holes behind the post where they were killed.

After coming off duty, I was lying alone in the straw, and just dozing off, when I heard someone stop outside the cellar. Sitting up, I saw the blanket slowly lifted and a head appeared in the dim light of the candle. I hardly repressed a scream of horror, and an icy numbness gripped me as I scanned—a blackened face, thick lips and acquiline nose, big eyes that stared at me, and a cap comforter drawn down almost to the eyebrows. It was the face of the dead man that I had buried.

For fully half a minute we looked in silence at each other, then he asked me if I could tell him what time the rations would be up. I laughed hysterically and made him come in so that I could dispel by conversation the awful fright that his appearance had given me. It was Corporal Harrison, his face blackened with wood-smoke but his every feature identical with that of the corpse.

March 13 We had only sufficient rations to give us a very small breakfast, and then nothing was left over for the rest of the day. But we did not mind, for we were to be relieved at 7 p.m., a thought which made us very bright and cheerful throughout the day.

At 5 p.m., as we sat in our dugout, a message in Playfair code was handed up by a signaller. It took some time to decipher and it was 5.15 p.m. when Holmes read out the following message: 'Our heavy artillery will bombard enemy front lines, commencing 5.20 p.m. Withdraw advanced posts.'

Of course it was impossible to withdraw our posts, which were half an hour's crawl away, and it would have been foolish to attempt it. So we resumed our various occupations, Holmes making out a report, Watkins packing his kit, and I drawing a map of the trench in my Field Message Book.

At 5.20 a series of thuds was heard in the distance. Holmes murmured 'They're off!' and we waited for the shells to pass over. A second layer then came, whistling and moaning at first then with a shriek and roar growing louder and louder until with devastating crashes they exploded—30 yards *behind* us!

As we stared at each other in horror, another salvo came—Crash! Crash! Crash!—with earth-shaking explosions on top of us. The air hummed with fragments and acrid yellow fumes rolled down into the cellar. Now they rained upon us; all along the trench we could hear them falling, as we sat with fixed grins upon our faces, trembling in every limb. Holmes grabbed a pencil and scribbled a message, but as he crossed to the signallers' shaft, a louder, fiercer screech swooped upon us and a terrific crash flung us in all directions and into darkness.

It felt quite pleasant to be dead. There was such utter quiet and peacefulness. Just a light singing in my ears, restful blackness around me, and a sense of absolute freedom and abandon. I seemed to be standing up, and stretching out my arms I encountered, with a slight disappointment, a brick wall. Childishly I commenced to trace the patterns of the bricks with my fingers; then I heard a loud crash 30 feet away and Holmes' voice saying 'Is anybody hurt?'

I just realized that my mouth was full of dust, and that there was a big patch of light showing through the roof, when Holmes struck a match and relit the candle. We had had a miraculous escape, for the shell had hit the corner of the cellar and blown it in. The flying bricks and shell-fragments had spattered the walls but no one had been touched except Browne—Holmes' servant—who had been hit in the back by a flying brick.

Our guns had now ceased fire, but we could hear them receiving a few shells from the Germans. I now found that during the few seconds when I had believed myself dead, I had closed my note book, snapped round the elastic and returned the pencil to its socket.

Well, all was quiet now, and it was 6 p.m. We had only an hour before our relief was due, so Holmes sent Browne along to the neighbouring dugout to fetch Sergeant Phillips for his orders, whilst Watkins and I commenced to plug up the

gaping hole in our roof with sandbags, to prevent the light
shining through. It was now quite dark.

After a few minutes Browne returned, rather white in the
face, saying that he could not find the NCO's dugout. This
was only ten yards away, and consisted of an unfinished shaft
of a few steps leading to a tiny excavation in which there was
just room for three or four men to sit. Holmes guessed that
Browne was shaken up by the shelling, so he laughed and
said, 'Come on then, I'll help you to search for it, perhaps
someone's pinched it.' And they set off together down the
muddy trench.

I was just finishing off the roof, when Browne came
tumbling in moaning and laughing hysterically. He stared at
me screaming 'Oh God! It is. It is.' Then we slung him in a
chair, gave him a tot of rum, and ran off down the trench to
the mine shaft which had been occupied by Sergeant Phillips,
Sergeant Bennett, Corporal Everett and Corporal Hollins.

The last of the shells had obviously burst inside the shaft,
for the entrance was completely blocked, and the top of the
shelter was lying across the trench. In the faint light that still
remained we saw the sandbags and pieces of timber half
buried in the mud. Holmes stooped to raise one of these short
beams, then let it go, with a shuddering exclamation, for he
had bent back an arm with Sergeant's stripes. There was a
narrow gap through the blockage and we shouted down
through it, but our voices sank into the wet earth, and there
was no sound from below.

So we returned to the cellar to discuss the matter and found
Browne, gibbering and chattering like a monkey. First of all
we wired off the casualties to Anstey in code, and then we
went for the next senior NCO of each platoon. We explained
to them what had happened and instructed them to take
charge of their platoons and carry out the relief without letting
the men know about the casualties. These NCOs were very
badly shaken by the news, and particularly by the deaths of
the two brothers Bennett in succeeding days; there is a third
brother in the Company who is due back from leave tomorrow.

We sent the NCOs back to their posts and then decided that as it was nearly 7 p.m. and the relief would be in at any moment, we would be foolish to start getting the bodies out in a narrow trench through which the two companies would have to pass. So we left them, and when Antony—the relieving captain of the 7th Warwicks—arrived, we told him about it. He not only agreed to leave them for the moment but infuriated me by treating the matter as a joke.

I had just finished handing over when Wales, the Brigade Trench Mortar Officer, looked in for a drink. He was going my way, so we set out together. As the trench was so bad, we went across the top, passing by the graves of Underwood and the other men killed in the raid of February 4th. I had just begun to realize how hungry and tired I was, and as I turned my back on the horrors of the line, I thought of the food and warmth and sleep that awaited me at the rear; my heart began to glow and my head sang: 'Out of it! Out of it! In two hours I'll be home!'

As we picked our way round shell-holes and barbed wire, we heard the 'pineapples' begin to fall along the line; so we paused to watch their vivid flashes, until a sudden glare in the distance, followed by a whirl and rush, planted a couple of high-velocity shells 50 yards away, and we pushed on, jumping into the support trench outside Company HQ.

Down 30-odd steps I found Anstey in a small, hot dugout heavy with the smell of steak and onions, which made my mouth water and my eyes bulge. I reported that my platoon relief was complete, and as I was supposed to depart, he called me back and said 'I suppose the bodies have been buried?' I explained, of course, how the situation had made it impossible. He agreed that it had been, 'But,' he added, 'it is not impossible now.' He said that they must be buried before we left, and rushed a runner off to the main trench to collect any men of our Company he could find and bring them back.

Meanwhile he invited me to share his steak and onions, saying that when Watkins and Holmes arrived, we would toss up which of us should remain behind for the gruesome task. I gladly accepted the offer of a meal, but pointed out that the others had been in the line for seven days and I only three, so with his permission we would let them go off in ignorance of the job in hand. He agreed, and when they reported Relief Complete, I said I was waiting for Anstey and they went on—home.

A few minutes later we sat down to the table, and a servant placed before us a wonderful plate of steak. At the same moment the runner returned, reporting that Sergeant Hughes and six men were waiting outside in the trench. Anstey gave them instructions to go and commence work, and I would join them in a few minutes. Then, with a thrill of anticipation, I drew my plate towards me: Alas, too near! The newspaper tablecloth stuck out some inches from the table and on to this I pulled my plate, which capsized, sending my savoury meal into six inches of mud and water around our feet.

I wanted very much to cry, and when Anstey offered me a share of his, I shook my head. I took a hunk of bread and cheese and had just broken off a piece when a voice came down the steps. 'Sergeant 'Ughes 'as sprained 'is leg in the trench, Sir, and can't move.'

I laid down my bread with a sigh and, gulping down half a tumbler of neat whisky, passed up the steps amid the stream of smoke which continuously poured out. As I gained the open air, and paused to choke down the lumps of disappointment that kept swelling in my throat, the parapet in front leapt up in a sheet of fire, with a double crash. They had started shelling again, and bending double I ran down the trench to where a group of men hugged the side of the rivetted firebay in dead silence.

I tried, unsuccessfully, to get Hughes to move. He said it was an old knee injury, and that he could not possibly move, but that if we left him he would crawl back to an aid post as best he could. I could not afford to leave a man with him, so I left him, and in a moment he was hurrying back along the trench, while we plodded in dreary silence up to the line we had left in such glee an hour before.

We started at once to pull away the wreckage of the entrance, and had just come to Sergeant Phillips, when Jerry started his 'blue pigeon' strafe. Amidst their flashes and crumps we pulled him out and laid him behind the parapet. He had been killed by the dugout falling in as he ran up the steps, for there was no wound on his body but his head was crushed by the weight of sand-bags and timber from the roof. Two men started to bury him while we returned to the more horrible task of excavation.

As we worked down the sides, we realized (in the darkness) that the beams and sides were splashed with blood and flesh. The stench of lyddite and fresh blood was ghastly, and the foulness of our groping in the dark cannot be described. At last we could stand it no longer, and regardless of consequences, we lit a candle and commenced working by its shaded light. This evoked a shower of 'pineapples' and bullets which continued to fall until we had cleared the shaft.

Of Corporal Everett we found no trace; he must have been struck by the shell and blown to atoms. Bennett was badly shattered and most of his head was gone, whilst Hollins, who had been sitting with his rifle between his knees, was unrecognizable and the twisted rifle was buried in the front of his body.

March 14 It was early morning when we got them all out. Anstey had arrived, and he helped me to remove their papers and identification discs; then we buried them in shell-holes and walled in the dugouts with earth and sandbags. When this was done we sent the men on home and went into our old cellar to have a long peg of whisky with Antony.

As we left the cellar and climbed out on to the top I was forced to pause and moralize, gazing over the vaguely visible line of trench: to think of the mad fate which dragged simple, kind-hearted men into these nights of terror and destruction. Mostly my mind was occupied with the third Bennett who was by now waiting at our transport lines. I pictured him returning with messages from home for his two brothers, and the terrible shock it would be when he found that both were dead. From where I stood I could faintly see the roughness of the ground which marked where they were lying a hundred yards apart.

Turning into the shallow trench, where I had been so nearly sniped during my first tour, we struck across behind 'B' Company's sector into a sunken road—the continuation of the Herbécourt Road. Here there was another German machine gun which fired occasional bursts. As it was now growing lighter, we hurried on, zigzagging round shell-holes and hugging the bank until we were quite winded. We rested for a few minutes in a trench which cut the road, and then attacked the final spurt which had to take us over the ridge before the sun rose. As we hurried on, our packs growing heavier at every step, the sky in the east grew redder and redder until it changed to the white light of dawn, and just as we could say that it was really daylight, we crossed the ridge and were *safe*. Stretched by the side of the road we found our burying party, thoroughly exhausted; we shouted a few cheery words to them and passed on.

At Herbécourt soup kitchen we paused for a rest, and I tried to swallow some cabbage soup. But as the only food I had had in 24 hours was a half slice of bread and a piece of bacon, the greasy liquid made me feel sick and I left it. The morning was clear, bright and delightful. Outside the soup kitchen was an ambulance, and a motor bus which had been converted into a pigeon loft around which the pigeons were fluttering and cooing. The drivers were asleep in the ambulance and there was no other sign of life.

Asking the cook to be kind to our fellows when they arrived, we set off again, warmed by the rising sun and feeling very happy. We were out of the mud and muck, away from the bombs and shells, the rain and darkness, the blood and smells. Out in the free air where we could walk erect and talk aloud. The wonderful freedom drove away our weariness and our hunger; with our heavy packs we ran and jumped over shell-holes, laughed and sang and drawing our revolvers potted at birds which shrugged their shoulders and flew off. When a GS waggon met us and the driver said that he had been sent to carry us back, we laughed merrily, telling him to go on and pick up our troops and we would be at Eclusier two hours before him.

March 15 Arose at 9 a.m., having slept the clock round. We did no work all day, but held an inspection of rifles, gas helmets and iron rations. In the afternoon we went into a quarry and potted at tins with our revolvers. Anstey had been up last night and got very tight. He was not at all washed out by the tour in the line, but I was very nervy and ducked every time I heard a sharp noise.

March 16 Did no work during the day, but at dusk moved up to Herbécourt to mend roads. I suffered from an extra-ordinary delusion on this occasion. Before we left, Kentish, who was to command the working party, showed me the map and pointed out the place where we were to work—the road from Herbécourt to Flaucourt. It was bitterly cold, and I was not pleased at the thought of standing about in the darkness for hours. But then the picture of Flaucourt came into my mind. I imagined our arrival there after working along the cold wet road. The warm glow of the windows, the smell of the coffee shops and *épiceries* and the rosy, warmly-clad villagers who would greet us. The picture made me quite cheery although in my sane mind I *knew* that the village is razed to the earth, being only just behind the line. Still, all the way up the Herbécourt road the image remained with me and kept me cheerful. The snow had returned, and the ground was covered in a thin white sheet.

In front of Herbécourt we commenced work: filling up shell-holes and levelling bumps. It was a very irritating task, especially as no smoking was allowed, and progress was very slow. At about midnight I went with Kentish to the soup kitchen to arrange for the men to have a meal when they had finished work. Here we found eight or ten men who had sneaked off from their work in the dark. Billy took their names and sent them back.

As we progressed along the road, it became evident that we would not reach Flaucourt that night, so leaving my men at work, I walked on myself to see my little Christmas-card village. The road here was more torn and pitted than ever, and after a quarter of an hour, I found myself standing on top of a trench system, which ran around the foundations and ruins of some houses. Not a single wall was standing—all was a jumbled mass of broken brick and twisted iron. This was my village and I could have wept with disappointment. As I turned to go, I heard someone coming through the village, and I waited so as to have company on my return.

It was a private of the 4th Gloucesters, slightly wounded and very jubilant. 'Do you know, Sir!' he cried, 'We've got their lines?' I told him I had not heard of any attack, and he shook his head knowingly. 'There was none, Sir! We thought, d'you see, that they was very quiet, so we showed ourselves a little bit at first, and nothing happened. Then we sent a feller out just before dark: he walked slowly across, waitin' for a shot to be fired, but none came. He went on over their first line, and over their second, and then when he reached the third line we all went over. There wasn't a Jerry anywhere except a few stiffs. They've gone clean back over the canal. And the trenches they had! Why, Sir! we was living in *muck* to them!'

I asked him how he was wounded if there were no Germans, and he became suddenly serious. 'Ah Sir!' he replied. 'We've lost a lot of good fellies. The trenches were left full of booby-traps. All I did was to pick up a Hun's helmet from the floor of the trench, and a bomb went off underneath. Lucky for me, Sir, that it was buried, and I only got it slightly. Ye'll perhaps know Mr Harcourt of the 6th Warwicks, Sir? Well he's bought it. They went over on our right at the same time and he went down a dugout, but as soon as he put his hand on the hand rail, the two bottom steps blew up, and took both his legs off. He died before they could get him away.'

Poor old Harcourt, he was bound for Blighty in a couple of

days time, though from what I saw of him he is booked for the best of Blighties.

When we reached my working party, I left the wounded Gloucester to tell his news to my troops. They did not betray the slightest excitement; with only a mild interest they enquired 'Plenty of souvenirs?' What to me was the glorious rout of the enemy and retreat of the Imperial Army meant to them 'more blank marching!'

March 17 At 2 a.m. we finished work and sent the troops back to the soup kitchen, leaving them to have a meal and a rest and then find their own way back to the billets. Then spotting an inviting glow from a dugout, Kentish and I went in to cadge a drink. We found that it was occupied by some officers of the Engineers who were on the point of departing to construct a bridge across the Somme Canal where the enemy had retreated. They told us that the retirement had been expected for a long time, and that they had had the bridging materials ready behind the line. When we reached our billets we learnt that 'A' and 'C' Companies had already moved up to the pursuit of the Huns. 'C' Company was at that moment—4 a.m.—preparing to take Péronne and we were to move up later in the day.

I slept from 4 to 9 a.m. and then got busy supervising the cleaning of billets, issue of rations and packing of kits. At 5 p.m. we marched up the Canal Bank Road, led by Anstey. It poured with rain and was very dark. Soon we followed Anstey into a little wood. We passed in single file beneath the dripping trees for a hundred yards, then halted in an open clearing. I heard no orders given but suddenly found that the troops had melted away. I was left alone, marvelling at the manner in which they seem to divine instinctively where their positions are and go to them without being shown.

I sat on a wet tree-stump, looking round at the snowing slush and the shell-bitten trees until Anstey returned, with Dunham, and I followed him to what appeared to be a trap-door into the ground. Descending a short wooden ladder we entered a gallery, lighted by the rays of a lamp burning in a small room with glass-panelled doors on the left.

In this dugout we found Captain Taylor, commanding 'A' Company, which we were relieving. Before he left he gave us a very longwinded account of the day's events. The Boche retirement—long anticipated by our HQ—had taken place just before dawn on the 16th. At dusk the 4th Gloucester and our 6th Battalion had gone over into their lines, but had been held up at the canal, as the bridges had been destroyed. Pontoon boats had then been provided by the REs, and 'A' Company had crossed at Halle, whence they marched to Sainte Radegonde where they halted at 5 a.m. 'C' Company, crossing in the same way, marched up past them along the main road to Péronne, which they entered—unmolested except for a few snipers' bullets—at 7.30 a.m. on St Patrick's Day. The positions which we were taking over now were in reserve, and Taylor was going forward to establish his HQ in Halle.

After Taylor had left, Anstey rose, saying that he had to return to Battalion HQ for a conference and would not return that night. So I proceeded to turn the dugout into a home by opening my pack and disposing around me my raincoat, some cigarettes and bits of chocolate, my *Palgrave's Golden Treasury* and some Harrison Fisher girls which I carried about to enliven such quarters as these.

March 18 Sunday. At dawn I tried to follow the posts by myself and for a long time was hopelessly lost—so I guess it comes with experience. At 8.30 Major Gell, the second in command, came along and fussed about our positions, wanted a Lewis gun covering this point, a sniper on that, a fire trench here and a grenade party there! I worked hard to carry out these redispositions and was just in the middle of reorganization when a runner called me to answer the field telephone. It was he again, speaking from HQ. I was to leave what I was doing and take one platoon to reconnoitre the road to Péronne ready for the advance.

So I detailed the platoon to get ready, and sat down to write a note to Anstey saying where I had gone. While I was writing, a runner came with a message *from* Anstey ordering me to take one NCO back to Feuilleres on the canal bank and there find billets for the Company, which he was going to collect and march back immediately.

It was a bright clear morning, and the country looked beautiful as I set off across the open fields with Corporal Sissaman. The place where we had spent the night was Bazincourt Farm, just to the left of Biaches. It was a high position overlooking the canal and the litter of cartridge cases on the posts proved that the enemy snipers had had ample opportunities of showing their prowess.

The gently undulating fields were very little shelled, and the fresh grass was only spoiled here and there by a circular mud-rimmed hole. But each field was liberally besprinkled with graves, in which we took morbid interest. Not one of them had been dug to any depth, and in each case some portion of the corpse protruded—from one a bleached and polished skull, from another a rotted puttee and boot, from another the ammunition pouches. In several cases they had only been covered with a few inches of wet earth which now was caked and hard giving the appearance of mummies, except where the burrowing rats had broken away the mud and displayed a patch of blue tunic.

There were a few unburied bodies about and I had much difficulty in getting Sissaman past them—he wanted to stop and examine each for wounds and souvenirs. As it was, I'm afraid we progressed very slowly and it was 2 p.m. when we slid down the bank into the sunken road beside the canal, where the littered dugouts and gun emplacements betrayed the hasty advance of our gunners. Following the canal, we came to Feuilleres where we found Battalion HQ in a large, badly-battered house.

They could not give me any assistance in my task, so I started off on my own to find billets for the Company. I had just found one wretched shelter in a field to hold six men, and a portion of a house which would take a dozen, when the Company marched into the village. Anstey led them into a field, where our cookers were preparing dinner, and here they sat on the grass and ate their meal, while Anstey and I fished some lunch out of our mess box. Before we could commence it, however, a runner came to tell us: 1) We were to stop billeting, 2) We were marching up the line again at once, and 3) We were to report to HQ immediately.

The only thing I did at HQ was to have a good lunch, but Anstey was told to return to 'B' Company as Billy Kentish had turned up to resume command of 'D'. I was wondering what had happened to Watkins, who has been missing since we left the trenches, and I learnt that he had returned to the Worcesters.

At 5 p.m. it commenced to rain; at 6 it was dusk and we once more set foot on the Canal Road. I don't know what possessed Billy to bring his horse with him, but he optimistically started off, riding at the head of the wondering troops. After about a mile, the road became a mere muddy track, which we had to follow in single file. Kentish had to dismount and at times, when we came to fallen trees, he fell over them and then spent five minutes lifting his horse over. Finally the road was so bad and the darkness so intense that we were in danger of walking into the canal, so Kentish led us off the road through a gap in the hedge into the fields on our right.

Here we wandered for half an hour until, hopelessly lost, still carrying his horse, and raving like a lunatic, Billy slung the reins to one of the men and plunged off alone into the darkness, leaving us standing in the drizzling rain. Twenty minutes later we heard his voice shouting to us to lead on, and we marched after his voice, which we followed to a decent road that brought us to a point on the canal where the REs were constructing a bridge. We crossed a Heath-Robinson arrangement of planks and string and formed up on the wet marshes beyond the river. What happened to the horse I do not know, but it was not with us, and I suspect Billy of having consigned it to a watery grave.

A short march up the marshy track, a turn to the right along a decent road, and in ten minutes we were in Halle. We halted here at 'A' Company HQ and Billy and I went in to see Sullivan, who had 'captured' the village. We found him very luxuriously accommodated in a room furnished with cosy armchairs, mahogany pierglass, bedstead, curtains and carpets which the Boche had left behind. On the walls of the rooms, the playful Hun had left many sketches and ironic messages. Two that we saw were 'Great British Advance. Many villages taken' and 'Haig takes Halle, 4,000 Germans captured—official'. Sullivan pressed us to stay, and we accepted a drink and a cigar from a box decorated with a picture of the Kaiser and listened to his excited account of the advance.

We finished our drinks and continued our march for about half a mile, when we again halted, this time before a darkened and lonely house, which we found to be our Battalion HQ. I did not enter, having a feeling that I was small beer in their esteem, but Kentish went in for a chat, and I expect a drink. He was not very long and again we set off 'nach Péronne'.

The road along which we marched was lined with trees, and through these, from time to time, we caught glimpses of a fierce glow in the distance. Then we came to a place where the Germans had blocked the road by felling a large number of trees and as we made a detour across the fields we came into full view of the fire that was raging in Péronne. During all this march I was very nervous. I had heard so many stories of booby-traps and delayed mines that I was terrified by the sight of any old oil drum or coil of wire, and at every crossroads expected to find myself sailing up into the black sky. Nothing of the sort happened, however, and after passing first a few scattered houses, and then regular rows, at 11 p.m. we marched into the principal street of the town.

We did not enter the square, but I got a glimpse of it as we passed the end, and I saw that at this far end all the houses were in flames. A few figures were silhouetted against the blaze and the lurid light danced and flickered over the rough shell-torn cobbles, and over all the rain poured steadily down.

We marched straight on down a short narrow road and then halted. Once again the troops melted into the darkness and I was alone with Kentish and the servants. Following them into a house close by, I found a large party assembled in the cellar. To one corner of the room Martin brought our mess boxes, but I was too excited and nervous to eat anything, so after a couple of drinks I went down the two steps which Kentish told me led to our sleeping quarters. This was merely another cellar, which the Boche had partitioned off into cubicles, fitted with wire beds. There was a filthy smell of decaying vegetable matter which I could not locate. Our room was very tiny with a bed on each side, and between them a stove from which an iron chimney passed out into the open air through the cellar ventilator.

Kentish came in a few moments later, and we both lay down, covered with our macs, and composed ourselves to sleep. Soon I heard the servants tramping overhead to their several sleeping quarters. One by one the officers retired and all was quiet save for the drip, drip, drip of the rain and an occasional bluster of wind in the courtyard over our heads. Kentish was already breathing deeply and regularly in the other corner.

Tired as I was, I could not sleep, but lay awake thinking of the events of the past few days. It seemed years since we had spent that nightmare day in the cellar in Biaches, but it was less than a week; and it was only ten days since Harcourt and I tossed for leave. Poor old Harcourt! It was such rotten luck to go through trench raids and attacks and then be blown up by a booby-trap mine. That was a terrible, unforeseen death and . . . Good God!—an icy hand clutched my heart.

Here was a perfect billet, dry, well furnished and comfortable. In the villages, tiny hovels had been blown up, entrances to waterlogged dugouts had been smashed in—why had this been left? Obviously it was a trap and, fools that we were, we had walked into it. The sound of Kentish's light snoring maddened me. I strained my ears, and above the dripping of the rain I fancied I could hear the tick-tock of a fuse. This grew louder and louder until I could stand it no longer, and by coughing loudly and banging the bed, I woke Kentish.

He sat up grumpily, rubbing his eyes. 'What was that blasted row?'

'Which one?' I said guiltily. 'There's lots going on.'

He listened for a moment and then lay down again growling. But I didn't intend to let him sleep. 'Did you hear about the booby-traps in the Boche lines?'

'Um!'

'You know Sullivan found several in Halle?'—no answer.

'How long do they usually delay before exploding?'— silence. I paused a bit and then asked timorously, 'I say, Billy, can you hear a curious ticking?'

He pulled the coat from off his head and said 'You bloody fool,' and snuggled down again.

I was hurt by that, for I felt that nobody cared if I *was* blown up, so I resolved myself to die like a martyr and then when we met in the afterworld I could say to Kentish 'I told you so!' The consideration of this possibility rather cheered me, and casting aside my fears I fell asleep.

March 19 I do not know how long I slept, but it must have been a couple of hours. I dreamt that I was lying there asleep, all being horribly quiet except for the drip of water and the wind. Suddenly through the rain and darkness appeared a huge figure stealing across the courtyard to the grating above me. He was muffled up in a great grey coat and spiked helmet. I struggled to wake Kentish and to shout, but I was power- less. I saw him take a bomb from under his coat, a smoking bomb, and slip it into the chimney. With a frantic struggle I overcame my paralysis and sat up shouting as a metallic sliding sound came from the chimney. Waiting for the explosion, I sat staring into the darkness with that apathy that comes when fear has passed its bounds.

But nothing more happened. Kentish slumbered on, and

feeling I could not stay another minute I slipped on my mac and went out into the rain. The morning must have been sending its first rays of light into the misty darkness for I could dimly discern my surroundings, which were ruined houses and piles of wreckage. There was no road left, for the houses on either side had for the most part been blown up, and now the place was one long pile of bricks, earth, broken furniture, old clothes and twisted ironwork.

Across this miniature mountain range had been worn a tortuous track which I now followed until I was back on the road running into the square. The rain was now very much heavier, but it was growing rapidly light and soon I was able to take a more detailed view of the town.

The crossroads at which I stood was fairly clear, only a few shells having torn up the cobbles, leaving small jagged holes at intervals. On my left the front of a house had fallen leaving the undisturbed interiors of the rooms exposed like a large dolls' house. Opposite me was a barn through the open doors of which I could see one of our 'cookers' glowing. Outside were a perambulator and two huge, wicked looking 'minnen-werfer' shells.

Walking down to the square where the houses were still burning, as I passed the town hall I saw the huge façade of two houses sway forward in the wind. I drew back and, standing under the colonnade of the town hall, watched the huge slice of masonry lean forward, pause, and then crash in a cloud of brickdust into the square. The interior of the house I saw, as I passed on, had been previously demolished.

I now found myself in the square, the general aspect of which was one of cruel and dreary devastation. All the houses on my left were in ruins, whilst those on my right, though still standing, were badly battered, all doors and windows being smashed in. Opposite me the whole side was enveloped in tremendous walls of fire.

Near the centre of the square, an iron paling surrounded a stone pedestal, from which the statue had been removed. I walked over to it, wondering what statue had been there, and then I stopped—sickened by the sight of a body impaled on the iron spikes. In a Frenchman's blue uniform, gaily bedecked with ribbons, he hung with arms extended along the railing, his head hanging down on to his bright-buttoned chest, and his legs dangling.

Sick with horror but impelled by curiosity I went nearer, and saw some straw sticking out at the knee. Then I peered into the face—a black grinning mask—and saw that it was a realistic dummy. Nevertheless, in the eerie half-light, with the flicker of flames on that scene of devastation, it was a gruesome spectacle, and walking on I stood for a while at heat-range from the flames into which the heavy rain poured with no effect whatever.

Then I returned to the vast pile of ruins beside the pedestal and started to explore. Reapproaching the town hall I saw, fastened to its side wall, an enormous blue notice board— 'Nicht ärgern nur wundern!'—'Do not be angry, only be surprised'. This in letters a foot deep.

People were now stirring in the billets and as I passed the corner I saw the cooks—'Blackie' Neale and Brakespeare—in the barn, cleaning dixies for the Company's breakfast. I stopped and had a real sergeant major's cup of tea with them, before climbing back over the brickpile to our cellar. I noticed that opposite us was an enormous rectangular building in a large courtyard. The gates were shut and locked, so apparently no one had entered. At the end of the street—a hundred yards away—I could see the marshes of the Somme Canal.

We had a rotten breakfast, for our servants had let the HQ staff collar all the fuel and cooking places and most of the crockery, after which we sat and smoked until lunchtime, when received a warning order that we would move again that night. In the afternoon, I went up to the square again with Thatcher; on the way he told me that when he entered the town, the dummy Frenchman was standing erect upon the pedestal in an heroic attitude. He had lined up his platoon and fixed a volley at it, bringing it tumbling down into the position in which I had found it.

At 5 p.m. we paraded and marched out of the town dead away from the square through the ancient arch of the Faubeurg de Bretagne, where high grass-covered slopes marked the old fortifications of the town. With the last house, the cobbled road ended, and we came to the junction of two poorly made roads; we took the right-hand one, filing round a long-dead horse that lay sprawled across the way.

Just as it became dusk, we reached the edge of a deep quarry, the whole of which was overgrown with bushes and sodden with rain. The ground was slippery with mud, but we descended by a beautifully constructed winding stairway which brought us to the mud-track at the bottom of the shrubberies. There was practically no cover, so the troops commenced to make themselves bivouacs out of their oil-sheets, whilst Kentish and I established our HQ in a tiny tarpaulin hut. This was quite bare and empty; the rain dripped through in many places and altogether it was most uninviting. So I dumped my pack and went out again into the murky downpour.

Quite close to us the Boche had constructed a kind of pagoda of rustic wood; it appeared to be full of rubbish and on it was chalked 'Reserved for Batt. H.Q.' There had obviously been a German battery here, and during their spare time the gunners had beautified the place exceedingly. In all directions ran flights of steps with rustic hand-rails; rustic tables and seats were scattered about; and a huge rustic cross rose above a little row of graves at one end. Most of the shelters, however, were burnt, so we had very little practical benefit from their labours.

Returning to the hut I found it looking quite homely after the rain and mud in which the unfortunate troops had to spend the night. Our valises were laid out and a couple of candles were burning; the troops had filled up the larger holes with paper and laid out supper, on which Billy had already made a fair start. Removing my boots I crawled into my valise; I was very wet but as my valise also was soaked through, it didn't matter. Then I made a hearty meal of bread, bully and jam, and lit a pipe while we supped hot rum.

Billy told me that we were in reserve to the front line and were in a quarry near Buire Wood. We were well within gun range, but clear of the enemy infantry. The mention of 'gun range' made me nervous again and I began to show it by asking questions. I was keen to know what cover we should take in case of shelling. He answered abruptly, 'There isn't any cover,' and blew his candle out. I followed suit, and pulled the clothes over my head to shut out noises, but in a few minutes I heard a thud in the distance.

'Was that ours or theirs?' I asked.

'Ours now!' And there was an impatient turn and snuggle.

Another thud! 'How far away was that?' No answer. It made me worse to think that he was going to sleep to leave me to face the danger alone. So I asked him: 'I say, if a shell got us, would it hit the top of the quarry first, or drop straight in?' At that he sat up in bed. 'You *are* a windy young b——— Vaughan! You've got to chance it wherever you are, so for God's sake shut up and go to sleep.'

I did shut up, but, though thoroughly ashamed, I was still windy, and long after the distant shelling had stopped, I lay awake waiting for more thuds. At last, however, the lack of sleep on the previous night did its work and I slept peacefully until the sun was well up, and breakfast was cooked.

March 20 Major Gell came along during the morning and commandeered my platoon (and me) to clean out the pagoda ready for occupation by HQ. I say he collared us to do it, but actually we hardly did a thing, for he is a most energetic man, and clad in motor cycling leggings and coat he dashed here and there carrying stoves and rubbish, seizing brooms to show the lads how sweeping should be done, and by tea time had the place clean enough for the meal to be served therein.

At sunset I went for a walk round the top of the quarry. There was, however, nothing to be seen but undulating slopes of grass, and as I had not the faintest idea where the enemy line was, I could not work up an interest. I turned in early and was a little less windy—although the Boche shells fell much closer.

March 21 Without any warning we were suddenly paraded at 10 a.m. and marched all the way back to Eclusier, via Péronne, Halle, Feuilleres and Frise. It was a long march and we were thoroughly tired when we arrived back at our original camp on the canal bank. The rain had stopped, and it was like coming home to get back into the old cubicles. We celebrated by sitting round a huge fire—the two of us—and drinking rum punch. I was beautifully sleepy and happy when I went to bed. Nevertheless I lay awake for a long time looking at the huge brazier throwing a vivid light over the room, and a flood of memories came upon me.

I thought of the people at home, and what they were all doing then; of the 3/8th Battalion, of Watkins and Thomas and our first tour up at Biaches—what years ago that seemed. And with Jerry retiring it was obvious the war was ended. I wondered if I should meet Watkins again. Or Thomas.

March 22 We were all sent along to QM stores to draw a new kind of gas helmet. A rubber face piece with a tube leading to a canister of chemicals; the whole installed in a square satchel to be carried on the chest. The troops are quite annoyed at having 'another bleedin' present for the Christmas tree'. We of HQ have also been dished out with new tin hats fitted with a rail and hanging chain mesh to protect the eyes. We spent the afternoon putting on the gas-masks to make animal noises at each other, and saluting to make the helmets clank.

Attended a lecture during the afternoon in Cappy. It consisted of instructions concerning the new gas helmets by the Divisional Gas Officer. Thatcher, Bridge and Sullivan also attended and on our way back we called at every mess to have a drink and look out acquaintances; also bought large quantities of tinned fruit. On the road met Private Davies of the Worcesters who had been Watkins' servant. He told us that Watkins had left that battalion and joined another division.

March 23   The Battalion marched back to Péronne today but I was left behind with 13 and 14 platoons to guard stores until the transport collected them. I wandered round the billets picking up oddments—French and German bullets and handbooks—until 3 p.m. when two GS waggons turned up. They could only take half the stores, so that we had to remain for the night.

March 24   I spent the morning with the two platoon sergeants—Hughes and Allsop—making out platoon rolls. During the afternoon the waggons rolled up and were reloaded and despatched. Shortly afterwards a small party of NCOs reported to me. They were Sergeant Major Chalk—of my Company who had first met me in Hallencourt—now returning from leave—Sergeant Wheeldon, Sergeant Corbett and Sergeant Foster. I told them that we were rejoining the Battalion on the morrow and they should wait and march up with us. From Dunham I learnt that charge sheets would probably follow them as they were ordered to remain at base for duty; being anxious to get back, however, they had broken camp and stowed away on a ration train.

They all seemed to be excellent fellows and with the exception of Corbett were coming to 'D' Company. He it appears was a splendid NCO until he was badly wounded on the Somme in 1916, after which he went quite silly. Whenever he gets into the line he goes mad, though he never shows any fear. At one time he secured a dugout, and if any stranger or undesirable visitor entered it, he hammered the fuse of a dud 9.2″ shell with an entrenching tool, until he was again alone. He had been wounded a second time in a raid and was now returning from hospital.

March 25   Sunday. Set off at 11 a.m. and plodded up the muddy roads through Halle to Pérrone, which we found very much cleaner, working parties having been busy on the roads; at 'dead-horse crossroads' we took the left road— merely a muddy track—and at 4 p.m. reached the outskirts of Driencourt. Here I saw a signboard indicating Battalion HQ, which I found in a trench. They told me that Hatwell had returned from leave and was now taking over the Company, now in the village of Templeux-la-Fosse, to which they gave me a guide.

As we entered the village, the guide cheered me up by telling me that Jerry had been shelling the village all day. The street down which we started to march sloped from the top of a hill, and in front where the houses stopped we could see that it rose again to the top of a green ridge at our own level. We marched for about 50 yards and then a sentry on 'B' Company HQ shouted to us to move along the houses in single file. We did this, but saw no reason for it as we heard no shelling before we pulled up outside our HQ. I went into a courtyard to find Hatwell, passing two men with dixies going to draw water from the well.

He was sitting just inside a doorway drinking whisky with Kentish; I poured myself a drink and reported myself. Two minutes later there were two sharp crashes nearby, then Anstey blew in with some more of his company and we all went into the courtyard to study the map. We had been there scarcely a minute when a distant 'bang' sent us flying to the door. I was last in and was sprinkled with mud as a shell burst a few feet from where we had been standing.

I said to Anstey in great apprehension, 'Would this wall stop one, do you think?'

He replied dryly, 'It probably will!' And then the party broke up.

I went out again with Hatwell and he pointed out, on the distant ridge, the gun that was doing the damage. It was a field gun worked by four men with an officer watching us through glasses and directing the fire. Then we went in and finished our drinks and he said 'Come along. I'll show you where to go and you can push off with your platoons.' He went out on the road and I, having stopped to put on my pack, followed him. As I emerged, there was a crash, and I ran round the corner to see him lying on his back in the smoke of a shell.

Corporal Newey was standing outside, and as he moved forward he said 'Hatty's a goner!' Whereupon Hatwell sat up and said 'You're a bloody liar. Come and lift me up.' We carried him into the house where we found two perfectly round and bloodless holes in his thigh. He had had a wonderful escape for the shell had burst almost at his feet. He wasn't a scrap disturbed by his wounds, but they made me feel faint and I had to go out for some air. In the courtyard I found Major Gell looking for me. He instructed me to take two NCOs at once over to the Bussu Road and find accommodation for the Company.

I obeyed him with alacrity, and as I collected the NCOs I heard that the two men who had gone for water had been killed at the well, and a third man blown down into it. It was dusk when we passed through the back of the courtyard, vaulting over the low stone wall, and hastened by the fall of another salvo of shells. Crossing the sodden fields we very soon struck the point shown me on the map, and struck round in the darkness for shelters.

In a very few minutes we found three large dugouts, each with two entrances, so I sent off a message to Gell and posted the other NCO on the road to guide the troops in. I then settled down in the centre dugout, which the Boche had evidently used as an HQ. It was divided into two parts, one of which I allotted to the sergeants, the other, with five wire beds, I made our combined mess and servants' quarters.

Here Kentish joined me at 9.30 p.m. and we proceeded to make ourselves comfy; sitting on German grenade-boxes, whiskies before us, a glowing brazier at the side, and with two or three sandbags wrapped round each foot, we were at peace with the world, and we discussed our probable future and the events of the past few weeks until 11 o'clock when we climbed into our wire beds.

I lay for a while on my upper berth, smoking and reading a book on trench warfare. Then I began to feel itchy, and the itchiness grew, and spread so much that I was unable to concentrate on my book. So I lay on my back looking at the timber roof a foot above me, and I wondered whether the saw-marks across the beams were the work of the Boche to ensure the roof falling in when a time-mine exploded. I was distracted from this thought, with its potential horrors, by the sight of moving insects. Raising the candle I found that the place was crawling with lice. During the night I felt them dropping onto my face, and in the morning I was infested with them.

March 26 As soon as I woke I went out into the open, where I was met by a delightfully fresh breeze. The sun had risen and the fields, trees and bushes looked beautifully sweet and green. There were no shell-holes, and the new grass of the fields was besprinkled with gem-like wild flowers. A few hundred yards away across the road was Buire Wood.

I filled my lungs with sweet air, and my eyes with restful green and then walked along to the next dugout to visit the gas sentry. I was unable to find him and my shouts down the staircase brought out Corporal Oldham who told me that Private Dredge was on duty. We found him halfway down the steps of the next entrance—fast asleep. Woke him with a few well-chosen words, and left him under arrest. Then I went along and chatted with the other sentries, and such NCOs as I found seated by the roadside taking stock of their surroundings.

Over breakfast I told Kentish that I had put Dredge under arrest for sleeping on sentry. He didn't quite know what to do, for if he had charged him officially, it would have to be tried by court martial and the penalty would be death. So he decided to have him in and frighten him, then let him go. While he was doing this, a terrific howling arose from a dugout which we had forbidden the troops to enter on account of falling walls. On investigation we found Swindon, a village idiot type of soldier, half buried by a fall of earth. He had gone in to look for souvenirs, and when we had dug him out, Kentish delivered a second lecture, this time taking as his text 'Be sure your sin will find you out'.

At 5.30 p.m. we fell in on the road in marching order. At the same moment, as usual, it began to rain heavily and it became dark quickly as we marched towards Templeux. After about a mile, when the roads were nice and slushy and we were wet through, we left the road and followed a faint track to the right which took us to Tincourt Wood.

It was now pitch dark, and we entered the wood in single file, keeping touch by holding the equipment of the man in front. I was last man, and after a short while, the party having halted, and a confused murmur of voices rising in front, I went forward and found that Dunham had fallen over a tree stump, let go the man in front, and so lost touch. I gave instructions that no one was to move, and then set off as fast as I could to find the leading half-company. I successfully lost myself and for about 20 minutes wandered about the black, dripping wood shouting at the top of my voice. Then I saw a faint light flashing in the distance and following it came upon Kentish and Sergeant Major Chalk, who, having led the rest of the Company in, had come back to find me.

Close at hand was a tiny tarpaulin hut which was now our HQ, and when we were seated therein with drinks, Billy told me that the Company was holding a line of posts in front of the wood, which we would have to visit by turns. Half an hour later he went out for the first tour, and I lay down on the floor and slept until midnight when Sergeant Hughes came in and wakened me.

March 27 We went out into the rain, which was now very much heavier, and followed a tape to the end of the wood. Emerging onto the open hillside, we skirted the trees until they ran straight forward to a point. Here we found a post and got down into the bit of trench; as, however, we were only a reserve line, there was nothing to be seen or heard except rain. It was so dark that we could not see each other's faces. Corporal Johnson gave us a guide who led us to the next post on the right, and so we continued along the line.

At 10 a.m. I was detailed to take the Company across to the Aizecourt-Nurlu road and there fill up an enormous mine-crater. It was very unsatisfactory work, for though 90 men were hard at it for four hours throwing in hundreds of barrows of stones and earth, there was not the slightest sign of the crater being smaller.

In their retreat the Germans have been very thorough, and mines have been exploded at every crossroads, and at such strategical points as this, on hillsides and in cuttings, so that transport is quite impossible. The engineers are finding it quicker to make new roads than to fill up the craters. In addition to this trees have been felled across the roads in hundreds of places, and most of the wells have been blown in or poisoned—in some cases dead horses and mules have been thrown in.

When we returned to the wood, I found Colonel Harrison there. He instructed me that as soon as it was dusk I was to take one platoon and patrol the road up to Villers Fauçon. Meanwhile we were to march on and take up new quarters in a small village called Longavesnes, which 'C' Company had taken the day before. So without resting, we followed him through the wood and up this village.

There was practically no accommodation here, and the troops had to set to work at once to make themselves 'bivvies' by fastening oilsheets together and fixing them to the tops of low walls. We made our headquarters in a chicken-run, in which we could just stand upright. Here I dumped my kit and then went forward to look at the roads which I was to patrol at dusk. There were two parallel roads running up to Villers Fauçon and I was to have a half-platoon on each. The weather had suddenly changed and now a light snow was falling.

As soon as I got back, I started to muster the platoon, but what with the issuing of rations and their being scattered all over the ruins, it was 9.30 p.m. before we moved off. The snow was much heavier now, and was lying thickly upon the ground. We walked slowly along the top of the bank, to avoid the mud of the road, and without any excitement came upon the first houses looming up in the darkness. Then in a few minutes we reached the crossroads where we were joined by the other half-platoon.

I asked Corporal Wood, who had led them, whether he had anything to report and he said, 'Well, Sir, there's a feller up t'other corner, as seems half cocked. I arst him a few questions and he answered like a village idiot.' So I went along with Wood and found a trooper standing in the middle of the road. I, too, questioned him as to who he was and where his regiment was disposed, but he made perfectly futile replies and grinned idiotically; so presuming that he was shell-shocked, I collected my troops and went on up the road to the right, where, turning a bend in the road we struck a weird scene.

First there was a Bengal Lancer chattering with cold, holding the bridles of about 20 horses. A little further on, right in the middle of the road, was an enormous brazier, with flames leaping about six feet into the air. Around it were squatting a circle of native lancers perfectly motionless. There was a strange appearance of a theatrical scene, with the lurid light shining on their turbans and beards and on the snow-covered ruins behind them.

I advanced to the group and asked if there was an officer about. Immediately an excited chattering broke out among them until I repeated my question. Then one enormous fellow got up and coming to me with an extraordinary dancing gait, sang in a nasal monotone 'Officier. Oui! Officier. Oui!' Beckoning to me to follow him he led me across some ruined gardens and broken walls to where a house was fiercely burning. Then turning, with an expressionless face he said 'officier là', and gracefully avoiding me he retraced his steps and rejoined the silent circle.

I was now firmly convinced that the village was full of

lunatics, so without enquiring any more, I went on up the
road until I came to another broad crossroads in the centre of
which was the entrance to a tunnel. Inside I found a room
wherein was a major commanding the 8th Hussars. I told
him that I wanted to know who was holding the village, and
what the dispositions were.

He proceeded to mark on my map the exact positions of the
posts around the village. Boasting of their courage and skill in
capturing the village, he asked me to see that they were
relieved at once as they were tired out. He was also very
windy and at every mention of shelling or a counter-attack
his voice rose to a scream. When I told him about the 'village
idiot' we had met, he said, 'Ah, that's a smart fellow. I've
given instructions that no information must be given to
anybody.'

When I left him I was laughing heartily within myself.
Firstly because the village was empty when he took it and not
a shot was fired, and secondly because, although he had
warned his troops not to give any information away, I, a
stranger, had walked in and asked the most important
questions and was leaving with a marked map. And he hadn't
even enquired what battalion I was or where I came from.

We returned to Longavesnes, repassing the Bengalese, still
squatting in the snow, and a number of limbers being
unloaded. At 1.30 a.m. I got back to my chicken run, made
out a report, and climbed into my wire bed.

March 28 There was nothing doing during the day, so I
had a good lounge about the village, being keenly interested
in deducing the life and dispositions of the Boche, from the
ruined houses and sign boards. The gardens had been well
kept and were full of flowers and vegetables which now were
overlaid with bricks and dust from the shattered houses.
There are hundreds of fruit trees—but every one has been
sawn through and felled.

At the crossroads was a well but this had been blown in, so
that our only supply was from our watercart—a waterbottle

full per day for all purposes—if we were lucky. Of course we did not shave and washed only if we could find a clean puddle, which was seldom. Just behind our billet was a large German cemetery, beautifully laid out. There were 575 graves, and nearly all had stone monuments or crosses. In the centre was a huge German cross of blackwood, but this had been struck by a shell and was splintered. At the far end was a 'calvary', a little mound arched in the trees with a life-size crucifix in the centre.

In the evening a fire broke out outside our billet; a haystack buried by a fallen house had been smouldering for two days, and now commenced to burn furiously. I was terrified that it would draw shelling and spent a couple of hours throwing earth on it—all to no purpose. So I left it; it was ignored by Jerry and burnt out during the night.

March 29 At dawn we were unceremoniously routed out and marched a few hundred yards up the Villers Fauçon road to the shelter of a steep ridge. The line in front was advancing and we were to support them if required. The cookers followed us up and gave us a good breakfast which we heartily enjoyed in the open air. However, we heard no sound of the fighting and marched back to billets at 11 a.m. Later I met the RC chaplain of the Brigade—living with the 7th Battalion. I did not care for him. He was a convert parson, had red hair and no sense of humour.

March 30 I was detailed to go up at 10 a.m. with Kentish and the CO to study the line. We proceeded to a spot in front of Gros Wood, where they spread themselves over a map. They ignored my presence, but by listening to their talk, and sneaking glances at the map, I gathered that they were merely identifying landmarks. We were interrupted by a terrific crash as a 'coalbox' burst overhead and the bullets ripped up the turf around us. Two or three more came and it was obvious that we were being spotted, so we ran back to the shelter of the woods, followed by half a dozen more shrapnel shells.

We were detailed to go up wiring in the evening and at 9 p.m. Thatcher turned up to act as guide. He led us up to Villers Fauçon and while we were marching through the town we heard an aeroplane approaching. It was a brilliant moonlight night, and we stood like statues in the shadow of the houses as he swooped down onto the street; he did not spot us and after circling round once or twice he went back again and we continued through the village.

We moved out on to the open fields in front and marched on and on in the snow, as I thought, moving in a circle. Actually Thatcher had entirely lost his bearings and had to leave us to find the spot we were to wire. After a time he returned and said we were on it, so I spread out the Company and allotted them their various jobs. It was frightfully cold, but clear and the bright moonlight helped us a lot.

Thatcher and I supervised the work from either end and very soon a double row of stakes was in position; then, as they started to run up the strands of wire, I went along to Thatcher who was delighted to see me produce a flask from my pocket. A tot of rum cheered us up a lot and I returned to my end of the line. Here on the top of a little hill, I helped with the wiring for a bit and then went across to where Corporal Breeze was sitting on a pile of stakes beating his hands.

It was a very quiet and lonely scene, the slope of snow down from behind us, nothing visible but the whiteness of the earth merging into the grey of the sky. The line of little men at their noiseless tasks and the cold moonlight over all. As I sat drinking in this scene, Breeze touched me on the arm, 'There's someone declared peace', he said and pointed across past the last stake.

Covered with snow, as with a sheet, lay the body of a Boche, looking calm and, I somehow felt, happy. Yet the sight of him made me feel icily lonely. It seemed such a terrible thing to lie alone, covered with snow throughout the night, with never a sound until we came along, and tapped and clipped and never spoke, and then went away for ever. It seemed so unfriendly, and for a long time I sat wishing we could do something for him.

At length I passed down along the line again to Thatcher who decided it was time to withdraw; so we passed along the word to cease work and the troops fell in. As they lined up, I could not help thinking of my poor Boche up on the hill, and I imagined a piteous look on his face as he heard us marching away, leaving him once more to silence and solitude.

In the front rank was a man called Bailey, and as I looked along them to check their wire cutters and gloves, I noticed he was carrying a pair of boots. I asked him where he got them. He said brightly 'Jerry up on the hill, Sir.' My poor poor Jerry. We marched back and left him.

March 31 I was not expecting any work today, but at lunchtime I received very vague instructions from Kentish: No 13 platoon had been sent up to a sunken road on the left of Villers Fauçon, to occupy some posts. I was to move up at once with No 14 platoon, wait on the road until a new battalion—name unknown—came up and relieved us, then march back the two platoons. We were to move in marching order and carry Lewis guns.

I at once fell in the platoon, then found that Kentish had forgotten to have the Lewis guns brought up from the rear. So he said, 'Alright, you go off without the gun teams, and I'll send them on later.' I asked him to lend me a map, but he would not, so I fixed the position in my head, and made a rough sketch of the positions he had marked in the sunken road. When I marched off, my 'platoon' minus Lewis gunners numbered Sergeant Allsop and six men!

I struck across to the left and followed the valley until I hit the road three-quarters of a mile to the left of Villers Fauçon; then I turned in towards the village. Arriving at the point where I considered No 13 platoon should be, I took Sergeant Allsop and Corporal Oldham across the field in front to find their posts. I was quite elated to see, almost at once, a fellow walking along the top of a trench. Below him two heads were

showing above the parapet. I called my NCOs' attention to
them and we made in that direction. We saw one of the men
get out of the trench and run across to another post where he
fixed up a machine gun.

Suddenly Sergeant Allsop clutched my arm crying 'I don't
like the look o' them Sir! I believe they're Boche.' I whipped
out my glasses, and sure enough they were Germans fixing
up a machine gun. We gave them no chance to use it, for we
cut back to the road as hard as we could go.

A little further along the road we saw some fellows erecting
a tin shelter in a field. Approaching, we found they were
troopers if the 8th Hussars, and they told us that the spot
where we had seen the Boche was the line occupied by our 13
platoon, so we decided to return and have another look. We
had only gone about 30 yards, when there was an excited
shout from the Hussars and one ran over with a message slip.

'From OC 8th Hussars. Warwicks posts on left have been
forced back and are occupied by the enemy. Take special
precautions and get into touch with their new positions.'

This put me in a frightful fix, as the relieving troops were due
in an hour's time. I felt that my duties were 1) to let HQ know
what had happened; 2) to find where the platoon now was, and
if necessary to take them to recapture their posts; and 3) to
ensure that the incoming troops were met and warned of the
retirement.

I considered it best, therefore, to send two men back to HQ
and a couple to right and left to try to get into touch with 14
platoon, whilst I remained on the road to receive reports.
The patrol from the left found nothing, but the one from the
right reported that higher up was a road which corresponded
to the one where my party should have been, but it was quite
empty. I went with them to satisfy myself that this was
correct, and on my return met the relieving troops.

I explained matters to the Company Commander and after
a powwow we decided that he should carry out his relief,
commencing from the right and working along the line. If his
left platoon could not find the posts, then we would take steps

to search the country for the missing troops. I remained with him on the road to pick up my party. I had no reply to my message to HQ.

I waited on for several hours in the darkness until the 'relief complete' messages rolled in. One, two, three, and finally four reports were received, and knowing that my platoon was found I breathed a sigh of relief and waited for them to come along. For an hour and a half I sat there and still they did not come, so I presumed that they had gone back by the other road in Villers Fauçon. Then I marched off back myself with my four remaining men.

I called in at an old sunken balloon shed where our Battalion HQ had been, but found that they too had been relieved and gone back. So in the pouring rain I continued my march to Longavesnes.

April 1 Sunday. At 12.30 a.m. on the outskirts of the village I met Billy Kentish, wet through and half mad with rage. 'Thank God! Where the hell have you been? The CO's been waiting and I've been lurking round in the rain for hours.' I asked him if the other platoon had reported OK, and he simply screamed a string of oaths. 'What! You haven't *brought* them! You ——!' As he was offering his congratulations Colonel Hanson came up; he waited to hear no explanation but as soon as he heard that the platoon was not there he became white with anger. He said nothing except 'Stay here until you find them.' Then he returned to Driencourt with his HQ staff.

Kentish had with him Corporal Kent (the post corporal) and Sergeant Major Chalk, and now we went up the muddy roads and across sodden fields yelling '13 platoon!' 'Corporal Wood', and Kent calling in a doleful voice 'Bobbee-ee! Bobbee-ee!' until at about 2 a.m. we heard an answering hail, and 13 platoon came trudging down the road which I had used.

They told us that they had not been relieved at all by the incoming troops. The position which they had occupied was not the one which was marked on Kentish's map, but was on another road further forward. The report that the Boche had taken their posts was false, though a Uhlan patrol had actually ridden up and down a wood in which Corporal Newey and his post had been hidden. The relieving platoon had taken up its position in the road behind, and it was not until Corporal Wood took a walk back that he found that he should have been relieved.

All this we learnt as we trudged back through the rain to Driencourt, where at 5 a.m. we entered dugouts on the road in front of the village. It did not take us long to get fixed up, and in half an hour we were lying in our soaked clothing, trying to drive from our minds the dire foreboding of the tick-off which awaited us on the morrow.

The tick-off came soon after lunch. The CO came round, and on the road outside our HQ commenced to grind me to powder, in front of Kentish. He told me it was a disgraceful thing that with two platoons at my disposal I had made no attempt to recapture the posts. In my own defence, I had to point out that I had only six men, and that my first job was to *find* the other platoon. Of course the absence of the Lewis gunners was brought out, and the CO turned his batteries on Kentish. Finally he switched back on me saying, 'Whatever the circumstances I consider that it has been a disgraceful show, and not what is expected from an officer of *this* battalion.' When he had gone, Kentish, smarting under his own reprimand, turned on me too, saying that it was a rotten thing to let my Company Commander down, and I should have kept quiet about the Lewis gunners. For the rest of the day I moped about, thinking that now my chances of shining were finished and longing for a return to the line where a bullet might mercifully end the disgrace into which I was plunged.

April 2   Moved up to Longavesnes, this time to a different billet. A town major had taken charge of the village, and allotted a certain portion to each company. In our section there was very little shelter, and after squeezing the troops in amongst the ruins, we could only find a tiny harness-room, about 9 feet by 6 feet, in which to make our HQ. There was no roof, and we were just stretching a tarpaulin sheet across, when there stalked up a great lanky lieutenant of the 4th Gloucesters who said he was the town major and this was his billet. So we had to clear out and, pending a further discovery, Dunham and I installed ourselves in an old boarded-up lavatory, and Kentish cadged a space in 'A' Company's cellar.

During the afternoon I was sent up with Major Gell to reconnoitre the country in front of Villers Fauçon. Here, as we stood on the forward slope of the hill, we saw the cavalry forming up for an attack on the positions in front of Epéhy. They had just got into column when the Boche spotted them and opened their artillery. This created a terrific panic, and they commenced wheeling and circling in an effort to writhe away from the zone of fire. There was great disorder and many of the horses bolted, although there were practically no casualties.

As we strolled along watching them we saw our divisional general, 'Dicky' Fanshawe, standing alone on a little knoll. He also was interested in the attack which started soon afterwards. It was a very pretty sight, and for a moment we were thrilled by the line of galloping horses and pointed swords in perfect order, but the excitement was soon spent for we knew that there were no enemy in front. We saw one or two fellows whirl out of their saddles from long-range machine gun fire, but then came a pitiful anticlimax, for on meeting with a few thin strands of wire, they were thrown into confusion, and as Fanny mounted and rode away, we started off too, leaving a line of dismounted troopers leading their frightened horses across the entanglement.

As we continued our reconnaissance, Fanny came galloping back and handed a packet of chocolate to Gell, saying 'This may be useful to you.' It is this benevolent habit that has earned him the nickname of 'The Chocolate Soldier'.

Having finished our 'decco' we returned to Longavesnes where I spent a most uncomfortable night, half standing half sitting in my tiny billet.

April 3   We had been very uneasy on account of a great swaying house-side which overhung our billet and some of the men's shelters. So I got my men together and, after working from 9 a.m. to noon, succeeded in bringing it down in a cloud of dust with no casualties. I also put in some good work on the town major. I said so much that, to save himself more, he consented to hand over the harness-room to us, and himself entered into my cubby-hole. Good luck to him! Billy and I gave him no time for a second opinion, but installed our valises and servants at once. Then we walked round the village, and found that last night a mine blew up at the crossroads and killed the padre of the 10th Manchesters who was in my old billet in the chicken run.

It was raining hard when we returned to our billet. There we found the CO talking to a tall, thin second loot, with a fair moustache and washed-out eyes. He wore a tin hat tipped over his eyes and looked very tired. The CO seemed relieved to see us, and murmuring, 'Ah, Holland, this is Kentish, your Company Commander,' he hurried away. The new arrival drew himself up and raised his hand in a long, slow stage salute, saying '*Sir*. I am pleased and proud to have the honour of meeting you in the scene of operations. *And* I can assure you that I will do my best to serve you, and my king, at a top rate. I've crossed over to *make good* and to help the old country all ends up.'

Billy was rather taken aback by this, and feebly replied, 'Quite, er—that's the spirit.' Then we took him into our billet and showed him *our* spirit. He was already very tight, having turned up with Major Townsend—this was an excellent fellow, late of our regiment but always tight so that he could not be kept in the Battalion. It broke his heart to be sent back to England, so now he had been given the job of Divisional Salvage Officer.

Holland talked without pause from the moment he came in. He told us about his exploits as a commercial traveller, in Birmingham and in Canada. And about his one brief visit to the trenches a year before, where he was slightly wounded in the shoulder ten minutes after entering the line. He was a dreadful bore, but his curious terms of speech and intonations made me shout with laughter.

After dinner he said he would build us a real good blaze, as the evening was chilly. So out he went into the rain and secured some oil-soaked rafters which he hacked into two-foot lengths. He piled these up in a corner close by our feet and lit them. All through the night he continued to pile on fuel until the place was worse than an oven. The wall was red hot, and I had to roll up my valise to save it burning. Worst of all, as there was no chimney or window, the smoke had to filter out slowly through the oilsheet-covered doorway.

April 4 I was driven out by the heat at early dawn. The others stuck it until 7 a.m. when Holland started talking. It had been raining hard so there were plenty of puddles, and we got a good wash. We had not shaved for days, and presented a very ragged appearance. Moreover I had developed a beastly rash over my body which Holland said was 'Gordam scabies'. Kentish had the windup and said he would not sleep with me any more till I had seen the doctor.

We learnt that the town major had spent the night walking about in the rain as our fire had made his cubby-hole untenable. Holland was detailed for Company Orderly Officer, but when we held a rifle inspection at 10 a.m. he was absent, and when he turned up at 1 p.m. he was very tight. He had been drinking again with Major Townsend. Billy gave him a choking off, whereupon he cried bitterly and promised never to do it again. Then he went off to the cookers to see the dinner issued.

He returned later with a mug full of lukewarm, greasy, half-cooked stew, floating with cabbage leaf. Upon this he proceeded to eulogize. He said that when he got to the field kitchen, the 'pontoon' was not cooked, so he had issued the jam pudding first. This he assured us was a 'downright treat', for he had sampled it before the whole Company to show them how good it was. Next he had drunk a mug of the half-cooked stew, to show them how good it was going to be. Then he had brought back a mug so that we might share his enjoyment. We declined it, and persuaded him to pour it down his throat—to stop him talking.

At 2 p.m. we paraded as a working party and marched to Saulcourt, followed by a limber bearing picks and shovels. We were to dig cruciform trenches on either side of the road junction to form a strongpoint in front of the village. First we marked out the position by means of tapes, then we commenced to dig, I with two platoons on the right, Holland with the other two platoons on the left of the road.

At the end of about an hour, apparently Jerry thought we had worked the union time, for with a fearful clatter a salvo of 5.9″ shells burst close by, followed at once by two or three more salvoes, dead on us. No one was hit, for we dived like rabbits into the sunken road or under whatever cover was handy. The guns stopped at once and after a few minutes we returned to our digging.

I climbed up on Holland's side and stood talking with him and Corporal Kirby for a few minutes until—Crash! Crash! They came again—right amongst us. As we ducked, I felt a hot blast behind me and went tumbling head over heels down the bank into the road. Kirby was a good second, and sat up with a look of pained surprise. A piece of shell had ripped his leather jerkin from tail to collar, shaved a bare patch on the back of his head, and smashed his tin hat—but he was not scratched.

Several more bursts came, and Billy, who had been lurking higher up the road, decided that it was impossible to carry on, and gave us the order to form up to march back. As we were stacking the tools in the limber, Holland's platoon sergeant said, 'Excuse me, Sir! Aren't you hit?' and pointed to a tiny blood spot on his shoulder. 'Blank Me!' said

Holland, 'I sure am.' A tiny bit of shell had gone into his skin half an inch from the last wound he got. He did not wait for a dressing, or sympathy or even to say goodbye—he just shot off down the road, while we followed at a more leisurely pace.

While marching back we saw four of our kite-balloons come down in flames. Arrived at Longavesnes. Billy put in a casualty report, but Holland had not reported back. We wired all neighbouring dressing stations and battalions but there was no trace of him. Finally at 6 p.m. Billy said we must go and search. I wanted to let him rip but Billy wouldn't. 'We shouldn't have let him go alone,' he said. 'He may be throwing a fit in a field this minute.'

This picture left me cold but out I had to go with a squad along one road, while Billy went up another, yelling and shouting—exactly like our night search for 13 platoon. Of course it rained, and at 10 p.m. we returned—tired, hungry and drenched to the skin—to learn that Holland had hopped on a limber and gone straight down to Péronne. We drank his damnation and good riddance in a hot whisky.

I tried to ring up the doctor about my rash, but could not get him so I walked to Tincourt through the rain and darkness to find him. He was out, and his orderlies told me I had scabies and should go to hospital. However, I pushed on to the 10th Manchesters to see *their* doctor, but he was ill himself and back I had to slog and turned in beside Billy despite his protests.

April 5 The doctor, an objectionable Irishman called Carroll, turned up during the morning. Told me that I had not got scabies—it was a rash caused by vermin and dirt. He also said that the CO was going to choke me off for ringing him up at such an absurd hour.

Later, Ewing, the young Scot from 'A' Company, turned up and took over the Company from Billy who was going on leave. He seemed quite a nice fellow, but very quiet and nervous on taking over command. I had not met him much before. He told me we were to move tomorrow.

April 6 Moved at midday up to Saulcourt, where we sat the troops down in a large courtyard while we looked for billets. 'A' and 'C' Company HQs had a fine cellar in the farm and we managed to squeeze our troops into the hayloft. For ourselves we could find no shelter, so we decided to have our meals in with 'A' and 'C' and laid our valises out in the corner of a cellar. The roof was blown away, so we just lay looking up at the sky. Fortunately the rain had stopped.

April 7 The Boche had shelled fairly closely during the night, but no damage was done. I didn't even get the windup. I turned out very early, thoroughly enjoying the fresh air, though it was very cold.

At 6 p.m. we were suddenly turned out and marched up to support an attack on Epéhy. We simply lay out in the wet grass and saw or heard nothing of the attack but a little machine-gun and rifle fire in the distance.

April 8 Sunday. At 3 p.m. Ewing came back from HQ in a great flurry, gave me a map and pointed out a crossroads three kilometres in front of Epéhy. He said that on the next evening we were to carry wire to that point, in preparation for an attack, and now I was to take two NCOs to reconnoitre it.

At 4 p.m., with Corporals Mackay and Wood, I took a nice little walk up to Epéhy. There was very little shelling, and as the ground was new to us, we found it rather interesting. The village was very badly smashed, and we did not see a single living person, though there were several dead Jerries and English. We passed straight on to the station, then followed the railway to the right past a ruined cemetery until we came to a patch of ground pitted with hundreds of shell-holes. We judged this to be the commencement of our road, and stopped to verify it.

As we decided that it was, the German guns opened and a dozen field shells fell around us, covering us with earth and enveloping us in a fog of fumes as we cowered in a shell-hole. During a lull, we jumped up and ran forward on to the hard road ahead which led on across the green slopes.

In a few minutes the clouds, which had been closing in as we advanced, opened to drench us with rain. This provoked a flow of choice language from the NCOs who had all this time kept up a continuous crosstalk of chaff and commentary. I had grown to like these fellows immensely and was now on very good terms with them. On we plodded, while the mist and darkness closed in, and we got thoroughly soaked and fed up, until at last we topped the ridge and before us saw a line of glistening earth hitting our road at right angles.

'There you are,' I said. 'That is the road junction and will be the dump tomorrow night.' Wood's sharp eyes detected a belt of wire on our side of the road, and as it was not marked on my map, we went forward another 50 yards to make sure. We were now about 70 yards from it and could see it clearly, so I jotted it on my map, and we made our way back with a better grace than we had left as we advanced.

It was pitch dark when we reached Epéhy and, following the railway, we had stopped to examine an enormous mine crater on the line, when I was astounded to hear Ewing's voice at a short distance away. I was so pleased with myself for having carried out a job successfully that I at once shouted and went after him. Inside the commencement of a deep cutting, I found the whole Company assembled and on enquiry learnt that they had moved up during my absence and relieved the 6th Battalion.

Ewing was the picture of childish rage; he was stamping, tearing his hair and almost crying. As soon as I approached he turned on me, screaming, 'where's my telephone, you damned slacker! What's the good of sending you on a job? I sent you up to take over the positions, and now I've no information and no HQ. If Kentish had come, he'd no ha' let me down . . . etc.' I tried hard to get a word in, but he ramped on like a madman, so I left him saying I would talk to him when he was in his senses and when there were no NCOs present.

I found Billy Kentish a little further on, sitting on a heap of mud, and looking a horrid mess. He had returned from his short leave in Amiens and was too fed up to sympathize with me. In fact he rather sided with Ewing. I helped them to fix the Company up in little cubby-holes dug into the embankment, posted sentries along the top, and finally found a little shaft leading about six feet into the side of the bank, where I left Dunham guarding my pack while I went to find Ewing, intending to have it out.

Returned with him and, with a lighted candle stuck into the earth, we sat down. The dignity of both of us was handicapped at the offset by the fact that we had to sit one at each end of a short board balanced on a bucket, and I could not forget for a moment the ludicrous effect that I would produce if I suddenly stood up and sent my irate Company Commander sprawling on his back.

I asked him to explain his remarks about my letting him down, and at once he assumed his blustering attack. He affirmed that he had instructed me to come up and take over these positions from the 6th Warwicks, ready to lead the Company in when they arrived. I was simply astounded by his cool prevarication, but I quietly handed him my map, and asked him to mark on it the enemy front line. After some hesitation he did so, and his line corresponded with the line of wire that I had marked in.

Then I pointed out the circle he had made round the crossroads when he told me that that was to be our dump, and I told him in hard, cold tones—still precariously balanced on the bucket—that we had actually walked in daylight onto the enemy lines, and that only the mist and the slope of the ground behind us, *and* the idiotic nature of our errand, had prevented us from being shot to ribbons or, at the best, taken prisoners.

I didn't rub it in too much, for he half admitted that he had been overwhelmed by the responsibility of taking a company up for the first time, and he looked so miserable that I considered it more blessed to forgive and producing my flask I gave him a swig of whisky.

A few minutes later an officer of the REs came along and claimed the dugout as his—built by his own servant. So out we turned into the cheerless cutting and, having nowhere else to go, we left Kentish on duty and climbed up the embankment at the back, to find the HQ of 'A' Company, who were in support a few hundred yards behind.

We found them in a tiny corrugated-iron shanty, where we joined them in a drink. It was fairly cosy, but I was terribly windy all the time I was there; perhaps it was because the shelter looked so lonely, right out in the middle of a field, or possibly because one side was riddled with bullet holes. Anyway I was heartily glad to get back again to the cutting, where 20 feet below earth level I felt safe.

April 9   At midnight I went on duty, and, as it was quite impossible for us to stay out in the open, with no HQ, we decided to establish one in the village behind, and remain one at a time on duty in the cutting. So Ewing and Kentish set off across the fields while I proceeded to make myself thoroughly acquainted with our position.

This was not difficult, for the Company was simply huddled in a line along the front bank. At our right the cutting ended at the vast mine crater, and our left flank rested on a bridge which had been blown up, and so blocked the rails. Along the top of the bank, fire-steps had been cut at intervals and on each a sentry was posted. Sergeant Major Chalk and one or two sergeants had fixed themselves a bivouac with their oilsheets, and with a brazier glowing inside they were quite happy. Sergeant Allsop had found a huge barrel in which he sat smoking and crosslegged like a goblin. The remainder of the troops had only such shelter from the rain and cold as their oilsheets provided.

I sent Dunham back to the village to locate HQ and waited at the demolished bridge until 4 a.m. when he returned with Kentish who relieved me. Returning to the village with Dunham, I found a house almost undamaged and of gloomy aspect from without. But entering under the oilsheets, I found myself in a cheerily lit kitchen wherein the servants were sitting by a roaring fire. In another room, amongst his satellites, sat Sergeant Major Chalk who had abandoned the bivvy in the cutting.

Descending the cellar steps I entered a cosy scene. It had been occupied by the Boche, and along one side were two wire beds on which Ewing and Johnny Teague lay asleep, and in a recess at the far end, my valise and Billy's lay side by side. There were two big armchairs, a *settee*, and a round table on which a lamp burnt, and my supper was laid.

I dropped into a chair and removed my sodden boots, puttees and tunic, then made a hearty meal of pontoon which Martin brought me. He also brought in a small glowing brazier and I sat beside this with a cigarette and a large hot rum, feeling luxuriously lazy and revelling in the thought that I had three whole hours, to eat or sleep or read, before I must go out again into the rain and cold to sludge about looking at tired and dirty troops trying to be cheerful. I even read a chapter of some sloppy book belonging to Teague before I finally crawled into my valise.

At 8 a.m. I was back in the line. It was quite light so I could not go across the open. Running past our billet was a road, slightly sunken, which led to the cutting, and I followed this. At its commencement stood a lifesize crucifix.

At 11 a.m., when we were getting nicely comfortable, the rain having stopped, there was a mighty crash as a 5.9″ fell smack into the cutting. One or two bivvies were hit by shrapnel but no one was hurt.

I was off duty from 12 to 4 p.m. At 5 p.m. I was feeling bored so I went up into an artillery OP (observation post) and spent an hour with the FOO (forward observation officer). It is his duty to observe and direct the fire of his battery by telephonic reports. On this occasion he was very successful, getting two direct hits on the beet factory.

We watched the heavies registering on Villers Guislain and saw and heard explosions both there and in Honnecourt, followed by terrific fires as if we had hit their dumps. The

German kite-balloons kept ascending and descending rapidly —probably they were trying to spot our guns.

Through our glasses we saw quite a number of men moving about, particularly in front of Canal Wood. The FOO got shrapnel on to them, and got most of them running, but one man stood still and after each burst signalled an ironical 'washout' with his arms.

During the night he peppered us very sharply with whizz-bangs and 5.9"s, but fortunately we had pushed our posts forward down the slope so that most of the men were away from the cutting when the shells came. I stood on the top of the embankment during the shelling and took bearings with my compass. I spotted three distinct batteries.

April 10 The firing slackened from 3 a.m. to 5 a.m. but then, just as it was getting light, about twenty 5.9"s came in a steady stream, catching the cutting with deadly precision. They were so horribly accurate that after the first one or two I took to my heels and ran forward to the troops in the advanced posts, leaving them to crash and pound into the empty cutting.

I waited until the shelling had stopped before I sent the troops back, and I must have let it get too light for as I withdrew the last post, and stood on the embankment watching them climb down, a crackle of bullets swept past me, some beside, some over my head. I dropped like a rabbit and rolled down the bank, grabbed a Lewis gun and climbed up again in time to see about a dozen Boche hurrying across to the left, a thousand yards in front. I gave them a couple of bursts and had the satisfaction of seeing several drop, while the remainder ran on and got into a trench.

I returned the gun to its owner and then started off for HQ with Dunham. I was too tired to go round by the road and decided to risk it across the top. We walked quite leisurely, expecting a burst of fire at any moment, but there was no sound and in safety we crossed the shell-pitted fields of Crucifix Corner.

Dunham went straight on, but I stood for several minutes gazing around me. The undulating slopes were beautifully green, save where concentrated shelling had left a brown burn. The sun had risen and was glowing on the red patched roofs of Epéhy and Pezieres. Crucifix Corner had been heavily shelled but now looked delightfully peaceful. The figure was untouched except for a shrapnel hole right through the heart, and two robins were singing merrily, one perched on the hand, and one on the crown of thorns.

I felt very calm and soulful as I turned away to walk up the road. Instead of going in to the billet, I passed it and went along to a little pond, where I sat on the stone coping, looking at the new shell-holes of the previous night, drinking in the sweet air of dawn and once more thinking of a number of things.

We were perfectly quiet all day, and I thoroughly enjoyed wandering round with Kentish and Ewing looking at corpses of Jerries.

Shelling recommenced at nightfall and caught our corner pretty heavily; the crucifix came down, smashing the figure to atoms. At midnight we were relieved by the 14th York and Lancs, who were most frightfully windy. They belong to the 42nd Division who have just returned from Egypt. After relief we marched back to Longavesnes where at dawn we took over our original billet in the chicken run.

April 11 I was wonderfully happy when I woke after a refreshing sleep. In the bright sunshine our tiny room looked very cheerful. There were two beds of wire netting, one above each other. Billy had wanted to toss for beds of wire, but I had flatly refused to sleep with his enormous weight hanging over me, so here I was up top. Then we had a tiny table and two boxes for seats; on the walls were saucy pictures from 'La Vie' and there was no door so we had plenty of air.

It surely was a happy day, for after a late and cheery breakfast, I went out onto the village road and saw Ewing talking to the one man I most wanted to meet again. It was Syd Pepper, who had been with me in England and whose parting words had been 'Remember, when you get to France, to say "I'm for the 1/8th", and don't let them put you to any other crush.'

He himself had come to France as a private in the Battalion, had got a commission on 1 July 1916 during the Somme attack, and had been shot through the stomach. He had nearly died, and I had left him a living skeleton— Permanent Home Service. He had never been happy at home, and after much agitating and rejection by medical boards he had enlisted an eminent surgeon to help him through. When his girl learnt that he had asked to come back to France she had chucked him, so he let her go, and here he was—back with the Batt. He was accompanied by a Captain Hoskins.

Our meals were very cheery, for we had to sit, two on the boxes, two on the bed, and one on the ground outside. After lunch Pepper and I went into the cemetery behind and looked at the inscriptions on the gravestones. In the evening we played 'Slippery Ann'.

April 12 We routed the Company out and played football near the cemetery before lunch and in the afternoon a crowd of us turned out with revolvers and potted at bottles. Of course we had money on it, and I was glad to find that my hand was still steady enough to rake in a few francs, though the CO carried off most.

They had shifted a battery of 60-pounders close to our billet, which kicked up a frightful din; also Jerry's heavy guns had been searching for it and we had a pretty breezy time.

The RC padre came in to dinner, and I arranged to clear a billet out for him to say mass next morning. I also told Sergeant Gunn of 15 platoon, who was an RC, to warn all Catholics.

April 13 After breakfast I strolled down to the well with

Gunn, and watched the REs trying to clear it and render it workable. Then we went on to No 13 platoon's cellar where we found the padre waiting. After clearing out the non-Catholics, we went to confession behind a blanket. Then he said mass on a bully-box covered with an oilsheet, and we went to communion.

In the afternoon Syd Pepper and I took the Company up to Basse Boulogne, via Villers Fauçon and St Emilie. The latter village was terribly battered; there had been several large factories which had been mined, so that the whole place had been littered with debris of shattered machinery.

We were working on road repairs near Quid Copse and having set the troops on the job, Syd and I wandered off into the ruined gardens and filled our haversacks with lettuces and other 'saladable' stuff. Returned after a few hours work.

April 14 We received a nasty setback this morning, in the form of orders to parade immediately and march back to the line where we would relieve 14th York and Lancs. Our troops were infuriated to learn that the 42nd Division had retreated from Guillemont Farm, which our 5th Battalion had captured with heavy losses. Now that division was so windy that we had to relieve them and at nightfall our division was to advance and recapture the farm and also Pigeon Ravine. We were to support the 6th Battalion on the latter sector.

Approaching Saulcourt we met the 10th Manchesters marching back, and our lads greeted them in no veiled terms. 'Make way for the soldiers!' and 'Here come the windy 42nd' were the mildest of their shouts. In daylight we entered the cutting at Epéhy and there were several free fights before the relief was carried out.

As soon as it was dusk we moved out of the cutting to the much-shelled crossroads, whence Woods, Mackay and I had commenced our famous reconnaissance of the Boche line. Two thousand yards up the road we came to the tiny ruin of Red Mill. The shelling here had been terrific, and the ground was a churned mass of holes. Need I say that the rain had started as we left the cutting?

From Red Mill we extended to the left in a straight line across the valley, and in the steady rain, in long wet grass, we lay for two hours before anything happened. Then the German shells began to fall, scattered at first along our line, then more and more heavily, particularly about the Mill where I lay with Sergeant Hughes. They were dead on our line, but luckily no one was hit, chiefly owing to the fact that the ground was so soft that they sank well in before bursting.

Then out from the darkness behind grunted a line of dumpy figures; overcoated with fixed bayonets, weighed down by their soaked clothing and loads of spades, sandbags and bombs, they passed through us like a comb, only an occasional greeting to an acquaintance breaking the silence. Then two minutes later a second line passed through into the rain and darkness, and we were left, with high-explosive bursts around us, to wait with bated breath for sounds of the attack.

A quarter of an hour of silence. The shelling had ceased, and we heard nothing but the swish of rain, when suddenly there was a sharp flash and crash of a bursting bomb, a dozen rifle shots and then the air was thick with bullets as angry machine guns spat fire along our line. The darkness was cut by the flashes of rifles and bombs, then from behind came the flames of German guns as a barrage was opened that sent hundreds of shells crashing amongst us and caused us to bury our faces in the mud and pray for respite.

In a few minutes, two figures staggered back, one with his arm gone, the other shot in the side; one collapsed and died, the other we patched up and sent back. After that, wounded and unwounded came running, walking, crawling back, all in utter despair. The show had been a ghastly failure, for the Boche had vacated their trench and from positions on the high ground behind had mown down our lads with bombs and machine-guns as they floundered about in the wire.

Along came the order to advance, and with beating hearts

we fixed bayonets and moved forward in a heavy black line, so like the lads who now lay dead in our path. But the gods were good to us, for suddenly the machine-guns stopped, the barrage lifted and unmolested we reached the belt of wire behind which the remnants of the 6th Battalion were digging frantically to prepare the trench for the counter-attack that must follow as surely as night follows day. We leapt in and worked beside them shifting sandbags and converting the parados into a parapet.

April 15 Sunday. At one o'clock a.m., as we waited for the first signs of a Boche counter-attack, we heard troops behind us, and learnt with delirious joy that it was the 10th Lancs who had been sent up to relieve us. Eagerly we handed over and made off down the ravine to the cutting. As I passed through the wire, I stopped to free a poor dying bugler-boy who had been caught and shot through the throat. I handed him over to the stretcher-bearers who were now busy amongst the wounded, who lay shrieking and groaning on all sides.

We moved straight back to Longavesnes where we learnt, before turning in, that the 5th had regained Guillencourt Farm with many casualties. It was estimated that there were 700 dead lying around the building.

We did not have much rest, for at 11 a.m. Syd Pepper and I again assumed the role of Stonecracker John and led the Company up to Basse Boulogne for roadmending. When we had seen the troops started, we took the servants along into the village. At the crossroads we found a small portion of kitchen standing and here we dumped our haversacks, *and* the servants with instructions to have a sumptuous repast at one o'clock.

Forgetting all we had learnt about advanced guards and scouting, we marched back to the troops and butted into General Fanshawe haranguing a group of our NCOs. At once he sent them away and commenced to devour us, as a more worthy prey. He was annoyed by a group of men who were walking about in the open near Quid Copse. Secure in his sense of innocence and righteousness, Pepper thought he could afford to be saucy. 'Those men, Sir,' he said, 'are Royal Engineers. We are the 1/8th Royal Warwicks.' This lashed Fanny into a state of fury. 'Oh! But I thought you were an officer. What's this? It looks to me like a Sam Browne belt! It's time you realized that you fellows are not in charge of platoons or companies, you are responsible for the whole army. They may be Engineers, but if they draw shelling, the Warwicks will get it as well!'—And some more.

We saluted, sent an NCO to drive away the offending REs, and knocked the Company off for lunch. Returning to the crossroads we found a dixie of tea awaiting us, and we attacked our sandwiches with appetites sharpened by the keen air. Crash! Up went a 5.9″ outside, and a bit more of our kitchen fell in. Five more crashes flung mud and stones over us and into our tea—then all was quiet. Then shaken nerves and foul language were the record of the REs' exhibition on the hill. I bet Fanny laughed if he saw them fall.

We finished lunch, and a 'cigarette cup', then whistled the Company together for the afternoon's work. At 3 p.m. a short, stout figure puffed up to Pepper and greeted him heartily. It was Major Townsend, with whom Holland used to disappear for his drinking bouts. We walked a little way with him, across to an old ruined sugar factory behind the road. There was nothing left of the building, and in a huge, green, slimy pool were piled bodies of men and horses in a ghastly putrefying swamp. The stench was horrible and we soon beat it back to the road, meeting a dozen high-velocity shells en route, one of which burst a few yards from Pepper as he lay grovelling in the mud.

Just after 4 p.m. we marched back to Longavesnes, the troops heavily laden with salad and vegetables which they had scrounged. I don't think they had carried out a *lot* of work.

April 16 A new officer, named Kinnel, had joined us, and he accompanied me with the Company to Villers Fauçon, where we were to erect Adrian huts. A mine had exploded here two days before in a house used as the HQ of the 4th Gloucesters. The CO, adjutant, second in command, padre, doctor and all the staff were killed.

The 7th Battalion were now in the village, so I went in to see the padre. The red-haired one had gone, and Fr Woodlock, a Jesuit, had taken his place. He was living with Jones their QM and I soon got very chummy with him. We strolled along to the church, where we climbed the tower which gave us a very good view of the surrounding country. It was interesting to watch the batteries working below us.

Descending again we found the skeleton of a kiddie about eight years old, blown out of a grave. The dear little, smooth, white skull was lying near the church steps and we picked it up and laid it with the other bones in the opened grave. Then we covered it in and gently patted the earth back. The padre grunted when I told her to go to sleep again. But it pleased me to think that she was a little golden-haired lassie and that she looked down shyly to say 'Merci, Soldats'.

Fr Woodlock is the brother of Mother Regis at Ilford, and he was in great distress because of a letter in the *Recorder* about children not going home sharp from school, or something. It really *is* a terrible war.

April 17 The Company was detailed to go up to Pigeon Ravine this morning to erect barbed wire. Ewing marched off three platoons, but I was left behind with No 13 cleaning Lewis guns. I had instructions to follow them when our job was done, and at 1 p.m. I moved up. I was very surprised to meet Kinnel on the road coming back on a stretcher. He told me that the Boche had spotted them working and opened up with shrapnel. There had been several casualties, and he had touched for one on the foot.

At the Epéhy crossroads, we found a huge cat squatting on the chest of a dead German, eating his face. It made us sick to see it, and I sent two men to chase it away. As they approached it sprang snarling at them, but they beat it down with their rifles and drove it into the ruined houses. Then we covered the body with a sack, and went on.

Up the old Red Mill Road we found the bodies of the 6th Battalion lying as they had fallen, and ahead, in the ravine, we saw a line of shellbursts flowering and fading in quick succession. This rather put the wind up us, and we were heartily relieved, as we approached, to see Ewing sending his men back towards us at the double. He had found it impossible to work under the heavy shelling, so we marched back.

At Epéhy we saw the sack we had thrown over the dead Jerry heaving up and down, and there was pretty pussy, still rending and tearing the body; so we shot it and continued our march to Longavesnes.

We had hardly taken off our equipment when we received orders to pack up again and return to Pigeon Ravine, there to relieve the 14th York and Lancs in the line. This we carried out at dusk, and we found ourselves occupying a line of detached posts across the valley, where we had lain out during the attack.

During the night the darkness was so intense that we had to arrange a code of whistle signals to guide us from one post to another. Company HQ was simply an isolated pit in the wilderness, which, during the long black night, we could only locate by a faint glimmer of light which Sergeant Major Chalk showed on the signal of a code whistle.

April 18 I established myself in a little trench with Sergeant Swingler, making myself a seat by scooping a hole in the earth wall. In my tiny cubby-hole I spent the afternoon writing a letter, with the water pouring off the oilsheet, which I had fastened over my head, onto my legs which stuck out below, and a candle burning on a bit of stick jabbed into the earth six inches from my nose.

We arranged the same signals as the night was again dark and wet, but at midnight the 1/4 Ox and Bucks came up and relieved us. We were filled with delirious joy to learn that we were going right back to Péronne, but unfortunately I had to remain in Epéhy to guide in a new detachment of the 42nd Division. So I brought my platoon into the courtyard near Crucifix Corner, then made myself comfortable in the old cellar which had been our HQ.

April 19 When the 42nd turned up, we showed them round the positions and then turned in for a little sleep before moving off. I had intended to march off at 8 a.m. but the new arrivals seemed windy and loathe to let us go, so that by the time we had answered all their questions it was 11 a.m. We marched to Saulcourt, where we had lunch in the soup kitchen, and were just going on again when I remembered that I had left my leather cigarette-case (a present from mother) in the dugout at Epéhy. I mentioned it to Dunham and, like a brick, he trudged off back for it without a murmur.

I went on with the platoon and had just settled down to a long weary footslog, when we were overtaken by a lorry. The driver not only consented willingly to give us a lift to Péronne, but took us back to pick up Dunham who had retrieved my case and was legging it like blazes to overtake us. Then we were borne back towards the rear, singing merrily. On the way my blackthorn, which I had brought out from England, fell out at the back, and we were travelling so fast that we were far away before I could stop the driver, and I had to let it go.

At Péronne, which we hailed with ringing cheers, we debarked in the market square, which was hardly recognizable in its present state; all rubbish had been cleared from the roads, the shell-holes were filled up, and the cobbles replaced. CQMS Corfield met us and directed me to our billet. This was down a side road near the corner which I had last seen in flames; here, close to the river, was a house practically untouched, in which I saw Ewing and Hoskins. The platoon's billet was practically next door; I took them in, saw them wash their feet and settle down, then went into our HQ. At the door I passed and saluted Colonel Hanson, but he did not recognize me on account of my scraggy ginger beard. Kentish was sitting in an armchair looking awfully seedy, and they told me that the doctor had ordered him to hospital with quinsy. He left an hour later.

The mess was ripping. The room I was in had been a shop, now it contained a settee, one arm and four other chairs and two tables. Behind it was a large kitchen with a big open fireplace, and then another room full of rubbish. On the first floor were three rooms and on the second, two more.

During the afternoon a new batch of officers arrived, of whom the following were posted to 'D' Company: Jimmy Harding, an oldish fellow, dry and wizened, late champion shot of southern India, who we forthwith nicknamed 'the Rajah'; Frank Radcliffe, an artistic, quiet middle-aged man, and a Doctor of Music; and then a very young chap named Hammond, an ex-Grenadier Guardsman of splendid stature and physique. All were excellent fellows and in half an hour we were a very cheery crowd. We split up bedrooms, sleeping in pairs, Hammond and I, Radcliffe and Harding, Pepper and Ewing. The servants took the top-floor rooms.

Our first dinner was a very jolly meal. Hammond and I went round to the canteen and returned laden with delicacies —curried prawns, tinned fruit and butter, tongue, port and liqueurs, etc. I exerted myself as mess-president and when we had had delightful baths, shaves and changes of clothing, we sat down to a six-course dinner that prepared us for a long sociable evening round the fire, with glasses of port beside us and coronas between our lips.

When we went to bed, I had a long talk with Hammond, who told me all about his home life, his fiancée who seemed very very dear to him, and then he astounded me by saying that they knew that they could never marry, in fact that he had not long to live, for he was eaten up with consumption.

April 20 We sallied forth in a body after breakfast, to make a tour of the town. We followed the river along towards the centre of the town and came to a large prisoner-of-war camp, there to a couple of big marquees which were the YMCA and the EFC. Here we turned up the street in which I had spent my first night in Péronne. Here, by the way, the REs were erecting a new bridge to cross the river to the station—the Huns had blown the old one down.

We went up into the square and examined several cellars, ending up at the Citadel, an enormous medieval fortress, where the walls of 20-foot thickness were chipped and scarred by shellbursts. The 5th Battalion were billeted in one part of the castle, and all the remaining rooms were empty except that in a tiny attic at the top we found an ancient arquebus. We dared Jimmy Harding to take this on parade, but he solemnly assured us that when he joined the army first, he used to use one. The vast moat had been converted into a rifle range, and as we went out into it, I met and exchanged a few words with Sergeant Foster of the 5th whom I had last seen in England.

We returned to the billet, had lunch, and then I went out into the garden behind. Here the rubbish lay waist deep; there were thousands of tins which had been thrown out by the Boche. Nearly all had American labels—Libby's milk, corned beef, pork and beans, etc—and there were large piles of old clothing and of decaying vegetation.

I resolved to clear this up and make a pleasant garden in which we could sit during our off-hours. So I started at once—with a long German mud-shovel—to hurl the tins over into the neighbouring garden, and lighting a big fire with paper and broken furniture I piled up clothing and rubbish which it consumed rapidly. It became rather lively after a bit, for amongst the muck were lots of bullets which exploded and made me skip. One hit a window of the billet and put the wind up the servants. At the end of four hours I had made very little impression, so after tea I went out again and worked until dark, by which time I had reached ground level on an area of about four or five square yards.

April 21 The Company was sent out for a rather pleasant

job today. We marched to the station where we filled lorries with stones, hopped on them and rode to a little village called Courcelles, just past Doint, where we shovelled the stones out into piles by the roadside, and returned for more loads. It was a beautifully bright, fresh day so we thoroughly enjoyed it.

Returned at 4 p.m. for tea, after which Radcliffe and I went round scrounging. We went through dozens of houses, climbing over roofs and knocking through walls, and ended up with lots of nice cutlery, salt cellars, glasses, etc. Our wallpaper was badly faded, so from another house I peeled the whole side and repapered our mess. We scrounged curtains for our glassless windows and some lamps and tablecloths, so that by evening, with our Harrison Fisher girls framed upon the walls, we had a very cosy mess.

April 22 Sunday. There was no work today and, as the padre was away, no mass, so I put in a lot of time in the garden. For a while we amused ourselves by shooting at bottles, until there came a loud howling from the platoon's billet. We dashed in to see who had been hit and found all the troops grinning. Someone had been fooling us, but we couldn't find out who it was.

April 23 We learnt that we were going to stay in Péronne for some time, so I thought it would be a good opportunity to have my teeth seen to, as they had been troubling me for some time. Ewing gave me permission to go sick, and having worked with the troops from 7 until 11 a.m. I went up to see Carroll. He told me that the only way for me to get dental treatment was to go to hospital; I told him I wouldn't do that, and returned to the working party which knocked off at 1 p.m.

As we were having lunch, I received a note ordering me to report to HQ at 2.30. Colonel Hanson was away somewhere and Major Gell was acting CO. I found him in the mess with the doctor, the padre and the assistant adjutant (Mortimore).

Without any preliminaries he charged me with being absent
from parade. He said he had visited the working party when I
was away and no one had known where I was. He would not
allow me to explain and said it was another example of my
damned slackness. He added:

'Look at your record since you have been with the Battalion. You fall foul of Brigade the first time you report to
them; you make a fool of yourself when you take a few men to
hand over a position; you lose yourself when you are sent up
to find your company HQ, and now you slink away from your
work. Now you take my word for it, Vaughan, these things
are all marked against you, and remember that if the day ever
comes when a company commander is needed, I will see that
you are passed over. And, moreover, if you don't pull
yourself together with a jerk, you will be sent back to
England as an inefficient officer.'

I was covered with shame and indignation at the injustice
of his remarks and at the sneering regards of the padre who
was a swine, the doctor who was a blackguard, and the
sympathy of Mortimore who was a damned decent fellow.
There was nothing I could say so I saluted and walked slowly
back to the billet trying to fight down my angry resentment
and depression. This was soon accomplished, but by the
other fellows who must, I think, have known why I had been
called to HQ. They kept up a cheery flow of conversation and
dared me to go out onto the marshes with Hammond in an
old punt. So off we went and punted about for an hour until it
filled with water and we had to scramble back through the
mud.

After dinner, Pepper, Hammond, Harding and I went out
to the nearby lock gates where we played like kids. Then we
played 'Pontoon' until bed time.

April 24 Was delighted today to be sent back with Pepper
to salvage the old trenches at Biaches. I had been longing to
have a look round our old positions from the enemy side, and
quite excitedly set off with the Company in single file along a

rustic pile-bridge which the Jerries had constructed across the 500 yards of marsh to La Maisonette. Here we were met by a Salvage Corps officer who set us first to move a light railway trolley across a wide open space to a little wood. This was a long and irksome job as we had only three pieces of rail which we had to lay in succession before the truck as we advanced.

When we had finished, we went on to Biaches where we had had such a rotten time in the line. The main road had been cleared and the shell-holes filled in, but otherwise it was untouched. The German trenches were in perfect condition, deep and beautifully revetted with high fire-steps and pumps. It was a higher site than ours and from their observation posts, every bit of our line was visible; we could also see that they had pumped all the water from their trenches down into ours.

Then we went down into our lines, and I at once made for our old cellar. But it was blown in. I got up on top and had a look at the graves of our boys, at the ruined boilerhouse in front and at the pump between the trenches which both we and the Germans had used. I found that at one point we had each had a machine-gun staring straight at each other with only 20 yards between. At the point where I had heard the Boche talking I saw that we had been standing against the wall of a cellar in which they were living.

All the time I had been wandering about, the troops had been collecting and classifying bombs and other objects. Now Pepper's whistle sounded as a signal to knock off for lunch, so we returned to the bomb dump where, sitting on two huge dud 'minnies', we ate our sandwiches and played with various French and English bombs. We had just lit our after-lunch pipes when two figures came towards us from the Maisonette Wood. I recognized Padre Woodlock, and the other seemed familiar; as I went to meet them I saw it was Mr Jones, my old form master, now a major and senior chaplain in the 42nd Division. We were awfully pleased to meet again and swapped news items about two old boys of Stamford Hill, but unfortunately he had to get back to his division and could only stay a little while.

Pepper and I spent the afternoon wandering about No Man's Land where we found scores of corpses in the last stages of corruption. They were mostly Frenchmen who had been killed during their attack in September 1916. The German wire was very thick and in many places he had arranged elaborate bomb-traps to catch raiding parties. I had a look at one old shelter behind Desirée and saw that the one from which Dunham had got ice for our tea, was full of green water in which lay a rotting Frenchman—yet our tea had tasted quite good.

April 25 I did a lot more work in the garden. The fire had been burning continuously and had consumed a vast quantity of rubbish. By the time I knocked off I had a large space quite clear and had struck a nice tiled path and flower bed with rose shoots still growing.

April 26 In the early morning Radcliffe and I took the Company up past Doint to the place where we had been unloading stones and started to fill up the shell-holes. It was 8 a.m. and bitterly cold so, leaving them hard at it, we went across to some small huts we saw over the fields. There were some transport lines, and only a few men asleep, but we found a canteen where we roused a corporal—ugly, frowzy and surly—who informed us that he had *no* tea, *no* coffee and *no* cocoa. Bitterly disappointed we bought a large stock of chocolate for the troops and came away. We worked until noon in a beastly cold wind and under a dull sky, so that when we returned we were very fed up.

There was great excitement during the afternoon. Saunders, the Company sanitary man, digging in the yard behind the Company's billet, struck a bottle of wine. Digging carefully he unearthed a huge dump, which provided the Company with food for thought! Several bottles found their way into our mess, but, of course, we knew nothing about it officially.

April 27 Harding accompanied me today on the roadmending party, and when we went on parade at 7 a.m. we had a terrible shock. There were numerous absentees and nearly everybody was tight. They were reeling about and laughing and presented such an extraordinary sight in two swaying lines that we hurried them off at once and marched unsteadily up the Doint road. They were immensely happy and greeted everyone we passed—including mules—with most amusing remarks. Corporal McKay in particular kept me choking with laughter, for he was very tight indeed. He kept trying to shout the step and mixed up his 'Lefts' and 'Rights' indiscriminately. But he and all the others were very good humoured and cheery.

When we arrived at our working place, we spread them out along the road, then discreetly retired to the soberest part, where, seated on an old 15-inch gun barrel, out of the corners of our eyes we saw them one by one lie down until only an occasional conscientious fellow remained shovelling stones into a shell-hole. About half a dozen lads came up at odd times and asked if they could go home as they were feeling horribly ill. We let them go and then I called up the sergeants and gave them a lecture, warning them to watch the troops more carefully in future. Luckily no one came along to supervise the work, so when we marched the fairly sobered Company back at midday, we said nothing to Ewing about it, though I had an idea that he knew.

After dinner, a fellow from 'C' Company named Samuel came in and asked me if I would go with him for a short leave in Paris. I had hardly spoken to him before so I was highly flattered when he said he wanted someone who would be quiet and intelligent. I told him that I was going into Amiens next day with Thomas for a couple of days, but if he would put in an application I would accompany him later.

April 28 At 7 a.m. Thomas called for me and we tramped through the empty streets until we found the washing lorry—which carried the Division's shirts back to Amiens. It was too early for us to be cheerful and we were fast asleep when he woke us outside the station in Amiens. We crossed the road to the Hôtel Belfort, where we had a bath and a shave and booked a room. Then we wandered round the town, taking a swim at the baths and drinks at the American bars.

After lunch at the Hôtel du Rhin, we floated along to my little flapper in the arcade, where we sat in armchairs with the gramophone playing while she brought us souvenirs and trinkets to inspect. We bought some and wrote notes to our friends in England for her to enclose with them, then had a sticky tea in a little patisserie. Finished the evening by a visit to a Divisional concert party and a stroll along the canal bank.

April 29   Sunday. Had breakfast in bed and, rising at midday, attended late mass in the Cathedral. After lunch made a tour of the town, eating ices in every café we could find. Also had luxurious haircuts and shampoos. We lunched at 'L'Universe' and dined at the Hôtel du France. Bed at 1 a.m.

April 30   Caught a train at noon from Amiens to Corbie where we had lunch at the club run by the pretty sisters, then lounged about until 5 p.m. when we got on to a little light railway that had just been laid into Péronne. It moved very slowly and often stopped for long periods, so that as we crossed the old battlefields we were able to get out and look round the trenches and graves, now overgrown with grass and weeds. It was growing dusk, and I was moved to moralize over the pathetic aspect of the deserted trenches which had once been filled with life and—if dangerous—had at least been cheery. It was dark when we reached Péronne and leaving Thomas I went on to our mess. I found everybody very amused by an incident of the morning.

Yesterday a new major had joined the Battalion. He was P. H. Whitehouse—brother of Willy Whitehouse who was sent home soon after I arrived. This one was not quite so objectionable, I was told, but being full of hot air he had ordered a Battalion parade for this morning. When he rode on parade, feeling a hell of a tit, his horse threw him and he lay grovelling in the mud before the delighted troops.

May 1   This was a glorious day. We were working on the road by Courcelles again so, having drawn rations for the troops, Hammond and I marched them off in beautiful sunshine, tunics open and lively songs pouring out in chorus. We got them started and then we wandered off to investigate a small house close by. It was a sad little place for, although all the furniture had gone, the floors were littered with kiddies' clothing, dolls and toys. There were lots of photographs of grannies, babies and rural weddings—all these had been cut across with knives and all crockery was broken.

We then went out again to the troops and as all the shellholes were now filled, we started them digging channels to drain the water into the ditch. While they were doing this, Hammond and I played at being engineers, I building up a reservoir in a puddle, and he constructing an elaborate system of locks and channels and waterfalls to drain it off into a puddle of his own.

We had just commenced to fight about it when Dunham came along with our lunch—two packets of sandwiches, a bottle of real *English* beer for me, and one of lemonade for Hammond who was a TT. So we set off to find a nice place to eat it, while Private Mayes, who had been watching our efforts with lofty displeasure, hurled reservoir, locks and all into the ditch with his mud shovel.

A little further towards Péronne we saw another larger house which we approached. It had evidently been a staff HQ, for the rooms on the ground floor had been cleaned and built up with three layers of large trees to make the cellar shellproof. We decided to lunch there and passed the word along the troops to knock off. They were all very happy working in their shirt sleeves, singing gaily and chaffing each other—pouring sweat under the sun's hot rays. We sent Dunham across to the surly corporal's canteen for more chocolate.

We went along to a verandah of coloured glass at the southern end of the house, intending to lunch there, but the rustling greenery of the garden called us and we went back into the sunshine. The grass was long and rough but, in the still heat, with no sound but the faint rustle of the trees, it seemed very calm and peaceful. The tiny grass-grown pool was unruffled and beside it, in the branches of a weeping willow, stood a statue of St Antony.

Against a high red wall 30 yards away stood a greenhouse, with a little glass left, and inside a tangled mess of vines, tomatoes and weeds. At one end a dugout had been made; lower down a tiny rustic bridge crossed a rapid brook on the banks of which stood a miniature rustic hut and occasional willow tree. Lying here on the soft grass we ate our lunch, basking in the hot rays of the sun and finding life sweet. Then smoking and talking we made brooches and bows out of sedgegrass and tiny flowers. In order not to desecrate the happy little ruin we buried our sandwich paper and replaced the turf (though there were dozens of empty tins lying round). Then we threw our empty bottles into the stream and raced beside them, each cheering his own craft—TT versus Toper—until after about half a mile they were caught in the weeds and we lay down and panted on the bank.

Strolling quietly back in silence, we found a dead pigeon and buried him, railing in his grave with little sticks and chains of plaited sedgegrass, and in his coverlet of pimpernels we erected a tiny white cross.

Then we went out on to the hot white road where our troops lay under the hedge, some smoking, some asleep. Most of them had pulled bunches of may and dogroses which bedecked their caps and all were very lazy and happy when we went along to distribute the chocolate which Dunham had brought. Then we continued our work until 4 p.m., when we marched back feeling that life was worth living and war worth fighting.

May 2 It was my turn off duty today so I did not march out with the Company; nevertheless I strolled down later to chat with Hammond and Radcliffe. There had been several changes during these few days. Colonel Hanson had returned and Major Gell had returned to the 5th Battalion (thank God!). Harper, the adjutant, had gone sick, and Mortimore had taken his place with Hoskins as assistant. Guthrie and several others had left—in fact we had lost nearly all the fellows I most disliked.

I was still working hard on the garden and by now had it half cleared and much nicer to look at. The mess and whole house were spick and span and we were more comfortable than anyone else in the town.

May 3 A few days ago the sentry on HQ did not salute the brigadier, so this morning the whole Battalion had to parade for drill and guard duties. In the evening we had a Battalion dinner, all officers dining together at HQ. We sent up several of our servants to assist.

The dinner was very loud. The food was excellent and the champagne flowed very freely. Nearly everybody got tight, Thomas being the first to succumb. While the CO was making a serious speech, recalling the history of the Battalion and toasting the memory of the fellows who had gone west, Tommy burst into maniacal laughter and collapsed on the floor. He was swept up and Radcliffe took the piano to accompany the various singers.

After a long singsong, a violent rag was started in which the enormous and disgusting padre offered to fight six subalterns. He knocked them about for a long time before he was debagged and spanked. Coleridge and Scales had a serious fight, but neither was hurt and they ended by kissing and crying over each other.

May 4 At 1 a.m. we broke up and returned to our messes, singing all the way in the moonlight. Pepper, Radcliffe and I went on to our favourite spot by the lock gates where we sat and droned sad choruses for half an hour before retiring. As I went up to my room I wondered if the servants were back, so climbed up to their quarters. Dunham and Martin were asleep but Willis was sitting up, swearing gently at his puttees. He was very tight and though quite respectful to us, he swore offensively at Marshall—who was not there.

Going in to Radcliffe's room, I whispered to him to come and help me find Marshall—a boy of 19 due for leave in a few days. Trekking back to HQ we found him lying by the side of the road. I picked him up in my arms and started back. After a few moments he woke up and started whimpering; I told him that he was all right and, recognizing my voice, he cried and begged me not to stop his leave. On the way back I had to assure him repeatedly that I would forgive him and not have him court-martialled. While we were putting him to bed, Willis delivered a long, solemn and more or less incoherent harangue on the evils of drink which was quite lost on Marshall who was by now fast asleep again.

May 5 The Battalion did no work today, so we spent our time bathing and fooling about in an old boat. I also did a lot of work in the garden which was now nearly finished. During the afternoon, Marshall came out and stood silent and hesitating. As I took no notice of him, he started working beside me then stood up and said, 'Mister Vaughan, give me a 'it over the 'ead with that 'ere shovel. Sir.' I said, 'Certainly, Marshall, if it will please you, but why?'

' 'Cause I'm ashamed of meself, Sir. I ain't never been like that before, and my muvver 'ld break 'er 'eart if she knew. It was the shampain what got me down, it's the first time I've 'ad any.'

Then followed a long expression of penitence and thanks for my looking after him, which I terminated by repeating Willis's lecture on the evils of drink and gave him my pardon.

May 6 Sunday. No work again today so I finished off the garden. Really finished it! Every bit of rubbish burnt, paths swept, rose trees cleared and beds weeded. I was planting flowers scrounged from other gardens when Ewing came out and I stood pointing at my handiwork with pride. He stood for a bit sneering slightly then said, 'Well, Vaughan, you know it's labour in vain don't you?' 'Why?' I asked. 'Because we're moving north tomorrow.' And with that he left me.

Gazing round at the result of my many hours of hard work, I felt inclined to cry, but I consoled myself with the thought that someone would get the benefit of them and, finishing the planting of the flowers, I called Hammond and set off to the YMCA to lay in stores, for heaven knew when we would again strike a canteen. Ewing was very fond of a new kind of lemon squash called Kia-Ora and when we had bought stacks of salmon, fruit biscuits, butter, prawns and other tinned stuff, plus much whisky, I thought how nice and kind it would be to buy a case, convey it secretly and enjoy his delight when it was produced at the other end. So we added on to the pile which the servants were coming to fetch.

Returning to the mess we set about the old game of sorting and discarding our property, and packing mess boxes. The Harrison Fisher girls and many of the pretty plates I arranged to take with us. My British Warm, French bayonet and souvenirs I packed up to send home. We all felt a great pang at the thought of leaving Péronne, for we looked upon it as our adopted town, and had grown very fond of it, more practically because our friendship and own closer knowledge of the men had grown there.

Going into the mess after lunch I found Ewing looking at the canteen bill which the servants had brought in. He looked up at me with an angry red face. 'Vaughan, you silly senseless idiot! Why!' he choked. '*Why* will you be buying a case of Kia-Ora when we're moving tomorrow. You *fool*! How the hell do you think you will carry it? Oh! I've no patience wi' you, you're past teaching!'

I was filled with disappointment at the misunderstanding but managed to blurt out a few cusswords, telling him that I was Mess President and not he, and could he mind his own bleedin' business. A long quarrel followed in which he, being

OC, got the better, and I retired into the kitchen to prepare what I intended to be the best dinner we had ever had.

With my own hands I did half the cooking and was very bucked with the results. At 7.30 p.m. I was slicing eggs for the *hors d'oeuvres* when Ewing's angry voice floated out asking why the hell dinner wasn't ready. So I wasn't able to make any mayonnaise. I served up an excellent seven-course dinner but it was a dreary meal. Ewing was a bear and we had hanging over us the depression caused by the knowledge that this was our last meal in the old town and, incidentally, the end of our rest. Radcliffe and I tried to keep things merry but it finally devolved into a 'shop' conversation regarding the possibilities of the future and our destination.

May 7   After a farewell look round the old billet and our happy playground at the lock gates, we fell in with the Company and marched to the Battalion parade ground on the road back to Sainte Radegonde. In a few minutes—at 7.30 a.m.—we moved off and swung out of the town towards Bapaume, striking the cobbled Route Nationale at Mont St Quentin. It was a very hot march, the sun was glaring and the pace was fast. The troops, too, were out of practice so that as I marched behind as second in command, I had a deuce of a job to prevent them straggling.

When we reached Sailly Saillisel, Ewing rode on ahead to see the adjutant, and I took charge of the Company. As we were marching down a sunken road towards Morval, the halt signal was blown and we fell out on the right of the road. The bank, however, was so steep that many of the troops could not get off the road, and when, a few minutes later, a cart came along they had to climb up the bank on the left to allow it to pass.

As they were thus scattered, a high-pitched voice came from behind the cart: 'Where's the officer in charge of this party?' It was the Brigadier riding with his staff, and I went forward and saluted. He was very peeved with us for being on the left of the road; it was 'dam' bad discipline'. He took my name and refused to hear my excuse, riding on to see the CO.

So I had to bow once more before injustice and rejoined my grinning troops who were just falling in to resume the march. After a short time we entered Morval where the head of the column halted by the broken wall. After a ten-minute standing halt, we were about-turned and marched out of the village to a field where we formed up in close column, piled arms and fell out.

We now learnt that we were to spend the night here. It was midday and, having sent the servants down to the road to fetch the mess boxes, we lay down to rest and await our lunch. To while away the time I had another awful row with Ewing about the Kia-Ora—which I had bribed the cooks to carry on the cooker.

We had a cold lunch and then Radcliffe and I went down to the village and wandered round the ruins. On our return we proceeded to rig up bivouacs from oilsheets. We erected two, one for Harding, Radcliffe and me, and the other for Ewing and Hammond. Pepper had gone on to Frémicourt to take over our next billets. It was very difficult to fix a decent shelter with our scanty material and we did not finish until nightfall. The troops did not worry to erect shelters, but lay on the grass wrapped in their oilsheets and coats.

May 8 We were all very wet when we woke, but soon dried as we breakfasted in bright sunshine. Then we packed our valises and mess boxes and sent them down to the dump on the road. An hour later (10 a.m.) we fell in and marched back to Sailly Saillisel, where we turned to the left up the Route Nationale, slogged on to Biencourt and thence to Frémicourt, which we reached at dusk. Having seen the troops into their huts and provided with a hot meal, we found our way to the empty huts allotted to us and dumped our packs on the ground. The servants went down to the cookers and got us some food which the troops had left and this we ate, though it was quite cold. We played about a bit in the hut but were fed up and went to bed early.

May 9 Depression was still upon us when we woke and having dressed we set out sourly to visit the troops in their huts. Cheery as larks we found them and ten minutes of jollying with them raised our spirits and we returned to eat a hearty breakfast, chattering like schoolgirls. Then we chased each other out again into the open to examine our surroundings.

Our camp is just outside the village of Frémicourt—a heap of ruins—and around us stretch undulating grass plains, relieved only by shell-holes and, in the distance, the partly destroyed village of Bancourt. Finding that there were a few empty tents standing near the huts, we decided to take them, and had our kit moved in. I am sharing one with Pepper.

May 10 Pepper went to Amiens on leave this morning so Jimmy Harding moved into my tent for company. I walked over to the 7th Battalion this afternoon to see Fr Woodlock. He was away, and I stopped for a while with Jones, their colossal quartermaster, who is very proud of two fat lumbering puppies which have just arrived—Jumbo and Punch. We have a nondescript terrier on our headquarters staff called 'Idle'. On my way back I wandered off to a small clump of trees where were a number of graves—Boche. Amongst them were the graves of three British airmen, each with a neat cross erected by the Germans giving details of their ages and regiments and date they were shot down. Their broken propellers were planted at their feet.

After mess, Hammond and I walked through the gathering dusk to Bancourt, which looks very pretty from the distance but is in ruins and overgrown with weeds. We wandered into a large garden but were turned back by a sentry who had orders that no one was to approach a large ammunition dump therein. As we walked we talked religion—Hammond being a strict low-church adherent who admires Catholicism from a distance.

May 11 An idle day; inspected troops and did a little drill.

Later wandered about the plains with Hammond. Early to bed.

May 12 Parade and gas drill during morning. In the afternoon played a cricket match against some ASC neighbours. They entertained us with tea and a very excellent concert in a marquee. One turn was particularly good: 'A sister to assist 'er'.

May 13 Sunday. We spent the day preparing to move up the line and were given maps of our new position, which is just below Bullecourt, in front of Quéant and Pronville. At dusk we moved off, I marching in front with Ewing. Following a track along the edge of a small wood, we passed another battalion lying down. We also halted until it was dark enough to proceed, then half an hour later we set off along the main cobbled road leading to Cambrai.

For an hour we marched in perfect quiet and then far ahead was a flash followed by the boom of one of our guns. Almost at the same moment we had to spread out to avoid a shell-hole. From there on the shell-holes became more frequent and the road was littered with the large, loose cobbles. The gun was firing at intervals of exactly two minutes until at last we reached its position and halted for a rest before striking off across the fields for the final stage.

The rain—of course—had started, and things seemed pretty miserable to me as I lay in the wet grass in full pack with the front line half a mile off. Pushing on we moved across a faint track and had just climbed on to an open plain when the order 'Gas Alert' was passed back. We got our gas-masks ready but save for a slight smell of pineapple there was no development.

Presently guides arrived and we were led away to the right whilst the rest of the Battalion carried on. Passing in single file through the long grass over several disused trenches, we had the usual trouble with our guide, who, not having any equipment to hamper him, was dashing on at a high speed in his anxiety to get the relief over.

At the trench wherein we learnt was the Company HQ dugout, we picked up one guide per platoon, and took our separate paths to the front line—I to the left, Radcliffe centre, Harding to the right. Hammond, Pepper and Ewing remained with 16 platoon in the HQ trench.

A gradual downward slope of 200 yards brought us to a trench barely 20 yards long. Here an officer greeted me and climbed up on top. I dropped Dunham, Sergeant Jowett and the reserve section and the remainder of us went forward to the line of posts in front. There were only two for me to hold and these I placed in the charge of Corporals McKay and Wood.

Having posted these sections we returned to the trench behind and climbed down the slippery earth steps. A small cubby-hole had been scooped into the front of the trench, and into this we crawled. There was just room for us to lie full length on the straw, with a candle stuck between us on a piece of stick jabbed into the side. Here I signed for the stores of bombs, Very lights, ammunition and petrol tins which I had checked, and I asked the officer if he had any tips to give me about the trench. He told me that everything was very quiet but that no one could move by day. At night Jerry had strong patrols out in No Man's Land, but his line was a thousand yards away.

May 14   Then we being mutually satisfied he led his platoon away and I despatched Dunham to HQ with my 'Relief Complete' message. I then took Sergeant Jowett and Edge (the runner) across the 80 yards which separated us from our left post. Here there was a steep bank about ten feet high running towards the enemy and in the side was a nice cosy dugout where Corporals Harrison and Newey were issuing rations to the men not on sentry. About ten yards forward along the bank were Julian and Haine lying in the grass. When I spoke to them they sounded very bloodthirsty! They said they were longing for a scrap, and showed me a small pile of bombs they were itching to use.

Then I went back to the trench, which although deep at the posts is only knee deep for the hundred yards which led to No 41 post where McKay had his Lewis gun team. They were also very cheery and Mac touched me for some tobacco—to the great amusement of Sergeant Jowett who told me that Mac had never bought a scrap of baccy, but was never without a smoke.

I then sent Jowett back and continued alone to the right following the barbed wire until in a few minutes I met Radcliffe coming to meet me. We walked back together to my posts and then decided to break the ice thoroughly by going out into No Man's Land. I felt awfully frightened and my heart beat very high as for the first time I passed through the wire into the silence and mystery of the unknown ground. The moon was giving a faint light through the clouds, which enabled us to see dimly for about 50 yards.

For about a hundred yards we walked slowly forward, seeing nothing but grass and occasionally a shell-hole. Then suddenly Radcliffe grasped my arm and pulled me quietly but quickly down into the long grass. Holding my breath I heard a faint but distinct rustle of knees ploughing through clover and then dimly in front I saw a small party of men approaching us. They halted 40 yards away and I lay frozen with fear and excitement. But Radcliffe was gurgling with laughter. I punched him in the ribs but he breathed gurglingly, 'They didn't reckon on my trench club!' and he shoved forward the thin swishy cane he had brought with him.

The party now moved slowly across to our left, jabbing the long grass with their bayonets, whilst we crawled swiftly backwards to the trench. We got McKay to bring his gun out in front but did not let him fire as the party had now moved on to the front of the Australians on our left. We left him on the alert and then went back to Harrison's post.

As we got into the trench there was a crack and a spluttering swish as a Very light shot up from the Australians' post, and burst into a vivid white flame overhead. A fraction of a second later there was a burst of rifle and Lewis gunfire and McKay's gun opened on our right. As a second light shot up, I just saw faint figures in front running and dropping, then there was quiet and a darkness more intense than before.

A minute later a long burst of machine-gun fire swept over us, sending us ducking to the bottom of the trench. Then there was perfect quiet and I took Raddy back to my little cubby-hole where Dunham had laid out my blanket, oilsheet, rations, cigarettes and a bottle of port.

We took turns at drinking port from a tin mug, then Raddy went back to his posts and I began to draw a map of the position and made out a report on the patrol. I was so pleased at having broken the ice that I felt quite anxious to get out again with a fighting patrol behind me.

I was awake all night visiting the posts, thoroughly enjoying the keen, fresh air, and the quiet moonlight. There was no more firing nor lights of any kind and at 6 a.m., when day had broken, I curled up in my cubby-hole with Dunham and slept peacefully.

May 15   At about 12 noon I woke and, while Dunham still slept, I wormed my way out under the oilsheet which screened the front of our hole, and standing erect in the trench I met a fresh sweet breeze and clear, warm sunlight that made me glowing and alert in a moment. Raising my arms in a luxurious stretch I rose on tiptoe and looked round the stretch of ground behind me—a slight valley of long coarse grass thickly strewn with poppies and dog daisies.

The sweep was broken only by a faint track which led back the slope to my left towards where Ewing had remained with the Reserve Platoon, and any occasional shell-holes. There was no sign of life and no sound save for the faint rustle of the grass on the parapet. Not even a bird was stirring, and I felt crude and coarse as I walked upon the broken rushwork of the trench floor, round the corner to where Jowett lay on his back in a cubby-hole, smoking and watching his servant Edge slicing bully for his dinner.

After saying 'Good morning' I sat down at his feet and in

silence lit a cigarette. He too was silent and for some minutes we remained so, puffing blue clouds up into the clear air above the trench. The calm and silence seemed as fragile, and the sky as dainty, as the picture on a Dresden plate and, when finally we spoke, his voice sounded harsh and grating—but it broke an uncomfortable sentimental spell.

It was a commonplace remark about the 'cushiness' of the sector and I answered accordingly, and then we went on to the ordinary military talk about the section formations and deficiencies of equipment. But even then I was picturing him lying thus and smoking in a deck chair outside a cottage in his beloved Hampshire village.

Leaving him and the cherubic Edge to argue with the bully, I passed on to the right, stopping to exchange a word with the occupants of each shelter, some of whom were reading an old copy of the *Birmingham Post*, some eating, some cleaning rifles. After a dozen yards or so the trench became shallow and suddenly ended. Leaning out over the parapet at the end I found Taylor.

Taylor is my black sheep. He is a Birmingham rough and is always in trouble, accompanied by Dawson who is his inseparable companion. They live, sleep, fight and get drunk together, and (I am certain) will die together. I have many times tried to get into Taylor's heart but he is as close as an oyster and sheers off whenever I talk to him. With Dawson however I have quite an understanding. I choke him off and punish him as firmly as is necessary, but after it is over we are just as chummy.

So I leant over beside Taylor and having made the obvious remark about the weather, commenced to study the view. I was very disappointed for I had hoped to see the Boche line, but the ground rose so sharply in front that I could only see about a dozen yards of foreground, and even my own posts were not visible.

And my surprise was even greater that Taylor should have been so wrapt in thought when there was nothing to study. I could not imagine him having any sentimentality which would drive him away to solitary reverie when sleep, cards or crown and anchor were available in his shelter. I therefore threw out a few tentative remarks, but he answered very abruptly then edged away and disappeared round the corner.

After a few minutes I followed him back to my cubby-hole where I dragged the sleeping Dunham by his ankles, up-braiding him for wasting such delightful sunlight—especially when I wanted my lunch. Then I went on round the other corner to see Corporal Wood.

'Bobby' was sitting in his shelter writing a letter and he grinned amiably when I appeared. 'Bit better'n Blighty, don't you think, Sir?' I agreed that there was less worry and certainly more peace, and he climbed out of his shelter to stand with me drinking in the atmosphere. It was indeed still. Not a sound could be heard but the tinkle of a button stick in the next recess, until without warning there was a mighty crash and a spray of earth and stones fell over us as we flung ourselves against the trench side.

A high-velocity shell bursting 30 yards in front had effectively broken the spell and as Wood climbed back into his recess, I hurried back to mine—not that these holes afford the slightest protection, except against small splinters, but as a rabbit seeks its burrow, so we each dash to our own hole for safety. Dunham was standing in the trench with a tin of pork and beans in his hand and a look of mingled surprise and indignation on his face.

His uttered opinion of Jerry was cut short by another and closer explosion, and again we grovelled until we heard the singing fragments pass overhead, when we rose and, climbing on to the steps, were in time to see the smoke drifting away from a fresh round hole around which the grass was covered with a thin layer of earth and pebbles.

Well, the best antidote to fear is food, so we sat on the mouth of our hole and shared a tin of bully and beans, and I drank port whilst Dunham made tea over a Tommy's cooker. The sides of the trench heaved twice more, but the shells were no nearer. However, the silence was dispelled, and the birds were now twittering with alarm. Voices were raised in song, talk and laughter and, as the afternoon wore on, the sky became darker and at five o'clock a few spots of rain began to fall.

At dusk it was raining softly. We climbed out and trudged through the long wet grass to the line where the troops were standing-to—all very cheerful. I saw the sentries posted and then walked out slowly to the right to meet Raddy, who I guessed would stroll along. As we slowly returned, everything became deathly quiet again, and it was so dark that we had to find our way by following the barbed wire.

We were still in the open near the right post when I grabbed his arm and we stood motionless. I had heard the faint crack of a 'grenatenwerfer'—forgotten since Biaches—and after a faint short swish the bomb burst with a sharp shattering crash and a spurt of yellow sparks—*overhead*!

Immediately a cold fear gripped me, for I realized instantly that there was *no cover* from these. It was no use lying down, for their burst was downward and they were immediately overhead. We waited for several minutes, and as the fire was not repeated I cheered myself by saying that this was only an accidental premature, and that the ground busters were quite harmless.

But this hope was soon shattered, for suddenly there came a persistent stream of them all bursting at the same height over our line. The fragments whizzed past us and struck the ground with horrid thuds, and our nerves were terribly racked. But reaching my post we found the troops taking not the slightest notice of them, so in feigned nonchalance we strolled along, chaffing the NCOs and questioning the sentries until the 'pineapples' ceased—15 minutes later.

Radcliffe was taking his patrol out from my right post, so I waited there while he went back to fetch them, then one by one we passed through the gap in the wire and crouched in the wet grass until the formation was complete. We advanced in jumps, Raddy and I creeping forward with a runner, scenting the ground for 50 yards at a time, and then sending

the runner back for the patrol. After a while we got tired of
this, so we left the patrol where it was and we two crept on
alone until we reached a junction of two roads that ran across
No Man's Land. The road was sunken and as we approached
we heard faint voices and, looking over the bank, there, hard
at work digging a hole, were eight or ten large Boche.

We were neither surprised nor alarmed. We just lay
watching them amusedly for a couple of minutes, then
crawled off back to the patrol. I was wondering what on earth
induced them to dig holes in No Man's Land, when a figure
almost upright hurried past us and was lost in the darkness
behind. So *we* stood up then and ran back to where our lads
were lying chilled, wet and fed up. Quickly we told them
what we had seen, and in a moment they were alert and we set
off together—out for blood.

Alas! When we reached the crossroads nothing remained
of the working party but a few chalky shovels. So we had to
be content with firing a few rounds down the road after them,
and then we walked back, laughing and talking, whilst four of
the silly asses marched the shovels between them with great
ceremony and exaggerated caution as though they were
enemy prisoners.

This little jaunt has left us with our tails well up, and I, for
one, am very keen on No Man's Land. I fully appreciate the
truth of the maxim that was dinned into us during training—
'Fighting patrols are the finest stiffeners of morale'.

May 16 The remainder of the night was uneventful except
for a breezy five minutes at 1.30 a.m. when one of our own
18-pounder batteries fired 24 shells straight on to our own
left post, and one 9-inch shell which fell 20 yards from my
cubby-hole. There were no casualties.

Still overcast and drizzling at midday when I woke. I lay
on my back watching tiny beetles running excitedly about my
earth roof and walls, until Dunham woke and lent me his
recently received copy of a Dorset local paper. I glanced
through the bloodcurdling description of local sewing-bees

and Band of Hope debaucheries, then I tried to write a letter but could not draw any cheerful inspiration from the drip-drip of the rain past the mouth of our hole, *nor* from the wet stretcher and bomb boxes outside. So I gave it up and told Dunham to join me in a whistle. In harmony we passed from 'The Minstrel Boy' to 'Marble Halls' but it was too exhausting and we relinquished that pastime in favour of an onslaught on a cold chunk of doubtful steak—covered with muddy whiskers of sandbag, followed by a tin of peaches.

After this sumptuous repast, I crawled out and threw the oilsheet, which had been my bed, over my shoulders and walked round the trench. With the exception of Dredge—who was gas sentry—everybody was fast asleep, and Dredge, being very deaf and *very* stupid, is no good as a conversationalist. So I had perforce to pace up and down the wet muddy crack, and yearn for a nice long exciting trench.

Evening gave us half an hour of faint sunshine which served only to accentuate the drabness of our surroundings. Darkness, chasing the sun down very quickly, left the sky behind us a strip of flaming red so that I judged it wiser to wait a bit before I moved the troops forward to the front line for stand-to. As I was gathering them together I heard the sentry shout a challenge which was answered by the voice of Colonel Hanson.

I climbed out and met him, receiving a terse choke-off for not having moved forward earlier. He may have believed my reason, but in any case he didn't approve it. I walked round my line with him; he had no remarks to make and having given him a guide to Radcliffe's left post I dropped into my right one, beside McKay.

I have never seen McKay depressed. He was always a fund of original humour, and seeing that I was fed up he set himself to cheer me by chaffing Corporal Newey about the latter's card losses during the afternoon. His cure was working well when I heard someone approaching from behind and went out to meet Samuel who had come up from the reserve company to look round the line. After a few minutes' talk he called my attention to a faint rumbling in the distance which we at first took to be thunder. But as it rumbled nearer and nearer we distinguished the individual boom of batteries and knew it for an artillery barrage swelling and deepening on our left.

The unrest spread across our front and soon short bursts of rifle and machine-gun fire came from Jerry's line, answered by fire from the Australians beside us. We thought we would walk over to the high ground on our left to see something of the battle that obviously was raging round Bullecourt. So we went out through the wire. We had just got in front of No 42 post when a machine-gun opened at close range and we flattened out under a stream of bullets.

It lasted about half a minute, during which time I heartily wished I was on the other side of Sammy (who is large and round). Then all was quiet again and we rose and doubled back to the line, forsaking our intention of visiting the Australians. Sammy lurched off to Radcliffe's sector while I took half a dozen men out in front.

May 17   We wandered about for an hour but it was wet and cold and miserable. We saw nothing and returned fed up to await dawn which came an hour and a half late owing to a thick fog.

I woke for lunch at 1 p.m., after which, the day being dry (though dull), I was allowing myself the luxury of a bath in a mug of warm water when a salvo of whizzbangs burst between my hole and Company HQ. Followed an uncomfortable 15 minutes while the brutes continued to crash about us—54 in all. They were directed at the little path which connected us—and damn good shooting too.

Stood to as usual after dusk and at 9 p.m. decided to wander up to Ewing's HQ for a walk. Followed the little path —now pitted by six direct shell hits—up a steep slippery bank to a trench whence a Lewis gun glared at me and a challenge was hurled. Further along the trench, by some earth steps, was the figure of our 'Little Treasure', Sergeant Major Chalk. He directed me to Ewing's dugout almost opposite the steps.

I sent Dunham off to see Martin and entered the shelter where Ewing was making out his reports by candlelight. He was not very thrilled on seeing me and having offered me a drink he went on with his work. I poured myself out a whisky and watched him for a couple of minutes until there was the rustle of an oilsheet and a clank of rifle on steel hat, and entered Quartermaster Sergeant Braham with a natty salute.

He reported rations delivered and asked if we wanted anything special from the EFC. Then flinging the cape of his 'wetter' over his shoulder he dived into his pocket for the last canteen bill which he handed to me with a grin. I was studying the items when there was a gasping and stumbling outside and as we sprang up with drawn revolvers a dishevelled figure rushed in and fell on Ewing's bed laughing and gasping 'Whisky! Whisky!'

We recognised him as Captain Melhuish of the 1/7th Worcesters and having supplied him with the required beverage we waited eagerly for his explanation of the mode of his entry. Laughing like an idiot he told us that he had come up to look round our line as he was going to relieve us on the 21st. He had declined to bring a guide, as the position seemed so simple to find, and accompanied by his servant he had left the main road and stepped off into the darkness in our direction. After walking for a long time, he had begun to think that he had gone wrong when he came to a large post full of troops. With a sigh of relief he had jumped over the edge and slithered down, to find himself sitting staring into the faces of a group of Germans!

He said that all had sat motionless with surprise for several seconds until his servant on top had spoken. Then with a frantic yell of 'My God! They're *Boche!*' he had cleared the hole at a bound and beat it followed by a fusilade of shots. He had not stopped running until he fell into our trench. When his tale was finished I said cheerio to them and followed Braham out into the trench.

We now noticed for the first time that the terrific rumble

had recommenced to the north and as we stood on the trench top we could see the sky lighting and flickering above Bullecourt. The breeze was laden with moisture and a few spots of rain began to fall as we started to return to our little home.

The darkness was intense and we had to feel our way along the strand of plain wire that led to my posts. It was raining heavily when we reached my hole and walking fairly fast I stepped straight into the trench—a sheer drop of six feet—checked only when the point of my chin hit the top of an angle iron picket which gave me a horrible jagged cut.

May 18 Walked about with a beard of bloody bandage all night. Fed up, did not go out on patrol. Trench full of water at dawn and we crawled into our cubby-holes miserably longing for the rum issue to recommence.

Horribly wet when we crawled out again during the afternoon. Water in trench over our boots. It got dark early and we were soon shivering in the line, watching our artillery pounding the German lines. This is their first decent effort during this tour, but it doesn't seem to worry the Boche any. Radcliffe did not come over during the night.

May 19 All quiet and uneventful. Message came up during the evening that we will be relieved tomorrow night. Cheers!! Raddy spent most of the night with me and we ate a lot and drank more—to save carrying things out of the line with us. Dawn was in consequence much rosier and I went to sleep feeling very cheery.

May 20 Sunday. I spent the wet afternoon checking the trench stores whilst the troops cleaned up the trench. All paper, tins, etc, were piled together ready to be buried at dusk; then they got their packs ready. At dusk, the tins being buried, I sent off all men not actually on sentry and waited until 11 p.m. when, after a steady approach of jingling equipment through the darkness, a very young and very raw officer whispered down for 'the officer in charge'. I hailed him down and he crawled very gingerly in beside me in my little cubby-hole, while Sergeant Jowett carried his platoon off to the line to relieve our posts.

Whilst telling the new arrival all about the geography of the position and getting his receipt for the stores, I plied him with whisky in his own tin mug. Then I took him round the line, collected my relieved posts and bidding him 'goodnight and good luck,' set off back to Ewing's HQ. On entering I found Radcliffe already there—our troops were lying on the wet grass up top—and shortly afterwards Jimmy Harding joined us. I was glad to see him again. It's only a week since I last saw him but it seems ages.

May 21   Bidding goodbye to Melhuish and his officers, we climbed out and in heavy rain moved the troops off in column of fours towards the road up which we had come in a week earlier. We did not strike it, however, for Ewing led us off to the right and for a long time we marched over the torn fields. The rain increased until it was a regular downpour, and when we were well soaked Ewing gave us the order to put on oilsheets!

As we moved on after doing so, I noticed that he glanced continually at his map, by the aid of a torch, and I guessed that he had lost his way. The troops guessed it too, and when he finally halted and confessed as much, a murmur of truculence arose which Radcliffe and I had much difficulty in quelling.

However, SM Chalk set off into the darkness and after a few minutes returned with the news that we were only half a mile from our destination. As we marched on again I ventured to ask Ewing what our destination was, but he snapped 'Ye'll know when ye get there!' It was Chalk who told me that we were approaching a ruined village called Morchies where I was to remain with my platoon while the remainder of the Battalion went into tents behind.

While we were talking we struck a broad wagon track which led in a curve to the left through a thick hedge and deposited us at what appeared to be a crossroads. In the darkness we could just distinguish a road straight ahead and one to the left. Here Ewing halted and his stragglers closed up.

It seems hardly credible, but he left me there with no orders other than that I was to stay with my platoon 'as escort to the guns hereabouts'. To my questions concerning the position of the guns, my duties as escort, the location of his HQ, where my kit would be dumped, etc, I received the reply: 'Don't waste my time now; get off on your duty.'

So when he had marched straight on, I took the only road and bore to the left. Here the road was sunken and into the steep bank were cut numerous dugouts. As these were unoccupied I told my troops to make themselves comfortable in them while I had a look around.

Dawn was breaking as I plodded up the road, and where the road was bounded by banks 16 feet high, the dugouts showed signs of occupation. Suddenly I was challenged in an unmistakably colonial voice and in answer to my questions the sentry (an Australian) indicated the officers' dugout—a large shelter built into the bank with a table, chair and gas-gong outside. I opened the door quietly and saw an officer sitting at a table playing patience by the light of two candles, a whisky glass beside him.

He looked up, and seeing me he spoke and acted simul-taneously: 'Come in and sit down', and a fist shot out with a clean glass. He poured me a whisky as I unbuckled my equipment, and I liked the look of him. He was remarkably handsome, with very large blue eyes and silvery white curly hair. He had no collar or tie and his open tunic bore the Australian badge on the lapels.

As I drank my whisky he told me that he was in command of that battery of Australian artillery and that he had been waiting up for me. I told him I had never heard of such an escort before, and could he tell me what it was and why. But he waved a brown hand at me. 'Tomorrow, sonny! Tomorrow. I'm dead tired, and you ought to be, so let's get to bed. Have you got your kit?' I told him 'No'. 'Oh, we'll soon fix that!' he replied and leaning back he yelled into what appeared to be an enormous grave which I had not noticed hitherto.

Two figures were squirming about and in response to his announcement of my arrival each handed up a blanket. I did not want to take them but he smothered my protests by wrapping them round my head and pushing me out of the door. Extricating myself, I followed him into a tin hut on the roadside where he lit a hurricane lamp and dragged the mattress from his bed onto the floor. Adding one of his own blankets, he ran out before I could argue and left me to settle in.

Waking to a bright midday sun, I lay looking at my untidy surroundings and wondering what the loud bangs were that I could hear. Only half awake, I thought they were the Australian guns, and that I ought to be escorting them! But as I jumped up I realized that they were crashes, not bangs— and uncomfortably near too!

I slipped on my tunic and went out into the road, bathed in dazzling sunlight. My side of the road was littered with evidence of troops' occupation—helmets, bully tins, buckets, wood, shell-cases, etc; the other side was bare except for a military well and a large crowd of troops who were lying flat against the bank. The reason for this was obvious.

Behind us was a village of mingled red roofs and trees, which extended to the corner where we had parted from Ewing last night. And at this corner now was a large cloud of red dust into which shell after shell was falling with deadly regularity and precision. The chunks of shrapnel and brick were falling about me, so I did not stand still for long—I grabbed my tin hat and joined my platoon on the bank.

When I realized that it was only *my* fellows who were on that side of the road, and that the few Australian gunners who had worried to come out were sitting on their own side, smoking and watching the shelling, I felt quite ashamed, and returned to my bedroom to put on my puttees before going into their mess.

I found the skipper with his two subs, one very small and dark—black eyes, hair and 'toothbrush'—known as Garry, the other a silent, dull-looking chap called Jack. They greeted me very hospitably, and chipped me about the windiness of my troops. While I explained that they had not been subjected to shelling for some time, and would have to get used to it again, Garry fished out a gramophone and we listened to some cheery revue records until a servant appeared with lunch. They were very familiar with this servant, and Christian names were freely interchanged.

During an excellent lunch I heard how some months before a party of 30 Boche had managed to get through our line to a battery of guns in this position. They had surprised and killed the gunners, spiked the guns and returned. They had been wiped out on trying to return through our posts, but ever since a platoon had been detailed to assist in defending the guns. The skipper pointed out to me a pile of shell boxes which he said contained a supply of shrapnel fused to burst at point blank, which he guaranteed would keep the Boche at 200 yards—if he ever did get so near again.

The shelling continued until 3 p.m., by which time we reckoned about 400 must have fallen. The troops had got used to them very early on and were walking about freely, but I noticed that they did not mix with the Australians; rather they acted on the popular distrust and kept a wary eye on their belongings.

At 3.30 I walked along to the troops' dugouts to inspect them. They were a wretched lot of holes and needed improving badly. So I made out an indent for 300 sandbags which I gave to Dunham telling him to go and find my kit, and to find HQ. Then I had the troops out for a rifle inspection and half an hour's gas drill. Then tea.

After dark Dunham returned wheeling a comic old trolley with my valise—soaked in water. He said he had found it lying where it had been dumped in a big pool. He was accompanied by Berry and Cooper, both of 'B' Company. They have only come for accommodation I think.

Cooper is a very young, childish-faced 2nd Lieut with a frequent mirthless laugh and idiotic conversation. He has already jarred my nerves by wandering about singing repeatedly 'Brown bread—well buttered', which are the only words he knows of some senseless song. Berry is a good-hearted chap but very foul-mouthed and loud-voiced. He drinks far too much and when he turned up this evening he was very tight. He is going on leave tomorrow.

I have been particularly struck by the niceness of the Australians' conversation. They never swear and their ordinary talk is very gentle and homely, the kind and intelligent discussions contrasting sharply with the coarse or harsh inanities that resound in the messes of most British units. They seem to have a tremendous respect and admiration for their skipper, too, although they are all so familiar.

As soon as Berry and Cooper arrived, Jack and Garry cleared their belongings out of the grave to make room for them, and I moved my valise in to the mess so that they could join their skipper. Then we all sat down to dinner.

May 22 When I rose for breakfast at 8 a.m. Berry had had his and was dressed in marching order ready to go on leave. He suddenly remembered that he had no money, so I lent him 40 francs. Then he shook hands and stumped off towards the village while I sat down to breakfast. The Australians are messing by themselves in future in the tin hut, and as Cooper was still asleep, I had breakfast alone.

Bridge and Pepper turned up during the morning and took over the grave, Cooper being pushed out to an ajacent cubby-hole. It was a frightfully hot day, and the troops wandered about the road playing pitch and toss or 'nearest the line', clad only in tin hats, linen shorts and boots.

The shelling was repeated at midday but was ignored by the troops except for a small clique (including of course

McKay and Newey) who arranged a small sweepstake as to which particular house would escape damage. I spent the morning overhauling my kit and putting out things for Dunham to clean. Pepper and Bridge wander about on their own and have very little to say to me.

I had a kit inspection in the afternoon and at dusk went with Garry to see the positions which we would occupy in case of alarm. Starting from the road junction on our left we pushed out through the hedge towards a clump of trees a couple of hundred yards in front. This proved to be one of those charming French 'calvaries': a horseshoe of bushy trees enclosing a small mound whereon stood a huge crucifix. One of the trees had been felled by a shell and a tiny graveyard behind was pitted with shell-holes. This had evidently been used as a ranging mark by the artillery of one side or the other.

The post which we were to work upon now, and occupy in case of attack, was immediately in front of the graveyard and commanded a fine view of the valley which ran forward towards the Boche. As I stood surveying the field of fire with the critical eye of the infantryman, my attention was caught by a salvo of pink shrapnel bursts at the far end of the valley. Then a crowd of troops appeared running full tilt down the road, relentlessly pursued by the pretty pink spitfires. The shelling stopped when they were about 300 yards from us, leaving me with the certain knowledge that the road is under enemy observation.

We then moved straight off to our right, visiting a series of similar posts at intervals, 150 yards in front of our sunken road. Just behind the posts stood the guns, absolutely in the open, and covered with camouflage sheets.

Since dinner I have been making out indents for my troops' deficiencies of kit and playing patience. Pepper and Bridge have gone off to one of the other messes and Cooper (thank God!) is in with the Australians.

May 23 Same old shelling, frightfully close but did no

damage. We are used to it now so we were not disturbed, but the village is looking very haggard and there is hardly a house left standing. We spent the afternoon doing gas-drill and rifle exercises—much to the disgust of the troops who do not like doing work when we are isolated and (as they imagine) uncontrolled. At dusk we went out to the 'calvary' post and did a little work. We were unable to do any wiring, which is really needed, as we had no cutters or gloves. When we returned at 9 o'clock we found that a hot meal had been sent up from behind. This being our first for a week caused great satisfaction to the troops.

May 24   I wanted to ask the adjutant to send me up some wiring materials, so early this morning I went in to the Australian signal dugout and asked them to get me through. When the old D3 receiver was handed to me, I heard Hoskins' voice at the other end. I said, 'This is Vaughan speaking. I want some wire-cutters and gloves sent up this evening for work on my posts.' He didn't seem to understand, so I said, 'You know I am acting as escort to the guns——' But here he shouted 'Shut up at once and ring off!' and put down his instrument, leaving me utterly bewildered. I left the signallers grinning at my embarrassment and returned to the dugout to send off the message by runner. I found Willis waiting with a message from Radcliffe—a cheery little note saying 'do come round to tea and cheer us up'.

At lunchtime another note arrived from Hoskins saying that I was wanted at HQ during the afternoon. I was very puzzled by this note, not having an inkling of what I was wanted for. Leave, promotion, special jobs—all kinds of ideas passed through my head as I dressed after lunch, making myself as smart and clean as possible—much to the amusement of Bridge and Pepper who kept up a running fire of criticism and sarcastic advice.

Finally at four o'clock, accompanied by Dunham, I set off with my tin hat at the exact angle, and an inch of green stocking showing above my highly polished trench boots.

There was no shelling in the village, for which I was indescribably grateful, for during a strafe it is a veritable death-trap.

It was a blazing afternoon and we found it hot work climbing round shell-holes and over the piles of brickwork that obliterated the road. Every bit of wall that was standing was scarred and chipped, and the whole village reeked of lyddite and stale brick-dust. Only the trees and bushes which have overgrown the place retained their freshness and the bright greenery gave a soothing touch to the awful scene of destruction. We only saw one man in the village—a military policeman—at the centre crossroads.

We passed right through the village and then Dunham led me off to the left along the very last wall which was quite un-marked, and close to which we found HQ. They were at tea outside their tents—Colonel Hanson, Hoskins, Mortimore and Captain Taylor (OC 'A' Company). The latter wore a brilliantly coloured silk handkerchief round his head, brigand-fashion, and all the others were in the last stages of *déshabillé*—shorts and shirts only, lying about on the grass or sprawled on boxes.

As I approached I heard the CO say '*who* on earth is this?' Whereupon all turned and stared until Mortimore said 'It's Vaughan!' and everybody laughed. I saluted and stood blushing with shame while they found nothing to say except 'good afternoon'. Then after a long awkward silence I stammered out that Hoskins had sent for me. The con-founded little pup said, 'Oh yes so I did,' as if he had forgotten about it. Then he drew me aside and said, 'I wanted to speak about your foolish remark on the phone this morning. You should know that it is a court-martial offence to say anything which could give information to the enemy. Every message is picked up by them.'

Now Hoskins is only a 2nd Lieutenant acting Captain, and he's never done any service in the line. So I was not inclined to take a choke off from him. I interrupted him furiously and told him that I knew all he did about *anything*, and that I had said nothing on the phone which could teach the Boche anything. There were batteries all over France and escorts too, and I might have been any one of them.

Under my tirade he caved in and changed to a conciliatory tone, saying that he had only meant to give me a friendly hint in case I did not know. I cut the conversation off by saluting the CO from a distance and making my way back to the road, being joined by Dunham, who all this time had been picking flowers through a hole in the wall. We returned to where the MP was on duty, then turned to the left; there were a few ruined houses on either side of the road, then it ran out into the open, screened on either side by a low bank. Just past the last house on the left was a small pond, whence protruded the grey-clad knee of a dead German. The water around him was green and on his knee was perched a large rat making a meal.

The bank nearer the Boche was honeycombed with shelters for troops. The first ones were occupied by Australians who took no notice of us. But they were very jolly and as they lay about basking in the sunshine we were accompanied by a buzz of talk and laughter as we traversed the few hundred yards that brought us to the whiter faces and cleaner billets of No 16 platoon.

All these lads stood up as we approached and each salute to me was followed by a greeting to Dunham who is immensely popular throughout the Company. He took their homage as I took their salutes—things to be expected as due to superior rank—and he acknowledged them in the same way. Dear old Dunham! His four-months association with the mess has made him feel a part of the Company administration, and in his dealings with the other men he shows a condescension and authority that many NCOs would do well to emulate, and which increase the respect with which he is treated. He had grown out of the stupidity which caused Hatwell to give him to me, and is now my most valuable possession.

The Company mess was the last cubby-hole in the road and entering I found Radcliffe and Harding—the latter fast asleep. Radcliffe seemed very glad to see me and arm in arm we went out into the sunshine and walked up and down the road. He told me that Ewing was becoming unbearable; being aware of his shortcomings and terrified of appearing incompetent as a company commander, he was continually strafing and fussing about, particularly harassing his two unfortunate subalterns.

I gave him a description of my life as 'escort to the guns', which made him very envious, then seeing Martin enter the mess with a teapot we followed him in and tipped Jimmy Harding out of his chair on to the grass-covered floor. Dear old Jimmy sat rubbing his eyes and in a tearful voice bemoaned the fact that he had no friend in the world, and that his forced acquaintances had no respect for his old age. We consoled him and coaxed him to sit at table with us, which he consented to do the more readily as a new tin of curried prawns had just arrived from the canteen.

I was just getting up, when Ewing himself came in. He was in shorts and carried his tin hat fastened under his shoulder strap, so I guessed that he had been reconnoitring. But as he sat down and commenced to eat in moody silence, we refrained from questioning him, and continued the light conversation that always prevails amongst officers—the recalling of past stunts, debating the present situation and surmizing the future. Soon the prawns began to whisper to Ewing that he was being unsociable and he ventured a few shy remarks. Eventually he told us that we were to move up to the line again on the 29th to the same sector, only that the positions of the platoons would be changed.

I remained until it was dark, and then thought it was time to rejoin my platoon. I routed out Dunham and set off back, Raddy and Harding walking with me to the crossroads. Parting from them I decided to take a short cut through the ruined houses and gardens, but having started I soon regretted it, for away from the road, and in the shade of the trees, the darkness was intense and we floundered about amongst shell-holes, piles of bricks, prickly bushes, broken ploughs and all sorts of obstacles. The excursion was, needless to say, a very profane one until we struck a fairly clear patch. Here we halted for a moment to take breath and there were four terrific and blinding simultaneous explosions. We flung ourselves to earth and lay grovelling in a panic until a shouted order and the clink of shell cases told us that we had walked on to one of our batteries.

With badly shaken nerves we hurried behind it and raced on until we dropped into the road that was our home. The battery kept up a monotonous fire long after I had settled my nerves with a stiff drink.

May 25–27   These three days were spent in a quiet instructive manner: mornings—watching shelling; afternoons—gas and rifle drill; evenings—an hour's wiring on the posts. My free time I have spent in perfecting myself in the use of the Playfair code, in making out new platoon roles and in drawing delightful little maps of the roads to Vélù to guide my section commanders thither when they go down for baths on the 28th.

Sunday 27th: Orders for baths cancelled late today.

May 28   The usual 'day-before'—inspections, returns of working strength, carting working materials back to HQ, etc. There was no excitement as we are familiar with the sector, but I believe my lads are quite pleased to be going back to the wild poppy-covered land of night patrols and daydreams. I know that there is that feeling somewhere in *my* mind.

Poor little Cooper has been trying very hard all this time to be friendly, and I have grown to like him quite a lot. He is a very decent boy and seems very keen to get up the line, this being his first time up. Pepper and Bridge allow no sign of their emotions to be seen, and simply prepare their kit with no comments other than dry discussion of the operation orders.

May 29   Everything was cleared up and I said goodbye to the Australians with real regret, thanking them from the bottom of my heart for their hospitality to me when I came, a stranger, amongst them. One of the most pathetic features of the war is this continual forming of real friendships which last a week or two, or even months, and are suddenly shattered for ever by death or division.

The remainder of the Company came up to us an hour before dusk, and we led them on, Ewing walking with me in front. He was in high humour and consequently quite communicative. The track that we followed skirted Lagnicourt, which is out of bounds to everybody owing to there being 2,000 dead lying in and around the village.

As we marched Ewing told me that an order had been circulated emphasizing the need for offensive patrols, in accordance with which each of our platoons was to carry out an all-night patrol in turn. I had a sudden inspiration and asked if I and my platoon might monopolize the honour and do them all. He jumped at the idea, as it will save him a lot of organization and we agreed that provided the CO and, of course, my men were agreeable, I should keep them in the reserve trench with HQ and employ them only on fighting patrols.

The journey to the line was uneventful and soon we were in the HQ dugout with Melhuish, drinking whisky and swopping news and small talk. It was obvious from their talk that they have done no patrolling and that Jerry has regained complete control of No Man's Land, for he has actually attacked their posts on more than one occasion during their tour.

When they had gone we made ourselves comfortable. Our shelter is merely a large square pit dug close to the trench and entered by a short passage. A few boards on top support a tarpaulin sheet over which is a light covering of earth and turf. On either side an earth couch about two feet high has been left and on these we have spread each his oilsheet and blanket and sandbag stuffed with straw. Between us a shelf has been driven into the earth wall and now supports our candles and couple of books. On the walls I have pinned my

Harrison Fisher girls, and in one corner is a fine heap of bombs, SOS rockets, Very lights and ammunition. By Jove! It's the most comfortable, cosy dugout we have had, and I am beginning to love Ewing a bit more.

In the front line, Radcliffe has my old section on the left, Harding centre and No 14 platoon on the right under Sergeant Allsop. Hammond, who commands the last named, is due back from a Lewis gun course tomorrow.

May 30 The troops have got excellent shelters, too, and when they had had time to settle in, I went along to put my patrol suggestion to them. They simply leapt at it, and I returned, well pleased, to tell Ewing. He had already received the acquiescence of the CO—so that was that.

At 3 a.m. I took my NCOs and three men out for a preliminary canter in front of the wire. I went out first to Radcliffe's left post, where I found him smoking and chatting in the large shelter. It was a faintly moonlit night and as he walked with me to Harding's sector, we could see quite a distance—about 50 yards into No Man's Land. I was rather alarmed at the long distance that separated the two platoons. Especially as there were several large gaps in the wire through which a Boche patrol could easily pass on a dark night.

We found Harding himself on his second post—a most important one, being at the actual and exact crossing of the two sunken roads which lead, one to Quéant, the other to Prouville. Everyone appeared to be scared at this point. They stood on the firestep talking in whispers, so we hurried on for fear of being infected by their windup, and reached their next post. This, being isolated and on rising ground, gave a feeling of indescribable loneliness to us as we passed with only a whispered countersign.

14 platoon had only two posts, the first obviously constructed by a lunatic—on rising ground with a view of about ten yards—the second close by on the bank of another road leading to Quéant. This one was excellently constructed and

sighted and we remained talking to Allsop for a bit before crossing the road to get into touch with 'A' Company's left post. When we had found this and walked back in front of the wire, it was nearly dawn so we struck back from Allsop's post to a pit whence a strand of plain wire led us back to HQ. Ewing was asleep, so I had a drink and rolled up in my blanket on the earth couch, which was luxuriously comfortable.

Breakfast came in at 9 a.m. and after just peeping out at the glorious sunshine we made a hearty meal, discussing the general arrangements for the tour which promises to be a long one. It is rumoured that several raids are to be made, but the dates and participants are not yet known. Probably it will be the reserve companies, as troops in the line are very rarely used for other work.

The morning was absolutely gorgeous; the sun was frightfully hot but there was a delightful breeze which just caught our heads when we stood on the first earth step. The grass is about a foot long and thousands of poppies are swaying along the lips of the trench, whilst among the stems of grass are multitudinous wild flowers.

It was very pleasant sitting at our dugout door or strolling along the trench chatting to the troops as they carried out their morning duties of shaving and cleaning buttons and rifles. Thus the day passed quickly and soon we were standing-to in the dusk while I detailed orders for patrol. Then the arrival of Braham with rations to divide and distribute occupied us until the sickly moon appeared.

By its faint light we climbed out and followed the plain wire down to Allsop's post where in bunches of six we passed out through the wire. As a preliminary we swept straight across our front in extended order, searching every inch of ground until we reached the left boundary of our Company sector. Then with infinite caution we advanced into the neutral ground of shadows and mystery, every sense alert for the faintest sign of a German patrol. With bayonets lowered and finger on trigger, crawling by inches up to every dark form (which turned out to be a bush or haycock), worming our way along hedges—for three hours we sought for an enemy patrol to surprise and attack, but although we advanced for about 400 yards we saw no Boche, and at midnight, in pitch darkness, I led the patrol back via Radcliffe's post.

May 31 I detailed six men to report to me at 4.30 and then dismissed them all to their dugouts where they had (as I had) a wonderful hot meal that had come up in food containers. These containers are a great boon to us, for the food arrives quite hot at the front line. In the past we have had to do any little cooking possible over a Tommy's cooker—if we had one.

At 4.30 a.m. I took my six men out again and scoured the whole area again. In such a small party we were able to move much faster and with less caution. We returned just before dawn and having waited for 'stand-down', I took off my boots and puttees, which were soaked through with dew from the long grass, and laid them on the parapet to dry. My breeches were also soaked, so I wrapped sandbags round me and rolled up to sleep.

I was disturbed for a long time by a mole which at intervals kicked earth down on to my face as he burrowed into the roof. I kept frightening him away but he always returned, until he thought I had had enough, then smiling evilly he went over to Ewing and gave him a dose. I fell asleep to the music of Ewing's broad cursing, which I believe included me—I don't know why.

Up at 9 a.m. and after breakfast made a delightful slow toilet, shaving and bathing in a mugful of warm water under a burning sun. As I was dressing, a British aeroplane came over very low; the Boche fired furiously at him and in derision he looped the loop over one of their strongpoints. For half an hour he flew low over their lines doing stunts until they gave up trying to hit him. Then he dived down and fired a burst from his guns. Rising from his dive he executed another loop then soared back over our lines as if he had suddenly remembered an appointment.

The night patrol was rather dull, as we swept the whole of No Man's Land without seeing or hearing anything of the Boche.

June 1 On the dawn patrol, however, we had a little excitement, for we ran suddenly into one of Jerry's patrols. We both opened fire together and, crouching in the long grass, blazed away in the half-light. Jerry retreated and we followed him up until we lost him. We had no casualties and we found no dead or wounded from his party.

During the morning an order came round that all patrols were to wear soft hats, to avoid the danger of the tin hats rattling against bayonets. We have placed so much confidence in these helmets as a protection against fragments, that my patrol rather jibbed at discarding them. To make matters worse I very foolishly turned out in mine this evening, because I had no soft hat with me. The result was that the troops were a bit surly and the patrol was only a half-hearted affair.

June 2 The aeroplane came over this morning and did exactly the same stunts. Pepper came along to take over second in command, so I have been pushed out of Ewing's dugout, to an empty cubby-hole at the end of the troops. It is very dull, damp and cheerless, so I shall not spend much time there.

I received a phone message summoning me to meet the CO this evening at 'A' Company HQ, in accordance with which I proceeded at dusk via our right post to a little tin shed sheltered by a high bank, wherein I found the CO with Coleridge and Captain Yalor. The CO gave me an aeroplane photograph of No Man's Land and pointed out on it a crossroads which formed one of Jerry's strongpoints. He instructed me to go out from 'A' Company's front and thoroughly investigate its position and approaches to assist 'B' Company to raid it the next evening.

While we were talking, a large shell fell outside and as

several chunks came through our walls we adjourned to a neighbouring dugout to finish our powwow. The strafe only lasted a few minutes, then I saluted the CO and went out with Coleridge, who had asked me to take him out to have a look at No Man's Land.

We walked over to our No 36 post and thence passed forward along the road. We were walking along the top of the bank about 50 yards out, when a machine-gun opened out at close range dead on us. Of course we were not seen, it was only a gun sweeping the road on the chance of catching somebody. We both dived together into a tiny shell-hole which just covered our heads and shoulders, and Coleridge laughed like the deuce while the bullets spat past our legs. When the gun swung away, we crawled out and spent a few minutes looking for his pince-nez which had dropped off into the hole. When we found them he said he had had quite enough for one evening, so we returned to the wire, where we found Sergeant Allsop bringing out a party to carry our bodies back.

June 3 Sunday. I was about to move off with my platoon when Radcliffe arrived with No 16 platoon. I was glad to learn that he had been detailed to accompany me, for it was likely to be a ticklish job. We moved immediately to 'A' Company's HQ and thence out through their posts. On our own front I knew every bush by heart, but this part was new to me, so progress was very slow.

About 80 yards out, we dimly discerned a group of figures and we prepared for a scrap, but crawling forward with Raddy I heard English oaths and found that they were a wiring party from Smallwood's company. For 500 yards we crawled inch by inch through the darkness, in two parties— each in diamond formation. The misty darkness seemed pregnant with enmity and time after time we paused to surround some dark form which all had seen distinctly moving but which proved to be a bush or haycock.

At last I judged that we should be immediately on the right

of the crossroads and, leaving a section to protect the flank and rear, I headed the patrol round to the left. As we moved on there was a sharp crack and a Very light shot up, flooding us in white light, and as a burst of rifle fire spat over our heads, I raised myself in time to see a white chalk trench a hundred yards ahead.

We lay motionless while more flares were fired and rifle fire continued, then half a dozen rifle grenades crashed amongst us and 'grenatenwerfers' and trench mortars began to pound the ground behind us. They had spotted us alright, but as our business was not with this post, I just made a mental note of its position and, when the rifle fire ceased, continued to crawl to the left until I reached the top of a steep bank almost overhanging the crossroads. The moon was now giving a faint light through the clouds and we could see across the road ahead of us a belt of wire guarding the dark holes which were the German posts.

Safe as we were in our present position, I was at a loss as to how I could further investigate the position. It seemed an impossibility for us to descend into the road and pass through the wire at the very muzzles of Jerry's rifles. However, it was a definite job and I resolved upon a desperate plan. Calling up the NCOs by a wave of my hand I breathed to them that a couple of us would slide down into the road and approach the wire along the grass. When the inevitable flares shot up, those on top were to observe the rifle pit positions while we searched for gaps in the wire. They were not to open fire unless the Boche came out to capture us.

It was a pretty plan, but quite wasted. Having extended the platoons along the bank facing Jerry, Bobby Wood and I together slithered over the bank and down into the road where we lay with faces crushed into the chalk waiting for the clatter of bullets around us. We waited for several minutes but nothing happened, so we began to toss small stones on to the wire to attract attention. This, too, failed to evoke a demonstration, and as the truth dawned upon me I stood up and in disgust began to hurl large chunks of chalk at the enemy trench.

The enemy post must have feared from the firing on their left that an attacking patrol was about, and retired to their day positions in rear. I called to Raddy to bring his fellows down and he and I in the misty moonlight executed a little dance of triumph, for this farcical development was far removed from our expectations. As we proceeded to move forward to inspect the post, a figure strolled out of the haze behind us and yawned at our muttered challenge. It was the Rajah! We hailed him with silent buffets then demanded in whispers to know what on earth he was doing there. In solemn tones he replied that learning that we two had come out on patrol, he had felt lonely and had set out to find us. He had been lying in the grass watching our little stratagem, upon which he complimented us.

Although it was a serious thing for Jimmy to leave his platoon like that, we were glad to see him and trusting that his absence would not be discovered we led on to where the road was blocked by a belt of wire. The gap was closed by a light 'knife-rest', which we flung contemptuously on one side in the manner of kicking open an enemy's door; then one by one we passed through, followed by our patient troops who had stood grinning while we embraced Jimmy on the road.

Once through the wire we linked arms and with revolvers drawn marched up the road with all the swagger of the Three Musketeers. Twenty yards along we found the first rifle pit, dug in the centre of the road and large enough for half a dozen rifles, with a perfect field of fire across the approach except for the side where the bank overhung the road. It was beautifully revetted, so with our wire cutters we destroyed the supports and dragged it down. Then we set the troops on the good work of digging out the sides with their bayonets to break the hearts of the working party who had made such a nice job of it.

Meanwhile we three continued along the road to the left where the main crossroads were. Here we found no rifle post but a deep shaft was in course of construction right in the centre of the crossing. A tripod of scaffold poles had been erected with tackle for hoisting buckets from the pit. We took down the tripod, cut up the ropes into short bits and hurled the pulley out into the long grass. Having dragged the ladder out of the pit we robbed it of most of its rungs, then, leaving a post to guard our rear, we moved on again with infinitely more caution.

In a very few minutes, crawling along in the dark grass of a bank, we were checked by the sounds and sight of the German main line. From a long traversed trench which stretched into the darkness on our left, a voice was raised, evidently hailing a friend: 'Peter! Pete . . r!' with a long wail, then several voices in conversation. After a few minutes of dumb show in which Jimmy professed to be having a conversation with the unseen Huns, we crawled back to the crossroads. There we gathered the troops and walked back in blobs, talking and laughing, for we felt that we had done a good night's work and were entitled to treat No Man's Land as our own preserve. The result was that we drew a few bursts of machine-gun fire, but no one was hit. Entering our lines at No 35 post we separated and returned to our various sectors.

It was then close on dawn, so I made out a very detailed report which Ewing despatched immediately to HQ, Berry's raid tonight being based on my information. We are all very excited about it because the General has sent a definite demand for prisoners to the front-line units, and we want to be the first battalion to send him some. Hammond has now returned and is taking over his old platoon—No 14—on the right.

As soon as it was dusk I set off to No 35 post alone, intending to accompany the raiding party as a spectator. I looked in at 36 post and had a drink with Hammond, but failed to persuade him to accompany me over to 35. As I crossed the intervening ridge, half a dozen shots cracked past me from close range. I dropped and lay doggo for a few seconds, then continued at a trot. I heard fire opened from No 35 post and in a couple leaps was among them, peering over the parapet into the darkness whence the shots had come.

Sergeant Allsop shot up a flare and we saw a slight movement in the grass 50 yards away. I added a few rifle grenades to the rifle fire from our posts and then took out half a dozen fellows to look for bodies. We were not gratified by finding any and we returned to the post and discussed the incident until Berry turned up with his platoon.

Berry had been drinking and he talked pretty loudly of what he would do to the German army. His party made a terrible din going out, and they appeared to me so unfitted to carry out a raid that I decided not to accompany them but to follow after a few minutes. Nevertheless, when I walked slowly out I reached the crossroads before anything happened. Then there was a single shot, followed by about a dozen which passed over my head. There was some confused shouting and as a flare shot up, a figure rushed past me shouting wildly, then the whole platoon tore past in confusion followed by rapid fire from Jerry. Last came Berry alone, and having called to him I walked back with him to the line.

He gave me his account of the fiasco in a high-pitched, almost hysterical voice. Having passed unmolested through the wire gap which I had reported, he had gone ahead with Sergeant Corbett, the half-mad fellow whom I had picked up at Eclusier. They were walking warily along, when, long before they reached the spot which I had indicated as the enemy post, they had heard voices on their immediate left. Perceiving an occupied post Berry halted to bring up the platoon; but Corbett had sprung forward on to the parapet. The sentry yelled 'Halte! Wer da?' and answering 'Anglais! You bastards!' Corbett had promptly bayoneted him. The post was full of Boche, who for the moment were motionless with surprise. Disregarding them, Corbett grabbed the equipment of the dead man, dragged him on to the top, smacked his face and then kicked him back into the trench. Meanwhile the German officer drew his revolver and shot Corbett in the side.

All this only took a few seconds and the platoon was still some distance away when Corbett ran back shouting 'Retire! Retire!' At the same moment the Germans opened a rapid fire. The platoon raced back in utter confusion as the first flare went up, and Berry could do nothing but follow. He was terribly sick about it and I did not envy him his interview with the CO, who was waiting to examine prisoners at 'A' Company HQ.

June 4 When I got back to our Company HQ, Ewing was out, but Radcliffe was waiting there with a very long face. An unfortunate little incident had occurred during my absence. Two of his fellows patrolling between his posts had seen figures moving in front. Receiving no reply to their challenge they had opened fire. They had been frightened to go out to look for the supposed enemy and it was not until Radcliffe was visited by an officer from the Somersets on his left, who had missed two men from a wiring party, that the bodies of two Tommies were found in front. Raddy seemed to feel himself responsible for the incident, but I cheered him up with a little whisky and by pointing out that he would probably have a couple of days out of the line to attend the court of enquiry.

I took the dawn patrol out in bright moonlight and we walked upright and talked freely, any attempt at concealment being useless. In consideration of my troops' feelings I have borrowed a cap comforter which I now wear in place of my tin hat.

Pepper was transferred to 'A' Company during the night so I have had my things shifted back to Ewing's dugout. Dunham, by the way, is having a royal time now; he does not do a stroke of work other than to help Martin with our meals.

During dusk stand-to I was fooling about behind the trench where I found a dump of German stick bombs, close to where a hole in the ground acted as a ventilator to our dugout. I was prompted to perpetrate a little joke, and later, when Johnny Teague entered the dugout to talk to Ewing, I unscrewed the canister of a bomb, removed the detonator, then pulled the fuse and dropped the stick just inside the ventilator shaft. With a fizz the fuse burnt for five seconds, growing louder and ending in a sharp dull spurt.

Putting my ear to the hole I heard Ewing say 'Good God! That was a near one!' 'Blinking good job it was a dud,' replied Johnny, whereupon I chuckled hugely and prepared half a dozen more. I waited a few minutes until they had settled down, then I dropped them in rapid succession. There was a faint groan from Ewing and I heard Johnny say in a puzzled tone, 'They can't *all* be duds.' Then I pictured Ewing's horrified face as he yelled 'They're GAS! Can ye no smell them?' I heard the rustle of their gas-masks and thought it was time to end the comedy, so I jumped into the trench just in time to meet them as they rushed out to warn the Company.

'Hallo!' I said. 'Have you joined the Ku Klux Klan? Or are you doing a little badly needed gas drill?' Ewing choked over his mouthpiece and gurgled 'Put on your helmet, ye fule! The air's a fog o gas!' And he coughed up what he imagined he had drawn into his lungs. I was quite at a loss as to how I should persuade them to unmask, when Chalk came along and stopped in blank amazement at the sight of the masked figures.

'Are the officers testing their masks, Sir?' he asked, 'because I wanted to speak to the Captain if I might.' Ewing knew that the 'Little Treasure' could not be wrong, so he pulled off his mask and asked, 'Is it a' clear now?' Chalk and I both denied having smelt any gas and after spitting all round the trench Ewing in bewilderment asked 'Did ye no' hear the shelling? They crashed wi'in a hundred yards, and the gas was strong.' Chalk declared that he had been standing in the trench for the last half hour and had heard no unusual sound, so they had perforce to abandon the matter and entered the dugout to discuss strength returns.

Little Teague, however, was not satisfied and when we entered, wondering at the phenomenon I saw his eyes wandering round the walls until they were arrested by the ventilation hole. Then they switched to my face in a searching scrutiny. However, he said nothing and a moment later Whitehouse and Mortimore came in and crowded into our beds demanding whisky. Whitehouse was in little drill shorts and his bare knees were plastered with earth owing to some heaven-inspired machine-gunner having caught him with a chance burst as he was coming across.

Ewing immediately told him *his* exciting story, omitting the denials of SM Chalk and myself, whereupon Whitehouse in great alarm fished out his gas-mask and asked Mortimore to show him how it worked, as he had never looked at it. Mortimore thought it was 'rather strange. I heard nothing as we came over. Did you, Major?' 'No,' said Whitehouse, 'that blank machine gun took all my attention, and I'm blanked if I come round the line again if this is what we get.'

Johnny sat quietly with a slight grin on his face, then suddenly changed the conversation by producing a letter. 'I say, Major, I've had a letter today from a girl who asks me if Major Whitehouse is still with us. I don't know whether she means you or Willy. Her name is Miss Dash, do you know her?'

'No, er no. I'm afraid not. Is she very sweet?'

'Very!'

'Then tell her *I* am here; tell her I'm young and handsome, very rich but very rude—that's it! Just say "rich but rude".'

Then he remembered that he had called in with a definite purpose and after thinking hard for a few minutes he slapped his bare knee. 'I *knew* I had a message for you Ewing! The General is going round the line tonight and you have to meet him at your right post at nine o'clock. Moreover,' he added reproachfully, 'as it's now 8.45 you'll have to put your skates on me boy.'

Ewing jumped up in a panic and started to put on his equipment, while I slipped out to call his runner. As I stepped into the trench, my belt was grasped from behind and Johnny's voice over my shoulder said 'How did you work

it, Vaughan?' 'Stick-bombs without detonators,' I gurgled
and my pent-up mirth escaped in a shriek of laughter. We
both leant against the trench side and howled at the memory
of Ewing's stricken face, until Whitehouse came out and
wagged a finger at us. 'Nasty-minded blighters! Sneaking
outside to tell them! Downright case of story-hogging.'
'Aye!' said Ewing following. 'And I'm to meet the General
and they're blocking the trench. Where's my runner?
Runner!' He climbed out and set off at a half-trot, still
muttering about 'meeting the General'. The others climbed
out and set off more comfortably towards HQ, while I went
off to collect my platoon for patrol.

We had a pleasant walk round, meeting no one, but enjoying the exercise after the cramping day in the trench. Returning by way of Radcliffe's post I sent the patrol home and
crawled in beside him in my old cubby-hole. We grinned at
each other over half mugs of port, then he asked 'How's
Ewing?' 'Oh, panicky as ever, but I'm beginning to like him
more.' 'No, I mean how's his knee?' I told him that the last
time I saw Ewing both his knees were working very efficiently,
and I asked if anything had happened to them while I was out
on patrol.

June 5 'By jove! yes,' he replied. 'I hear that he had to meet
the General—what are you grinning at?'

'Nothing. Go on.'

'Well, he was dashing across to No 35 post when he ran
against the spike of a screw picket sticking out of the long
grass, and tore a great hole under his knee.'

I was really sorry to hear this but could not help thinking
that from what I saw of his speed over the ground he was
lucky to have any knee left.

I found him waiting for the stretcher to take him down the
line, with sweat pouring down his face and evidently in great
pain. 'O Vaughan,' he said, 'it's a nasty hole, and I missed the
General— he went round by himself. Look after my kit for
me, and redirect my letters won't ye?' I felt sincerely sorry

for him and his last appeal made me realize that I would not
see him for a long time—perhaps not again—and I know now
that I liked him a lot.

After he had gone I sat in the dugout for a while, then
smote myself upon the chest saying 'Company Commander
me!' Whereupon I made out the report 'situation unchanged'
and signed myself 'OC "D" Coy.' before anyone could arrive
to deprive me of that honour. I was none too precipitate
either, for very shortly Syd Pepper arrived to take command.
I greeted him with joy, for I had had visions of Smallwood or
one of the other outsiders being sent. But Syd is the one
person I would have chosen from the whole regiment, and I
foresaw long hours in which we could recall days at Chelten-
ham and on the Plain.

After breakfast the aeroplane came across to perform his
matutinal stunts over Jerry's strongpoint, but as he had done
the same things every morning of the tour I did not worry to
rise from the trench step on which I was seated watching
Pepper stark naked having a bath in a mugful of warm water.
We were talking about fellows we had known in the 3/8th
Batt when a group of Archies burst overhead and a large
chunk came whirling and buzzing to land with a smack in the
trench between us.

'Oo! Jerry,' said Pepper, lifting up his leg. 'Here you are; just
in the soft part, please.'

'Would you really like a blighty?' I asked. 'I think it's
much more fun out here.'

'No, I wouldn't really,' he replied. 'For two reasons: first
because I wouldn't survive another one, and second because
this is the only country where a bloke can feel really at ease.'

I knew that Pepper was pretty fragile, because he was
nothing but skin and bone, but now he told me that his
stomach wounds had nearly finished him and when he had
refused to stay in England the Medical Board had warned
him that any further wound would be fatal.

During our conversation I told him about the several
occasions when I had got into hot water in the Péronne

sector, but he already knew of them and he read me a long
lecture which was very open and, I thought, unwarranted.
For I felt that I had honestly tried to carry out my duties
creditably, and my errors had been due more to ignorance
than to slackness. Also I had tried to be civil to the other
officers, most of whom I disliked, though I was forced to
admit that therein I had failed so utterly that I was hardly on
speaking terms with any but my own Company. However, he
did not spare me, and remembering the precept concerning
the criticism of friends I endeavoured to mark his points for
future guidance.

'Do you remember, Vaughan, when you were coming out
to France I told you to insist on joining the 1/8th? Well, I
wouldn't have done that if I had not believed that you would
be a credit to the Batt. And, honestly, I thought, there's a
damn good youngster who's sure to make good with them
because you were keen as mustard then and were doing well
in the third line. So I was jolly sorry when I came out and
found that you were in damn bad odour through the Batt.—
and I don't think you even faintly guess how bad that odour
is. The CO is always asking for reports about you, and has
seriously considered sending you back to England. In addition to that the officers of the other companies despise you for
your arrogant unsociableness and look upon you as an
inefficient young officer.'

I was thoroughly shaken by this, never having dreamt that
matters were so bad. I pointed out how hopeless it seemed. I
had conscientiously tried to do my job, but hitherto had not
had the instruction or support I had expected from my
several company commanders. 'And,' I argued, 'surely I can
choose my own friends?'

'No you can't!' he said, almost savagely. 'Remember that
you are an inexperienced urchin out here; you've seen
nothing and you've done nothing while these others—whatever their characters are—have sweated out here for months
or years and so are entitled not to your friendship but to your
respect. Anyway, you've got to live with them for the rest of

the war, and the only fun we can get here is what we make between us. There is no room for personal dislikes; if our social relations are bad, we will never work together and the Battalion will lose the leading position that it has always held in the division.'

He paused for breath. 'And what the devil do you expect your company commander to do for you? Wet-nurse you? You've had your training at home and now you have to apply it here by using your brains. What you lack is initiative; *do* what you like so long as it is definite and consistent, but for God's sake don't wait to be shown.'

After which we had lunch, I very much chastened and he very self-conscious, when his vehemence had subsided and he realized he had been chucking a lecture. Towards the end of the meal, however, he poured a little oil into the wound by saying 'It may soothe you to learn that Colonel Hanson is very pleased with your patrol work, particularly because you volunteered. And, by the way, Berry's platoon is being attached to yours to get used to working in No Man's Land.'

He also told me that Berry had failed in his raid by disregarding my reports and leading the party off the road to the right of the mine-shaft. This certainly did revive my drooping spirits and to myself in a deserted bay of the trench I swore I would be the model subaltern.

Berry's platoon arrived at dusk and, as we were putting them into empty shelters, a box of Mill's bombs exploded— probably owing to a rusted safety pin. Fortunately only one man was hurt. I took half a dozen of these fellows out with my patrol.

June 6 I found on reconnoitring Jerry's line that the posts previously occupied were now empty and that others were manned. This confirmed my early conjecture that to puzzle possible raiding parties he changed his positions nightly or bi-weekly. This I entered in report, and at dawn I received a note telling me to report to A Company HQ at dusk to meet the CO.

Wondering why I was thus summoned, I attended the rendezvous with mixed feelings. After a peg of whisky the CO produced an aeroplane photograph and a map and told me to describe in minute detail my patrol work and its results. I pointed out on the map the exact positions of the posts and the mine-shaft, described how his outposts had been placed on successive nights and hazarded my opinion that the hole which we had found under construction on our first patrol was to be another mine-shaft like the one inside his wire.

A close examination of the aeroplane map confirmed my reports in every detail, with the exception of the new mine-shaft which had apparently not been commenced when the photo was taken. The CO told me to go along after dark to have another look at this, adding that he thought that these points would be electrically mined in case we should attempt an attack on this front, which he was rapidly consolidating as the Quéant-Dricourt Switch.

As I rose to go, he checked me and my heart leapt as he congratulated me upon these patrols and their results. 'Keep on like that and you will do well,' he added and I saluted and walked back on air to the HQ trench.

Gathering my platoon I added another six of Berry's men and set out for the road junction. Knowing every inch of the ground, and recognizing every bush and shadow, I quickly reached the objective and rushed it in the hope of surprising a working party. No one was there, however, and I proceeded at leisure to examine the work. Very little had been carried out, but there was sufficient to indicate that this was to be a mine-shaft too; it was probable that our nightly patrol had prevented them from continuing their work there.

June 7 I now decided to break new ground so led my patrol up the road to the left. We examined the whole area carefully, finding three dummy trenches and one pukkha post, but no Boche. On my return I found that these were already marked on the map.

Operation orders received during the morning notified our relief during the evening by the 1/7th Worcesters, after which we were to return to our old camp at Frémicourt.

June 8 The relief did not arrive until 10.30, with the result that the last platoon was not clear until about 1 a.m. I sent my platoon back with the Rajah's and waited to accompany Pepper, who finished handing over and joined me on top at 2 o'clock. We followed the old track to Morchies, through which we passed in silence, for the gaping holes and ruined houses looked ghostly in the moonlight; we did not meet a soul, and there was no sound but the light tramp of our feet which woke soft echoes in such little barns as were still standing.

In my mind I reconstructed the scene in peacetime and a hungry little pain grew in my heart at the picture of moon-flooded lanes, deep shadows of cottages wherein were blanketed by sleep, the tiny troubles, joys and hopes which composed the gentle lives of the villagers and perhaps in the black shadows of the churchyard some little tragedy of pastoral love.

Still in silence we passed through on to the open road leading to Beugny. The moon paled into the dawn and as we reached the main cobbled road and turned to the right, the sun arose with delighted colourings of pink and blue. Here a groom met us leading Porky, the 'C' Company charger, which had been sent out to meet Pepper. He mounted and would have walked in beside me, but I forced him to ride by larruping Porky's sleek haunches with my stick.

I followed slowly, stopping to look into the ruined houses and climbing up to a pile of bricks and masonry in front of the shattered church. The blue starry sanctuary was intact save for a small hole through which a shell had passed. The ruins straggled on either side until I was in Frémicourt where they thickened again. There I turned off the road into the open fields behind the village where our camp lay.

There was no sign of anyone moving, but their columns of

smoke indicated the cookers, and thither I went at once. Blackie Neale and Walliter were preparing the troops' breakfast and grinned amiably at me as I sat down on an upturned dixie. I did not dare to look at the condition of a tin mug which was produced from a sandbag, but gratefully took it when filled with steaming tea. I begged another mug for Pepper, then stepped carefully with them to the line of Adrian huts which I guessed to be the officers' quarters. Pepper was undressing in one where Radcliffe, Hammond and Harding were asleep on the floor. Our valises were laid out for us beside them. Very soon we were delighting in the gentle caress of clean pyjamas after ten days of khaki—and then came sleep.

I woke at 1 p.m. just as lunch was brought in. Everyone was up except Pepper and I pranced round the hut exchanging mutual greetings. Standing in the doorway I was dazzled for a few seconds by the brightest sunshine we have had this year. The tents were all astir and on all sides the troops were casting down button-brushes, rifle-rags and pull-throughs before falling into the queue for stew. I slipped on my mac over my pyjamas and strolled across to watch the issue. They were all very cheery and quick with repartee.

On every side stretched velvet plains with gentle slopes and clumps of trees. The villages of Bancourt and Frémicourt were brilliant in red and white ruins set in fresh foliage.

On my return to the hut I upbraided Pepper for his laziness but he continued to eat stolidly and took not the slightest notice of my remarks. Martin had provided an excellent lunch and we added to it a continual chatter of witticisms and repartee. It was a merry meal indeed, and when we had finished Pepper and I dressed and we all went across to the troops' lines. We were joined there by the CO and we stayed for half an hour talking to our various platoons.

We spent the remainder of the afternoon in Frémicourt climbing about the ruins and examining the old school and account books lying about in them. After tea, the weather being so glorious, we secured tents and moved our valises into them. Radcliffe, Harding and I took one, Pepper and Hammond the other.

June 9 We held an inspection this morning and did a little drill; the troops were very clean but their drill was, of course, rather rusty. The rest of the day we spent writing letters and talking as we strolled round the camp. It had clouded up badly at dusk, so before retiring we deemed it advisable to slacken our tent ropes and lace up our flaps.

June 10 Sunday. At midnight a terrific storm broke over us; the rain descending in sheets drove straight through our tent and ran in streams through our belongings, which like us were lying on the ground. The noise and wet, however, did not prevent my sleeping soundly until 7.30 a.m. when I woke to find the sky blue and the sun warm. We dragged our valises into the open and dressed there, spreading out our blankets and other things to dry.

Pepper, having dressed with meticulous care, set off again for a couple of days' leave in Amiens while Anstey assumed command of our Company. Hammond suggested to me that we should go for a ride during the afternoon, and not liking to confess that I could not ride, I sent a note down to transport asking for Porky and another horse to be sent up at 3 o'clock. Porky had always seemed to be very quiet and docile when Pepper and Anstey rode him.

I borrowed Anstey's spurs and taking my riding cap I went to meet them so as to get mounted before Hammond came out. I boobed first by not knowing which was Porky, then by trying to mount the wrong side and finally had to be pushed into the saddle by the groom. I had just got my feet into the stirrups when Hammond, swinging into his saddle, headed his mount across the road. I grabbed a handful of reins and shouted 'Don't run!' but he had already started across country. Porky swung round so sharply that I lost a stirrup, then with a snort he set off, bumping me up and down and moving faster and faster until, dropping my gloves and crop, I clung to the saddle with both hands.

Instead of following Hammond, he swung off to the left. I slithered from side to side and slid gently up his neck, until shooting over a little ridge he thundered into the transport where he pulled up and I lay exhausted over his ears with the wondering gaze of 20 grooms centred upon me. Out of a mist the transport sergeant approached and asked if anything was wrong, to which I murmured shakily that I had lost control for a moment and grabbing one rein I tried to make Porky turn. This he refused to do until the sergeant took him by the snaffle and led him a couple of hundred yards out of the enclosure.

Then he let go and with a great swing and bound Porky set off and returned at a gallop to the centre of the yard where the grooms were rolling about with laughter. I then saw that Richards, the Transport Officer, was with them. As he approached grinning, I climbed down, and Porky began to snatch wisps of hay from a hanging hay net. Hammond, too, rode in carrying my gloves and crop. I was the centre of a ridiculing crowd when Richards said, 'The first time you came in, I thought we had discovered a jockey. But perhaps you would like the corporal to give you a few tips?'

I humbly assented and was led out on a pack pony for a little riding instruction, while the sergeant mounted Porky and rode away with Hammond. After an hour's instruction I pocketed my spurs and returned in a chastened frame of mind to the mess. Hammond, like a brick, did not say a word about my exhibition, otherwise I would have been chaffed mercilessly.

After tea I walked over to the 7th Warwicks to talk to Fr Woodlock, and after dinner, as it rained heavily, we played 'Slippery Ann' until midnight when we raced through the downpour to our tents which were already thoroughly soaked. I was asleep in two ticks and woke at reveille wet to the skin.

June 11   The morning, however, was gloriously warm, so

out came our valises into the sunshine. All subaltern officers had a lecture this morning on 'Discipline'. It was given by Captain Taylor of 'A' Company, whom I detest. He wears a quite superfluous eyeglass, is very supercilious and speaks to no one below his own rank. Having rehashed all the old wornout maxims that are delivered weekly at every training school in the army, he made them even less tolerable by frequently addressing himself to 'you younger officers'. The poor thing! We took great pleasure in increasing his nervousness by exchanging grins and whispers, and we were delighted when a few shrapnel shells burst overhead and caused him to terminate his harangue.

I had more riding instruction after lunch which left me sore and shaken so that I retired to bed early, having borrowed Sergeant Jowett's tin of Fuller's earth cream.

June 12 Went out on a quiet pack pony for a ride with Hammond. I was bumped terribly but thanked my stars we chose a place where there was too much wire to permit of Hammond's galloping. After tea he and I walked up to Bancourt where the gardens are overgrown with wild flowers and the creeper-covered walls are masses of blooms. On our return we found operation orders for a return to the same positions in the line.

June 13 The morning was spent in inspecting rifles and gas-masks, the afternoon in cleaning camp, then before dusk we moved off by companies to Morchies, Anstey leading. When we reached the village, the sky was dark and heavy; limbers rumbled up the roads which were swarming with troops. In many houses we saw glimpses of fires where troops had gathered to rest on their way down the line and the guns around the village were firing occasional rounds. We were not sorry to leave this turmoil for the freedom of the track, for we feared retaliation from the Boche gunners, and to be caught in the village which he had registered so thoroughly would have meant swift and certain decimation.

The relief went off very quickly and I took up my old position in HQ trench with Anstey. I am not doing any patrols this tour as 'A' Company are having a turn. We slept the greater part of the night, which was very wet, and woke to a misty dawn.

June 14 The mist soon cleared and we had a glorious sunny morning which drew the wetness from the flower-sprinkled plain and songs from my cheery lads as they lay about the trench. I find Anstey very good company in the line, where he treats the whisky bottle with great respect.

The grass is now so long that we are safe in climbing up on to the steps to have a look round so that we spent a long time examining his lines through our glasses. We also had a wonderful time crawling through the long grass playing Indians. As we growled at each other and spoke in the pidgin English used habitually by all the best braves of fiction, our troops were firmly convinced that their officers did not stand the strain of war very well.

Soon after dark I was standing on top, rapt in my own thoughts of war, when from far on my left came a terrible rumble of guns and I saw a line of red and yellow fire; almost immediately hundreds of Very lights shot up, bursting in to flares of red, green, white and mixed stars which wriggled and dipped, crossing and blending along the lines of flame. Then everywhere there showered the golden plains which formed the German SOS.

In a few seconds the barrage was doubled as the German guns got to work and it was obvious that another attack was taking place at Bullecourt. Anstey and Chalk now joined me and for half an hour we stood admiring the spectacle, and pitying the poor blighters who were in the thick of it. When rations arrived I had some hot pontoon and went to sleep.

June 15 The morning was again very misty, so long after daybreak I was able to wander about on top. The old dump of stick-bombs caught my eye, and I resolved to give Anstey a 'gas attack'. But I was not quite as successful as I had been with Ewing for I had dropped in three or four fuses when he gave a loud roar 'Blinking Hades!' and rushed into the trench. Unfortunately he leaped straight up the steps to see where the 'shells' had fallen, and spotted me at the ventilator. With another roar he cleared the trench at a bound and rushed at me. I brandished a bomb to check him then fled into the mist, where by running in a circle I shook him off and returned to the dump. He was too breathless when he joined me to inflict chastisement, so in perfect harmony we commenced to throw the bombs into a large shell-hole where they exploded with terrific crashes that brought the troops out to see what was happening. As a grand finale we arranged about a dozen to be exploded together and as Anstey was kneeling down, tying them with wire, I dropped one of my patent fizzers behind him and yelled 'look out!'

Poor Anstey, white as death, bounded a couple of yards and dropped flat with his face between his hands pressed into the wet earth. As the fuse fizzled out, I shrieked with laughter and raced for the trench, followed by Anstey who had jumped up with his face muddy and his clothes wet. Roaring with rage he pursued me round bays and traverses past the astonished troops. From an empty cubby-hole he snatched a filthy old cardigan-jacket, which he waved round his head yelling 'Haha!' Turning to see what weapon he had seized, I ran into a traverse, smashing my wristwatch to bits. In a moment he was upon me, enveloping my head in the filthy rags and trying to stuff lumps into my mouth while I hammered his ribs with my fists.

Then the sun broke through the mist and disclosed our savagery to a gentle sky. Also Dunham's voice floated down the trench asking in song 'Oh where and oh where can our officers have gone?'—which we knew was an indication that he had taken in our breakfast. So we declared pax and returned to the dugout, only stopping to offer the cardigan as a gift to one of my youths—who declined it.

The barrage at Bullecourt started again immediately after

dark and for a long time I stood wondering what was going on under that hail of shells. I tried to imagine how I would behave if I ever were engaged in an attack, and the thought made me tremble all over, so that I was forced to go into the dugout and dispel the images with a whisky.

June 16   Jerry broke all the regulations by sending over a few 4.2s this morning, but fortunately they went well over, apparently near BHQ. In return our guns bumped his strongpoint. We thought these exhibitions of enmity quite uncalled for and were worried lest the nasty noises and smells connected with war should come to upset our little rest sector.

Night was quite uneventful except for the firework display at Bullecourt. I went for a walk round the line, visiting Radcliffe first. Lastly I visited Hammond who told me that at 11 p.m. tomorrow, 'B' Company are going out from 35 post to attack the enemy post at the crossroads and to sweep the wood behind it. There would be a preparatory barrage. The officers with the Company would be Bridge, Berry and little Cooper (Smallwood, the Company Commander, was conveniently sick).

June 17   Sunday. I was greatly excited all day and at dusk dashed down to 35 post to see the fun. At 10.30 p.m. the attacking party arrived; while they were passing through the wire, I saw three people smoking out in front. These lunatics were Whitehouse, Coleridge and Smallwood—the last-named loud in his regrets that he was unable to lead the raid. They appeared to forget that no one had yet cleared No Man's Land and that they would be spotted at once by any Boche who happened to be out. But they retired very quickly to 'A' Company dugout in anticipation of Jerry's retaliation.

Bridge was quite calm and stolid, Berry loud and excited, while poor little Cooper was a bundle of nerves and very frightened. This was his first taste of fire of any sort. At 11 o'clock our 18-pounders opened rapid fire, sending a stream of shells over our heads to burst on the crossroads, while every few seconds a heavy would gurgle over into Prouville.

After a minute or so, the crackle of rifle fire and quick crashes of bombs told us that the raid had commenced, but at the same moment a shell crashed into our wire. Then another hit the parapet, spattering us with earth and stones and with water from a petrol can on top. It was one of our guns firing short and our ducking and dodging kept us busy for ten minutes until the barrage stopped and all was quiet save for an occasional heavy lobbing over into Prouville. For another quarter of an hour nothing happened and then, hearing voices in front, I went out through the wire. It was an enormous Hun prisoner escorted by two of our fellows. He was very unhappy.

Then the raiding party began to trickle through, all very pleased with themselves, for they had only seen four Germans, of whom they had killed one and captured the others. One or two of our fellows had been slightly wounded by bombs and I was talking to them when I saw a stretcher party struggling through the wire. When they had gently lowered it down the bank into the road and laid it down for a rest, I approached and asked who the wounded man was. 'Mr Cooper, Sir' replied the bearer; then, in a low voice, 'well away, Sir'. Cooper had heard my voice, and greeted me very faintly. I sent someone to fetch Hammond who had been one of his pals in England, then, sick at heart, bent down to say a few words to him.

A large chunk of shell had entered his back and he was only half conscious, but when Hammond came he rallied a little and said Goodbye. As the stretcher-bearers raised him, we grasped his hand and Hammond said 'Cheerio, Cooper, I'll see you in Blighty again.' 'No, Laurie,' came the faint voice, 'I shan't see Blighty again.' And he was right, poor little chap; he died on the stretcher. When all the party had returned I said goodnight to Hammond and slowly made my way back to HQ, thinking all the time of how I used to be irritated with Cooper for singing 'Brown bread—well buttered'.

June 18 Anstey and I were interested this morning by a new order regarding trench construction. We were to commence digging short lengths along our front forthwith, and the dimensions were to be seven feet deep, *eight* feet wide at the top and a three foot fire-step. Eight feet wide! and our present three feet seemed about ten yards when there was any shelling! We passed some very scathing remarks about the johnny who had circulated the scheme, and hoped that one day he might occupy one during a strafe. The orders also stated that I was to relieve Hammond on the right at dusk, and commence digging a post on the new plan immediately.

Anstey told me that great interest had been aroused by the fact that the large prisoner from the raid had had a dum-dum bullet in the chamber of his rifle. This was alleged to be the first red-handed catch of the war.

At dusk I took my platoon over and relieved Hammond on 35 and 36 posts. Leaving two men on duty in each trench, I took the remainder on to the ridge behind 36 and started them digging on a rectangle of 20 feet by 8 feet. They all firmly believed that they were digging a gunpit until they had got down about a foot; then I showed them how I wanted the sides sloped. Bobby Wood scratched his hat into one side, asking 'Might I ask what we're adiggin', Sir?'

'Why! a trench of course,' I replied casually.

'Goin' ter get the cavalry in, are we sir?' came the pert reply and set everyone grinning. Despite their incredulity the troops worked with a will until dawn, when we covered the excavation with grass and branches and retired to the trenches for stand-to.

June 19 My cubby-hole was just large enough for one, so Dunham had to sleep with the rank and file! I have a little earthen couch covered with straw, a six-inch shelf, a 'candlestick' stuck in the side and innumerable large, brilliant beetles that run excitedly up and down the walls and over my person. There are also many large, unenergetic caterpillars.

Daybreak was beautifully clear, and at 4 a.m. leaning over

the parapet I had a fine view of Jerry's line and got my first real sight of Prouville by daylight. A charming little village, nestling in a slight hollow, its red roofs framed by lines of dark poplars and clumps of bright foliage. Searching with my glasses I could discern figures moving in the streets. Sweeping the horizon to the right I spotted a lorry, a hand cart, three men on foot and one mounted. Presently they commenced carrying sacks to the lorry and noting a tree beside them which was clear to the naked eye, I borrowed a rifle and had a few pots at long range. I did not, of course, hit them, but the mounted man galloped off while the others ran to clamber into the lorry which drove at once to the village. After this little attack on enemy morale, I re-entered my cubby-hole and breakfasted off tinned herrings and sherry. Then I went to sleep.

From one o'clock to stand-to I employed writing a couple of letters, staring at the hot landscape and marvelling at the idiocy of war. Everything was so calm and still that one almost expected to hear the bells of Prouville begin to peal and to see the women hanging out washing or driving their cows into No Man's Land. Needless to say, nothing of this sort happened, but hundreds of more or less brave men on our side and ditto on theirs continued to hide in holes fearing observation. Whilst landscape, weather, church and all wasted their sweetness on unresponsive militarists, save where an isolated individual like myself succumbed and was held for a few moments before returning to the atmosphere of patrols, reports and working parties.

June 20 Midnight saw us well down our new trench, and being tired after half an hour's digging I was lying in the long grass staring up at the stars when I heard a challenge from No 36 post, to which the CO's voice replied and asked where I was. 'Over by the sunken road, Sir.' 'But there's no road over the ridge,' said the CO, and walked over rather angrily. I jumped up and met him, whereupon he demanded to know why my men had not been made acquainted with the ground surrounding the posts. I explained to him that 'sunken road' was the troops' name for the new trench, which tickled him, but he became quite cross when I ventured to voice an opinion of the usefulness of it.

He was very pleased indeed with our work and said that it was easily the best in the line, so when he had gone the work continued with redoubled energy—but it is purely show-work, for I am sure no one would ever remain there during a barrage if there were a nice cosy shell-hole nearby.

The day was dull and we had a little rain, but that did not worry us as our shelters were watertight. Nevertheless the trench got sloppy and the grass wet us to the knees when we went over to our 'sunken road' at nightfall. The night was very oppressive and the troops worked bare to the waist even during the light showers.

June 21 Dawn again was glorious and I stood for two hours in the bright sunshine and made a panoramic sketch of Prouville before going in to breakfast and sleep.

Jerry dropped a few shells round us during the afternoon but did no damage. These startling demonstrations at un-expected moments worry us more than regular shelling, and I was quite nervy for the remainder of the day.

At dusk I saw two men wandering about in front of 35 post. Going out with a couple of my fellows I found they were Australians who had been taken prisoner by the Boche. They had escaped the previous night and come through into No Man's Land.

We completed our 'sunken road' just as the CO came along with the subalterns of 'A' and 'C' Companies, to whom he held it up as a perfect piece of work. Our pride knew no bounds as he voiced his praise and satisfaction, and when he had gone we replaced the turfs over the new earth, then retired to the posts to smoke until dawn. At 2.30 a.m. a runner arrived with a note detailing our relief that night.

June 22 I got everything ready during the day for handing

over, so that when the 6th Warwicks turned up, we had the
relief completed in half an hour. It was raining heavily as we
filed back along the track to HQ, with our oilsheets glistening
in the dim light of distant star shells. At HQ we were quickly
joined by the other platoons and soon Anstey climbed out,
swearing at the rain as he slithered about on the greasy steps.

As we started to march I felt terribly tired and was quite
pleased when Anstey told me to bring up the rear as second in
command. We plodded on and on along a bad road that was
new to me until we struck the Route Nationale and halted for
a rest. We had only come three miles but it seemed far more,
probably because we did not know where Anstey was leading
us. I lay on my back and let the cool rain run over my face and
down my back until the stir and rustle of oilsheets warned me
that the front of the column was moving, and I hastened to
shepherd the rear.

A few hundred yards along the cobbles and we swung to
the left down a deeply sunken and frightfully muddy road.
The sides were honeycombed with dugouts, in which we saw
the cheery blaze of candles and fires where fellows were
sitting drinking tea, or lying snugly asleep. A cheer broke
from the troops, which I echoed in my heart, but it died away
as we passed the last shelter and found ourselves out on the
open plain, plodding through the rain and mud and darkness.

Next we passed through a black and ruined village where
we met no one and saw no light. At the far end we halted
again and lay on the roadside for ten minutes. Up and on
again, oilsheets discarded and the rain soaking through our
tunics and shirts, for the heat was unbearable. At last the
column halted. Nothing seemed to happen, so I went on
ahead and found the leading section halted beside a ruined
house. Anstey had vanished and we stood waiting for ages
before a shout came to 'about turn', and retracing our steps
we turned off through a pair of huge iron gates and slogged
along a muddy track in single file.

After a few hundred yards we turned off on to a slippery
path through thick trees and after sliding and crashing down

with clatter of rifles and tin hats and loud cursing, we at last spied the glow of cookers above us among the trees, and were met by Braham who was waiting to guide the troops to their bivvies. Thankfully we followed him inch by inch up a slippery bank to where the cookers stood promising hot pontoon.

June 23 I was the last to climb the greasy bank and had just reached the top when my feet slipped and down I went, rolling over and over until I was messed with sticky mud from head to foot. I cursed loudly and foully as I recovered my tin hat from a pool, and had another shot at the bank. I finished the last part on my knees, and by the time the cooks had directed me to the troops' bivvies, they were already installed and the other officers had gone on with Braham to their quarters.

So savagely I decided to be a martyr, and I stopped to see the troops draw their pontoon. Standing by the cookers like a brown ghoul I watched the troops one after another file into the flickering light of the fire which played on their muddy clothes, the black faces and dirty ducks of the cooks and on the dripping tree trunks. Over all the rain fell with a steady swishing through the leaves.

I waited until all the Company were served, then had a mug of stew, after which I set off through the trees in the direction indicated by the cooks as the officers' lines. The mess was very cheery to the gaze of a tired young man; it was like a large packing case 8 by 12 feet, open at one end, where a long panel of trelliswork was covered with pictures and extravagantly lighted by numerous candles, while a small brazier was drawing steam from the wet clothes of the other officers who sat at a table spread with pontoon, tinned fruit, whisky and Bath olivers.

Pepper was with them, having returned from Amiens during the day. They started to jeer at me for my muddied appearance but I assumed a superior attitude as I told them that I was the only one who had remained to see the troops comfortable. Then I howled 'Mess!' and Martin appeared with a huge plate of stew. As I ate, Martin stood watching me and chaffing me about my 'muddy look'. Being Martin he was allowed to do so, but when he commenced to pick bits of mud out of my hair I had to get cross and send him away. Even then he returned several times to fire off other remarks that occurred to him on his way back to the mess kitchen.

When coffee came in, we pulled our forms along on either side of the fire and sat there for a long time drinking whisky and drying our clothes. We were too tired to talk and at last, as the first glimpses of dawn filtered through the trees, we rose, grasped our equipment and followed Pepper to where our tents stood 20 yards away. Radcliffe, Harding and I crawled into one, and in two minutes were snugly asleep in our valises.

We waked to a hot sunny noon, and throwing open our tent flaps we leaped out in our pyjamas shouting 'good morning' to the world at large. Pepper was sitting stark naked on an oilsheet, having a bath from his canvas bucket. Naturally we flicked him with our towels until he was a mass of blotches; he defending himself by whirling his sponge at us. Then we washed and dressed, more or less, and attacked a lunch-breakfast in the mess. A very merry meal at which much Kia-Ora and whisky was drunk. Anstey went back to 'B' Company now.

Lunch finished, we dressed in the highly polished belts and boots and clean tunics that our batmen had laid out, and set off to visit the Company. How different our surroundings now looked! The bright sun poured onto a charming forest dell, where wild flowers grew in profusion and soft moss invited the sprawling figures of the troops. The boys were all happy and pressed upon us samples from the parcels that had just been distributed by the post corporal. We could not refuse the hard-boiled eggs, cheap cigars and cigarettes that were generously offered, nor had we the heart to take note of the Crown and Anchor boards that some of the old sweats were working among the bushes.

After tea Hammond and I explored our surroundings. We were in the grounds of Vélù Château. Parts of the stables were still standing and over the stalls in small frames were the names of the equine occupants of happier days. The long drive was a welter of grass and mud, where many feet and limbers and horses had passed on their way to the bivouac, and the overgrown lawns and ragged bushes gave such an air of desolation that we were glad to return to our little hollow where all was untouched by war's hand save for an occasional shell-hole.

Dinner was long and cheery, chiefly owing to the high spirits of Radcliffe who did not stop chattering for a minute. Then until midnight we played Slippery Ann, followed by a private contest between myself and Raddy at patience. I won 60 francs.

June 24 Sunday. Up at 8 a.m. and climbed trees for an hour. My energetic nature prompted me to construct a rustic seat, for which I borrowed a very small blunt axe from the cooks. It took me all day to chop down two small trees. We were surprised at lunchtime by the appearance of Ewing who had returned fit for duty. He took over the Company, but Pepper remained as second in command. Hammond was transferred to 'A' Company.

June 25 I was rather discouraged in my woodwork by Ewing, who disapproved of it and frequently told me so—'a foolish waste o' time, and labour in vain!' None the less I had fashioned one tree into a seat and the other into a pair of legs by dinner time.

We were joined at cards this evening by Coleridge, Anstey, Samuel, Bridge and Teague. I had marvellous luck, calling the bank blind time after time and never losing. I had won everybody's cash and had a pocketful of IOUs when we packed up.

June 26 Finished my seat and was exhibiting it with great pride when some fool sat on it, when, of course, it collapsed.

Finally rendered it stable by fixing struts at all angles. Then four of us sat on it, waiting for people to pass and envy us; unfortunately the only person who came was the CO, when we had to stand up!

During the evening Johnny Teague came in and surprised us by wishing us goodbye. He was gazetted to the Indian Army and leaving tomorrow. He was very cut up at leaving us and we were all sorry to lose him. He was a great little chap and very plucky.

June 27 Went over to Frémicourt in GS waggons to play the Gloucesters at cricket. A very pleasant afternoon but were spotted by an aeroplane who directed a few shrapnel shells on to our pitch. They did not affect the match, however, which ended in a severe beating for us. They gave us a splendid tea and kept the CO and one or two more for dinner while the remainder of us went home in the waggon.

June 28 Up the line tomorrow so Hammond and I had a final wander round the grounds through the tangled growth of raspberry canes into the green wilderness of the kitchen garden, where a large reservoir was camouflaged by an enormous canvas painted with circles of primary colours. Into the orchard heavy with green fruit and out onto the road beyond where in a little hollow we came across Coulson, the Town Major, reading an ancient newspaper outside his tin shanty. We returned via the flower garden where masses of flowers were blooming in confusion and overrunning the paths.

Far into the night we sat at the entrance to our mess, gazing into the starlit forest and wondering at life as it had closed upon us. A spell lurked in the ghostly trees, in the gleam of the cookers and in the stillness of the night, broken only by the distant rumble of the guns—a spell which kept us silent and held us from our prosaic blankets until early morning.

June 29 At dusk we marched back to our old sector and I again took over 35 and 36 posts. The night was perfectly quiet, not a single shot or star shell broke the monotony, nor did anybody visit us.

June 30 At dawn I received a message from Ewing telling me to extend my front to the right—across the road—there to form my HQ and man another post. This I did at dusk and found the shelters—long unoccupied—dripping with damp and beginning to fall in. We picked out the best ones: mine was quite large but very wet and full of frogs.

July 1 Sunday. During the morning a couple of 'A' Company runners loitered outside my shelter. I chased them away as soon as I noticed them, but an hour later a salvo of 4.2s crashed about us, two hitting the trench. They continued to fall at intervals throughout the day, and I was very nervy when night fell.

July 2 Light shelling as yesterday, no casualties but much windup. A machine gun from Inchy also dropped a few long-range bursts into the trench. It rained heavily all day so that several more shelters fell in. Dunham and I sat in my dripping cubby-hole and tried to whistle. We were not very successful, so I wrote a cheery letter home and went to sleep. I had a ghastly dream about the tinned rabbit that had come up in the rations. I woke, bathed in perspiration. Seeing that I was awake, Dunham asked me if I was ready for my rabbit, whereupon I swore at him and crawled out into the rain to wander round the trench until dusk.

Glad tidings arrived during the night that we would be relieved tomorrow, and the rumour also spread that we would not be returning to this sector. Consequently as we worked on trench cleaning, etc, we were full of wild conjectures as to our destination.

July 3 Soon after dawn Jerry opened fire again and in a few minutes two of my men were hit—one rather badly. I therefore thought it best to take the fellows out into the shelter of the bank behind us, where we lay for an hour while he plastered our trench. Then the shelling ceased for the remainder of the day. We were all ready to move out at dusk, but we waited for hour after hour before the relief arrived.

July 4 It was 3 a.m. when the 5th Gloucesters turned up and it was daylight before we had got back to Morchies. Here a guide met us and led us down the narrow road towards Beugny. About 200 yards before we struck the main road, we came to some shelters where he told us we were to kip down. We were the first platoon to arrive and as there was only very little accommodation I sent my lads scrounging for timber and corrugated iron to increase the shelters before the others came out.

When the whole Company was assembled it took us another hour to get everyone fixed up, then we started to fix up a mess. I found some oilsheets and tarpaulin on an old shelter half a mile away, and these we rigged up over a large hollow which we cut out of the bank. We did not finish until 10 a.m., when we had a good hot breakfast and turned in.

We slept through the warm midday and woke at 5 p.m., all very cheery except for Ewing who was in a pig of a temper. The troops were busy washing and improving their shelters. After dressing we wandered about the fields playing leap frog and 'catchers'. We sat up late playing cards and talking; the night was delightfully warm and it was very pleasant to lie smoking in our valises with the front of our mess entirely open to the night air.

July 5 Marched this morning down to Lebuquière where we had hot baths. Met Berry there—very tight. Radcliffe and I after lunch scrounged round the fields for a couple of miles looking at old dugouts. On return, I was told by Ewing to take an RE officer up to Morchies to see the reserve positions. He was a very quiet fellow—hardly spoke to me until we reached Morchies when he flatly refused to enter the village because it was being shelled. Even when we skirted it by a couple of hundred yards, he was very windy and kept dropping flat every time a shell burst. So when we struck a company HQ of the 6th Warwicks, I handed him over and returned to our billet.

July 6 Ewing went up to a conference at HQ and returning said we were to move at 3 p.m. Accordingly we marched off and re-entered our previous billets at Vélù Château. We know now definitely that we are going back for a long rest. Slippery Ann in the evening.

July 7 Had a big kit inspection discovering an appalling list of deficiencies. Orders received to move tomorrow.

July 8 Sunday. At 2 p.m. after a final stroll around the grounds, we fell in on the road outside the walls in pouring rain. 'B' Company was very late at the rendezvous, which started us off in a bad temper. We marched straight up to Frémicourt where we turned to the left along the great Route Nationale to Bapaume. It was a horribly dreary march; the shelling had torn up the cobbles and thrown them all over the road, the poplars were splintered and blown down beside their ragged stumps and the rain continued to pour off our glistening oilsheets.

When we reached Bapaume, the rain ceased and the prospect lightened considerably as we turned up the North road to Sapignies. Shortly afterwards we climbed a small hill into the village of Gomiecourt. A quarter of a mile further on we entered a field where tents were already erected. Having seen the troops installed, and feeling a little depressed and soulful, I went for a walk alone, returning to Gomiecourt as dusk fell. I passed through rows of cheerless empty houses and scraggy trees and entered a ruined barn which had once been used as a troops' theatre. Upon the stage was seated a desolate Tommy (the only person I saw in the village). He told me that he belonged to the 2/4th Londons and had returned from hospital expecting to find them here. As this is my brother's battalion I was anxious to help him to find them. I therefore took him up to our HQ, but we could only learn that they had moved out to some destination unknown.

July 9   Played football against 'A' Company. We lost 2–nil but I had the satisfaction of knocking that little beast MacFarlane about. We are moving tomorrow, destination unknown.

July 10   Marched out in high spirits at 10 a.m., the only drawback being the fact that we were carrying a blanket each and the sun was very hot. The troops sang heartily and unceasingly during the first hour as we swung down sunken country lanes and through deserted, battered hamlets. Song after song was started and taken up by the whole Company, Cole and Taylor being the leading choristers.

Towards the end of the second hour the sweat began to pour and the spirits to flag. A few of the old crocks like Bishop and Dredge were limping markedly and rifles began to shift restlessly from shoulder to shoulder. The singing died away completely and at once we began to get busy. Up and down the ranks we went, joking, encouraging and cursing. I could hear Radcliffe's voice singing a forlorn solo in front and Harding was already carrying two rifles. Ewing had sent his horse to the rear of the Company and was trying to pull the leading platoon together. We managed to keep every man in his place until the next halt when we flopped out by the roadside.

We had to enforce rigid discipline to keep the waterbottles corked and several names had been taken before we fell in. We moved off with the crocks weeded out and placed in rear of the Company, and a song was started in the leading platoons. This soon died away, however, and the step broke. Soon we came upon a man from 'B' Company sitting by the roadside, then some of 'A' and more 'B', and then there was a sudden rush from our platoons as men fell out to join them.

We pounced at once upon them and cursed them back into the ranks, but the effect was heartbreaking and our work was doubled. I finished that hour carrying an additional pack and two rifles while the other officers were doing more or less the same. Three packs were slung from Porky's saddle and a limping soldier grasped each stirrup.

When we dropped exhausted into the edge of a cornfield, Ewing came down the column telling the troops that we were almost at our destination. This cheered them somewhat, and when we got on to the road again all eyes were fixed on the horizon where our village was due to appear. Cresting the hill ten minutes later we saw a small village a mile ahead, and a quiver of relief ran down the column; on reaching it, however, we found that it was in ruins and a notice board proclaimed it to be Monchy-au-Bois.

A cyclist met us here and reported to each company commander that the Brigadier was waiting just ahead to see us march past. So we bucked up the troops a bit and swung past him in great style, only to fall to pieces again on emerging from the village on to the open plains. The whole Battalion was now silent, and everywhere could be seen the strained looks, bent shoulders and straggling sections that denote whacked troops. And thus we crawled across the plain for another 20 minutes, when suddenly from No 13 platoon the voice of Private Cole arose in a lovely and very vulgar song: after a few lines, Corporal McKay joined in, then Taylor and Kent and a few more until the whole Company was roaring out the song with their last breaths.

The effect was magical for the whole Battalion pricked up its ears and after a few shudders and syncopations, shook down to a good stride and curled steadily along the winding roads until we reached a charming cluster of trees, through which shone the red roofs of Berles-au-Bois.

A burst of cheering rose from the troops at the sight of the quartermaster sergeants who were waiting for us on the road. And it was repeated when Braham, having fallen in beside Ewing, turned and called out 'Oeufs boys! and bags of Biere!'

All our weariness was forgotten as we passed through the rows of farms and shops with their advertisements of *chocolat menier* until, on the west corner, we installed the troops in the barns and stables attached to a small estaminet.

In a cottage close by, one room was allotted to us in which to sleep and eat. We sent the servants for our mess boxes, dumped our equipment and returned to the troops' billets. But they were already almost empty, the whole Company being inside the estaminet consuming beer. On the road I saw a fellow with 6th Battalion shoulder marks, staggering drunkenly along. As I approached him he fell headlong and I recognized him as Private Richards whom I had last seen, also in a dead faint, on the rifle range at Perham Down. We disposed of him and returned to the mess.

July 11–25 We spent two wonderful weeks in Berles, training or (more accurately) fattening up for our entry into the projected advance at Ypres. The weather was perfect and our days and nights were spent in unalloyed content. The civilians in our house included a very aged couple of whom the old lady sat always in a chair motionless. I never saw her move or heard her speak. We always referred to her as 'Priscilla'. Huddled up in thick shawls, she sat and trembled with vacant eyes bent to the floor. The old man stumped feebly about, always restless but never appearing to do anything. A middle-aged man who may have been their son appeared once or twice during the day but did not live with them. I think it was he who tended the cows and worked the horses in the fields.

The house was run by a pretty wholesome girl named (of course) Marie. She was very quiet and rather sad. She had nothing to do with the troops and rarely spoke to us. Sometimes, when we carried a bucket or worked the pump handle for her, she flashed us a sudden dazzling smile, but she never encouraged conversation.

The courtyard was, as is usual, mainly occupied by an enormous midden whereon strutted a dignified company of fowls, but behind the stables was a charming little orchard where we were wont to lie beside a tiny flower-ridged stream, dreaming away the hot afternoons. Many delightful walks we had too, along the shady lanes or through the thick grass of the plains. We heard no news of the war, nor of our next move, and we did not give a thought to either. In the evenings, when we returned to the mess after a twilight stroll, Radcliffe and I would play patience at a franc a card.

After we had been settled a few days, Thomas, in the absence of his company commander, was told to take his company for a route march. He returned after about 20 minutes leading his horse and complaining that he 'couldn't make it go'. This led to a riding class for junior officers over which Richards presided. We were mounted on draft horses and taken to a field where we were taught the 'parts of a horse' and given a certain amount of riding instruction. It ended abruptly, however, when we were trying to trot with stirrups crossed and folded arms. Thomas's horse decided to make for stables, and headed there at a canter. All the other mounts followed and the whole village was startled by a cavalcade of shaggy horses clattering through the main street with purple-faced young officers clinging to the saddles. We had no more riding instruction.

On the same day, Hammond came in to say goodbye. Consumption had got him down and he was returning to England.

After a couple of days' drill and discipline, we started practising attacks and sectional rushes by companies. We rather liked this training but we so organized it that our rushes took us to the fields of potatoes and root crops. The troops were very careful to assume the prone position and lie completely doggo. The vegetable rations during this period were exceptionally good.

The second week of the rest was devoted to massed attack practices, sometimes by brigades and once the whole division took part and tanks and aeroplanes were engaged. These took us over the old Somme battlefields, and were very approxi-

mate to true conditions. During one show, when I was a
'casualty', I kept Taylor, the black sheep of the platoon, with
me in order to have one more shot at winning his confidence.
He is always in trouble and I had never been able to get onto
the same terms with him as I was with the rest of the platoon.
On this day, however, he seemed to be softened by the
wonderful weather and the life of ease, and suddenly he
became quite responsive and in a burst of confidence told me
of his youth in the charge of a drunken aunt, his several spells
in prison and his feeling now that he was a dog with a bad
name.

Out of all this welter of bitterness and despondency I
grasped one silver thread. He betrayed an almost sacred
respect for womanhood but passed that sex over as though he
were too unclean even to aspire to a girl's affection. But I
played upon that trait, and hinted at the different appearance
he would present in Birmingham if he kept straight and
returned, as he could, with his stripes up. Before we returned
to Berles, he was quite cheery and had even smiled in-
dulgently at some of my poor jokes. From that day on we
were fast friends and he and his pal Dawson were two of my
smartest men.

Ewing and I learnt to understand one another and became
good friends. Our temperaments were very much alike, and
all the time we had been together a slight hostility had been
increased by our nervousness and self consciousness. This,
however, was now cast aside and we lived in perfect harmony.

Radcliffe and I had one childish little quarrel though. We
were discussing the forthcoming sports with two or three
NCOs and someone had suggested an 'over-forty' race.
Jokingly—but foolishly—I said to Raddy 'Oh yes, you'll
want that, won't you?' He snapped 'Are you trying to be
funny, or merely rude?' I was so hurt that I nearly cried in
front of the NCOs. I walked out of the village and for four
hours wandered about the fields. For a long time I sat in the
edge of a wood wondering what our life was going to be like
now that the halcyon days were over. Raddy and I going into

action as enemies, and snarling at each other over every meal. I returned after dark and there was an uncomfortable silence for a few minutes, then Raddy said 'Oi! I've been waiting for you to play patience.' So that was that!

The sports were held a couple of days later and went very well. The colonel gave the prizes which were, of course, hard cash. The result was a terrific blind, and the troops presented a sorry spectacle next morning. I heard unofficially that Corporal McKay had, on returning to his muddy stable from the estaminet, laid out his oilsheet with great care and much cursing, then laid down beside it in the mud.

On the whole there was very little drunkenness. Radcliffe got out of hand one night and insisted on visiting every mess in turn, getting tighter and tighter and, I'm afraid, being musically vulgar.

A drunken young Frenchman called one day—for the rent I think. He was very supercilious and so bullied the terrified old man that one of our servants slung him out. He returned to kick and received a neat lift on the chin that resulted in his departure.

I had an interesting talk with a woman in one house. She was a war widow and had had German officers billeted with her during their occupation. With dramatic gestures she told me how a young fellow on receiving a certain letter from home had shot himself after a night of weeping. She told the story and indeed tinged all her conversation with a sympathy for the Boche. They had always treated her well and it did not matter to her how the war went or how long it lasted.

The only other females I talked to were two darling little girls in a coffee house in Souastre, to which village I walked one day. I intended to go alone, but the hateful MacFarlane joined me on the road, and remembering Pepper's advice, I refrained from being rude to him.

July 26 Ended are our happy, carefree days, and we are on our way to the Salient. For one regretful half hour we lay on the grass of our little orchard, then having liberally tipped the old couple we said farewell to our peaceful village and marched north on to the Arras–Doullens road until we reached Pommera. Here the troops were packed in a large barn while we officers took one tiny room in a cottage.

We were restless and unhappy at the termination of our jolly holiday and the uncertainty of the future. To Radcliffe came the bright idea of visiting Doullens, but I was the only one to respond to it. So he and I hopped on a passing lorry which took us the odd four miles and set us down in the square. We were frightfully disappointed with the town. No shops were open, there were no entertainments and no maidens to while away the time. We had perforce to choose the best hotel—a dull prim establishment—there to dawdle over a champagne supper until dark, when we hopped another lorry back to Pommera.

July 27 I was detailed today to take 13 and 14 platoons to Authieule station as loading party for the Brigade. We marched there at 3 p.m. to the music of a mandolin which one of the troops had scrounged. Here I reported to the Brigade Transport Officer—Edgerton—under whose instructions we commenced at once to load stores and limbers on to the trains standing in the sidings. General Fanshawe arrived after a while and subjected me to an exhaustive catechism regarding the names, numbers, ages, civil occupations and private lives of my men. He was satisfied with my replies and presented me with a slab of chocolate from his never-empty haversack. I got on very well with all the Brigade staff officers except Powell, with whom I had quarrelled on my first night in the trenches.

Edgerton and I spent the night on stretchers in an ambulance but were disturbed continually by runners bringing messages concerning the entraining. A terrific crash brought us out in the small hours—a train had shunted back in the dark and overrun a dead-end.

July 28 The entraining of the troops went off like clockwork and at 6 p.m. Edgerton and I, each with a bottle of champagne, climbed into the last train which carried the final consignment of stores and my two platoons. We talked rather solemnly about the possibilities of the future as we jolted slowly through the gathering dusk. The scenery was rather monotonous and depressing and as soon as we had finished our bubbly we lay down to sleep.

July 29   Sunday. I was in a heavy sleep—probably owing to the champagne, when Crash! Crash! Crash! and something ripped through the roof of the carriage and smashed a window. In the pale light of dawn I saw Edgerton stooping to lace his boots. 'What was that?' I asked, following suit. 'Shells or bombs,' he replied. 'We must be somewhere near Ypres.' The train was at a standstill and as we climbed down on to the deserted siding, a dishevelled RTO hurried along the train. 'Poperinghe' he said in reply to our enquiries. 'There's a guide waiting for you on the road; get away as soon as you like, they have been shelling us all night.' Nothing loath, we hurried our troops on to the cobbled road and marched away before any more shells fell.

We were struck very soon by the different appearance of the landscape here. It was perfectly flat, devoid of trees or hedges and only relieved by compact, tangled hopfields. For a while we passed ruined brick houses, but later we came across little bungalows built entirely of packing cases and beaten out tins. After about an hour's march we came to a tiny village around which were clustered numerous canvas camps. Into one of these our guide led us and we found ourselves being greeted noisily by the other platoons who were dressing in and around their tents.

Braham directed me to a dirty little hut that stood in a belt of trees, and there I found my brother officers in bed. I soon had them out and we washed, shaved and sat down to breakfast in high spirits. The air was again charged with electricity, and we chattered noisily about the rumours that had reached us of the fierce fighting and terrible conditions that lay ahead.

Rubbish! We knew. The line was the line all the way along, and our little family would sing its way through our spell here until we were sent back to the dear old Dricourt Switch.

A company commanders' conference was held during the morning, and during the session Radcliffe and I took our troops down to an improvised range to pot at bottles. Then he and I blew into 'A' Company mess for a drink. While we were there Pepper returned from his conference. Under his arm he had a bundle of papers and he played the fool for a bit—assuming the manner of a commercial traveller—but we could detect the excitement and nervousness that underlay his levity. We finished our drinks as he pinned a map on the wall and returned to our hut. But before we left we heard Pepper say 'and those red squares are concrete pillboxes, reinforced with iron and absolutely shellproof'.

This cheerful explanation caused Raddy to pull a long face at me and we discussed the possibilities of its truth as we walked over to our mess. Ewing was sorting out maps for us, and as we gathered round a large-scale trench map of Pilckem, he said he had no very definite news for us. He only knew that in about a week or ten days, we would be taking part in an attack somewhere along the Steenbeck stream. But he confirmed Pepper's statement that the German defences consisted of enormous concrete blockhouses so situated that the guns mutually enfiladed each other. I felt a terrible sinking inside when I heard this, for it appeared that any attack must be unsuccessful, but when we had discussed it exhaustively we came to the conclusion that the reports must be exaggerated, and we decided not to worry about them.

After lunch, Raddy and I walked to Poperinghe by a short cut across the fields from our camp in St Jans-ter-Biezen. We reached Pop at about 4 p.m. and found it a very busy little town. An incessant stream of motor-lorries, horses, limbers, guns and troops pours through its square, moving up and down the line. Nearly all the houses are empty but one or two shops are still open and do a great trade with the liberal Tommy.

It is well within range of Jerry's guns and the station and square receive frequent reminders of the fact. The old town hall on the corner where the road swings round to Ypres is now the APM's office and bears a huge black notice board which indicates whether the wind is 'SAFE' or 'DANGEROUS' (for gas). The church is damaged by shellfire, but mass is said there on Sundays.

After a preliminary wander round the town we went into a shop near the APM's office called Ypriana. We were surprised to find a large stock of English books and gramophone records, 'Swan' pens and all kinds of English goods, in addition to a splendid range of stationery and souvenirs. Five girls took turns in serving in the shop, the eldest about 25. Two of them were twins and told me that their parents had been killed by a shell some time before.

Along the Ypres road, opposite the station, we found the officers' club—a most inviting and comfortable place with a verandah in front where we lounged in deck chairs and drank whisky whilst watching the chains of vehicles crawling past towards Ypres. The station opposite we eyed askance, for it was very near and the buildings were almost entirely demolished by shellfire, while the much-worn rails were surrounded by shell-holes and debris.

Back in the square I saw a notice 'to the RC Chapel', and dragged Raddy down a little side street to a deserted convent. In the pretty chapel, with blue walls supporting clustered angels, we moralized aloud upon our presence in war-stained khaki on the spot where gentle nuns and children had so often knelt at benediction, their thoughts never straying to the possibility of an upheaval such as had now scattered them to different corners of Europe.

Our next visit was to a café in the square—La Poupée. The two rooms were full of diners but we found a table in the glass-roofed garden. A sweet little sixteen-year-old girl came to serve us. I fell a victim at once to her long red hair and flashing smile. When I asked her her name, she replied 'Gingair' in such a glib way that we both gave a burst of laughter. We had a splendid dinner, with several bottles of bubbly, and Ginger hovered delightfully about us. Over our cigars and liqueurs I offered her my heart, which she gravely accepted. At 10.30 we rose to leave, and at that moment everybody ducked at the whizz of a shell which burst outside. Then another went into the station, and as we walked home we heard them falling all over the town. Still more did we marvel then at the pluck of these young girls who were carrying on in such danger.

July 30   A little drill and PT this morning, not too strenuous, then I devoted myself to crayoning my maps to show the contours of the ground. Raddy followed suit, and the Rajah persuaded me with soft words to do his too. This occupied me until teatime, when I suggested to Raddy another trip to Pop.

When we arrived in the square we found that we were just in time for the commencement of a show by the 'Frolics'—the concert party of the 61st Division, our second line. We attended and I came across a lot of fellows on the 2/8th Warwicks and 2/4th Gloucesters whom I had known in England. After it was over a crowd of us went across to the club and had a jolly good dinner. Raddy got a little the worse for fizz and as we started for home he kept voicing his desire for a 'lark'. I had no idea how he imagined a 'lark' could be carried out in such a godforsaken spot, and I told him so tersely.

When we were a little way from Jan-ter-Biezen some evil genius prompted him to knock at the door of a dark, empty-looking house. The door was opened immediately and he was inside before I could stop him. I followed him and found we were in a kind of secret bar. Seated about were a sergeant, a police corporal, several privates with two or three girls and—horror of horrors—MacFarlane with his arm round a much-painted woman. Radcliffe struck an attitude and called to the stout woman behind the bar: 'Madame! Biere! Biere pour tous! *Bags* of Biere!'

The pots were circulating and Radcliffe was trying to force large rums upon Madame, who firmly refused to take more than the correct charge, when there came a heavy knocking at the door. In an instant the police corporal opened the back door and Madame swept the pots under the counter. We all slipped out into a barn where we remained while Madame was questioned by a party of French and English police. They appeared to be satisfied by her replies and when they had gone I told the other fellows to come away, and we all set off through the darkness. I soon found, however, that Raddy and I were alone. MacFarlane must have slipped back with the others when they were sure the coast was clear.

July 31   There was a heated argument amongst the officers of all companies this morning. One officer of the Battalion was due to proceed to England on leave and Holmes was the one due. Smallwood, however, was sick, and Holmes being temporarily in command of his company, had been told that he could not be spared. He wanted very much to go, and we were divided in our opinions as to whether it was fair of the CO to keep him back. Thatcher was next due for leave but he was on a Lewis gun course; after that we did not know how the roster stood.

Our company was solid for Holmes, and we were sympathizing with him after lunch when Hoskins—the adjutant—came in. He said abruptly, 'Vaughan, do you want to go on leave today?' As abruptly I replied, 'No thanks.' He raised his eyebrows superciliously and asked 'What do you mean by that?' 'Well,' I replied, 'we all think it jolly unfair to keep Holmes back.' Whereupon he strode out saying 'you can tell the CO that'. Shortly afterwards the CO sent for me and patiently explained how impossible it was to let Holmes go. Furthermore he gently implied that my absence would not greatly affect the efficiency of the unit, so that five minutes later I returned to the mess with my ticket of leave.

Having packed my necessaries, I said cheerio to the fellows and set off to Pop. On the way I overtook Samuel who in his capacity of Intelligence Officer was going up to Brigade HQ. We stopped a staff car and got a lift into the square where we spent an hour buying more souvenirs before we separated, I making my way to the officers' club.

Here I learnt that the leave train was due out at 9.30 p.m. and I decided to have dinner there so as to be handy to the station. I got a drink, carried it on to the verandah and had just sat down when there was a whizz and a crash as a high-velocity shell burst in the garden behind. I beat it into the dining room as half a dozen more arrived. The fact that two hit the next house and brought half our ceiling down speeded the departure of most of the drinkers. When all was quiet I went out again with another fellow and resumed my seat on the verandah.

A train at this moment drew up in the station and we smiled to each other as, on the sound of a whistle, a detachment of brand new artillery men tumbled smartly out and ranged themselves 'in fours facing the train', according to the drill-book. They had just received the command 'Right' when a shell landed smack in the middle of them and we turned sick to see a fountain of dust, smoke, bricks, khaki and equipment spurt up from the panic-stricken column. Great confusion followed, men running away from the scene, wounded men struggling into the club or dropping on the road, officers dragging wildly at the reeking contorted bodies and a stream of shells pitching into or around the station.

There were 16 dead and many wounded, all of whom were quickly despatched in ambulances while the remainder of the scared tyros were marched off to their camp. At about 6.30 a notice was posted in the mess room that owing to the shelling, dinner would not be served at the club and that the leave train would start from Peselhoek station instead of from Pop. So I went along to La Poupée and placed myself in the dainty hands of Ginger. It was half an hour's walk to Peselhoek so I set off at 9. Shortly I was overtaken by an SAA cart which took me to the station. A dismal empty train was standing at the platform and I was told by a Tommy of the

RTO's staff that this was a ration train returning to Calais. My leave warrant was made out via Boulogne, but when he told me that my train would not leave till well after midnight I decided to risk the wrath of the red hats, and stowed away for Calais.

August 1 Sleeping soundly until 6 a.m. I woke to find myself on the quay. I proceeded at once to the club where I had a shave and haircut followed by a rattling good breakfast. I learnt that the boat was leaving at 11 a.m., until which time I strolled about the town. Then evading the harassed Embarkation Officer I slipped on board the *Prince George* and so, at noon, to England. A Pullman was waiting on the quay at Dover to rush us up to London. At teatime I burst in upon my astonished relatives who, of course, had no idea that I was on my way home.

August 1–7 Leave.

August 8 There was no occasion to risk the wrath of the Transport Staff on my return, so in accordance with my orders I reported to the EO at Southampton. I was told that owing to the presence of submarines in the channel, we would not sail until tomorrow and I had to spend the night at the hateful, uncomfortable, ill-administered rest camp about a mile out of the town.

August 9 I kicked my heels in the cheerless mess until dusk when I was detailed to march a party down to the docks for embarkation. Our boat was a filthy old tub called *Viper* which, after a very calm night crossing, landed us at Le Havre at dawn.

August 10 After drinks and ices in several of my old places of call, I caught a train at 11 a.m., from which at 5 p.m. I alighted to turn my step to La Poupée once more. Ginger was sweet to me and gravely listened to all my talk of home and

England, in return informing me that life in Pop was becoming more hectic. Shelling was heavier and officers much more badly behaved. Every night there was a small riot when drinks had been flowing, and through it all the guns, the lorries, the ambulances and the troops rolled steadily through the town to Ypres.

When I reached Jans-ter-Biezen, I found the Battalion on the other side of the road, sharing a large field with the Brigade Trench Mortar Battery. I received a cheery welcome and we had a happy little dinner of celebration, to which we invited Sullivan who is now with the TMBs. Later a Boche plane came across and dropped a lot of bombs—fortunately into the other camps. We were untouched but the night was rent with crashes, by the screams of archies and the frantic spluttering of Lewis guns.

August 11 After lunch Samuel came across and asked me if I would take a trip with him up towards the line. A large-scale model of the front had been fashioned somewhere near Pop, and he wanted to find it so that he could take parties of officers to examine it. We went up on push-bikes, but foolishly did not ascertain where Divisional HQ was. We left our bikes in Pop at the APM's office and wandered about the open fields near the ruins of Vlamertinghe until we arrived at Dirty Bucket Corner without having found the HQ or the model.

Returning to Pop, we had dinner at La Poupée where Ginger told us (in strict confidence) that there would be a big advance in less than a week. This, by the way, is the first rumour we have had. It was very dark when we claimed our bikes and started to pedal back to camp. As we left the town, a string of lorries swung round the corner and we dismounted to let them pass. One after another they throbbed slowly past, painted in iron grey, wreathed in dust, buses with sleeping troops on top, all silent, dust-covered rifles projecting and no flicker of light seen—I had a vision of the dead armies of Ypres stealing back to the battlefields to help us in our next push. Sammy too felt the eerie influence, for when the long column had passed, he mounted and we rode home without exchanging a word.

August 12   Sunday. We had sudden orders in the forenoon to move up nearer the line, and after a hurried packing we marched off at 2.30 p.m. Straight up to Pop and out on the Ypres road with my nerves tingling, unable to talk for excitement and drinking in the real atmosphere of war. We were part of the never-ending stream now, welling up into the great reservoir behind Ypres which was swelling and deepening until the dam should be loosed and all the men and guns and shells should pour out on to the enemy lines.

Far above us little swarms of aeroplanes circled among the pretty pink shrapnel puffs, on either side were shattered poplars and barren fields, and meeting us were straggling lines of ambulances and tired troops. After about a mile we turned off to the left towards Dirty Bucket Corner and shortly halted outside a wood wherein our camp lay. It was a nondescript camp consisting of bivouacs, tents, huts and tarpaulin shelters into which we stowed the troops as best we could. For our combined mess and bedroom we had a small hut with a table and a couple of forms. It was a baleful place for the shell-holes and shattered trees bore testimony to the attentions of the German gunners. Amongst the trees was a great concentration of tanks—and the name of the camp was Slaughter Wood!

We regarded each other rather ruefully as we unpacked our valises in the hut, and I thought that Harding looked suddenly much older. Ewing it was who rose to the occasion now and with unceasing Scots chatter he raised our drooping spirits until we became our cheery selves. As we were having tea, a fellow in sergeant major's uniform came in and asked if we could find room for him to sleep. He had just been commissioned and posted to 'C' Company. We had plenty of room so we took him in.

We know now that our attack is fixed for the 16th but that

is all the information we have. We became so dull and serious over dinner that we decided to go to bed at once before we depressed each other further.

August 13   We heard this morning that we are moving up again tomorrow and that on the 16th we will be in support to a battalion of Irish Rifles at St Julien. The imminence of the attack made me very frightened and I trembled so much that I could not take part in the discussion at first. But after poring over the map for a bit and passing on all information to my platoon, I grew calmer. Before noon we had learnt every detail of the ground from the map and, incidentally, had been issued with private's clothing.

After lunch Radcliffe, Harding and I went down to Pop for a farewell dinner. We have heard so much now, that we know what we are in for. We found the trench model quite close to Slaughter Wood and we stopped to examine it. At La Poupée we had a most wonderful dinner with many drinks so that when we started back through the darkness, we were all a little unsteady. When we got back into camp, Radcliffe and Harding were asleep in no time, but the champagne and the excitement of the attack prevented me from lying down even. I felt that my head was bursting, so in pyjamas and slippers I went out again into the wood. A gentle rain was falling and the mud came up over my bare ankles. I had walked about 30 yards from the hut when without warning there was a blinding flash and a shell burst close beside me. Staggering back I hurried to the hut as three more crashed down among the trees. Kneeling on the steps I groped along the floor for my tin hat; at the same moment another salvo fell around us, chunks whizzed past my head and I heard the splintering of wood and a clatter as if the table had gone over.

Then I heard a voice screaming faintly from the bushes. Jamming on my tin hat I ran up the track and stumbled over a body. I stopped to raise the head, but my hand sank into the open skull and I recoiled in horror. The cries continued and I ran on up the track to find that the water cart had been blown

over on to two men. One was crushed and dead, the other
pinned by the waist and legs. Other men ran up and we
heaved the water cart up and had the injured man carried to
the aid post. I took the papers and effects from the dead men
and had the bodies moved into the bushes until morning.
Then soaked with rain and covered in mud I returned to the
hut.

August 14   The others were all astir and excitedly examining the walls and roof which were literally riddled with
shrapnel. Each of us had had a miraculous escape. Over each
bed was a hole through which had passed shrapnel and had
any of the others been sitting up they would have been hit. A
chunk had gone through my valise and would have gone
through me had I been in bed. Three separate chunks must
have missed my head by inches, for the biscuit tin, tobacco
tin, whisky bottles and a Tommy's cooker on the table were
all smashed to bits.

The papers showed that one man was an HQ man, the
other a sergeant from the Trench Mortars. His papers were
chiefly indecent postcards and we had just burnt them when
the padre came in. I handed him the remainder of the effects,
put on some dry pyjamas and went to bed.

From dawn onwards we received a constant stream of
visitors to whom we displayed our shell-splintered hut with
great pride, enjoying considerable notoriety. Then after
lunch we packed up, and taking various little zigzag roads in
an easterly direction for about two miles, we found ourselves at
Dambre Farm near Vlamertinghe. Here we marched into a little field furrowed with deep channels full of water with knolls
and shell-holes everywhere, and a few leaky old tents into
which we crammed the troops who were in a rotten temper—
induced chiefly by the rain.

Bennett now went back to 'C' Company and the remaining
four of us took one tent and settled down to a terrible night of
anticipation. After dawdling over a miserable dinner, we lay
on the ground wrapped in our oilsheets and listened to the

rain beating on the tent and the booming of the guns. We talked a bit and drank a lot until Radcliffe fell into a nasty mood. He said that we were all implying that he had windup; then he told us one at a time and all together that *we* had windup. Finally he cried and said we were all brave boys and none of us had windup. Then he went to sleep.

August 15 I could not sleep, but lay awake thinking and wondering about the attack, fancying myself blown to bits, or lying out on the wire with a terrible wound. It was not until dawn that I dozed off and slept fitfully until 9 a.m.

The whole day we were busy, examining gas-masks, rifles, Lewis guns, field dressings, iron rations, identity discs, etc, and trying to joke with the troops despite the gnawing apprehension that was numbing our minds. Early in the evening I changed into Tommy's uniform and tried to prepare for every contingency—spare laces and string in one pocket, spare pencils in another, scissors in my field dressing pochette, rations and cigarettes in my haversack with my maps, small message maps stuffed into my respirator satchel, and a pocketful of revolver ammunition. I also saw that my rosary was sewn into my tunic with the sovereign that Marie had given me for luck, and that my holy medals were firmly attached with my identity discs to my braces. We handed our money and decent cigarette cases over to CQMS Braham so that if anything happened to us Jerry would not have them. Then we mingled with the troops and talked lightly of tomorrow's excitement.

August 16 At 2 a.m. a guide led us out of the camp in an easterly direction. We moved in column of route, in silence and with no smoking. I was leading with Ewing, but it was pitch dark and as our guide led us, sometimes on a hard road then on to mud then again on a sleeper track, I could not follow our direction. At last we arrived at a canal, with a steep bank on either side and a towing path. We crossed a rough bridge and Ewing gave the order to fall out.

We were at Bridge 2A of the Yser canal, a few hundred yards north of Ypres. The air was poisoned by a terrible stench that turned me sick. In the dim light the water appeared to be a dark-green swamp wherein lay corpses of men and bodies of horses; shafts of waggons and gun wheels protruded from the putrefying mass and after a shuddering glance I hurried along the towing path to clearer air. The bank was honeycombed with dugouts, chiefly occupied by REs. At one point I saw a fingerboard 'To the RC Chaplain'.

Our cookers now rolled up and the cooks carried a hot meal over to our men. For my part I had lost my fear now, and in spite of the imminent attack and the fearful mass below me, I ate a hearty breakfast of sausages and bacon. Then, as the sky grew light, I walked along the path to where Sergeant Major Chalk was standing on the bank, silhouetted against the sky. I climbed up beside him and stood gazing across the darkness of the earth into the dawn. After a few minutes of silence he said 'what is the time, Sir?'

'Four forty-five' I said, and with my words the whole earth burst into flame with one tremendous roar as hundreds of guns hurled the first round of the barrage. An instant's pause, then far in the distance we saw the faint line of fire where the shells were falling. Now the guns began crashing and pounding, keeping the air alive with shells screaming in different keys while the line of fire crackled unbrokenly in the distance. Spellbound I saw a line of coloured lights shoot up from the Boche and then Chalk tugged my sleeve to indicate that our Company was lining up on the towing path.

Scrambling down I slipped on my equipment as I ran forward to fall in beside Ewing. Then in file we moved forward through a gap in the bank on to a trench-board track. My nervousness was gone now; trembling with excitement, but outwardly perfectly reasonable, I drank in every detail of the scene almost with eagerness. To the east we moved along the winding track between batteries of heavies that belched smoke and fire as we passed. The light grew rapidly, and the line of fire changed to a line of smoke. Around us and ahead of us was earth, nothing but earth—no houses or trees or even grass—just faint shapeless humps from which the great guns hurled their iron death.

I was astounded that there was no retaliation; not a shell fell near us until we reached a sleeper track which Ewing told me was Buff's Road. Here we formed up in fours and marched on and on, the troops now singing lustily until I began to distinguish a different kind of crack and looking up I saw the horrible black curls of heavy shrapnel. These shook me a bit, but none came very near, and we approached closer and closer to the barrage that was now hidden from our sight by a slight ridge. The road had now almost disappeared and we were marching over shell-holes around which was scattered debris and wreckage at which I now dared not look. I kept my eyes fixed on the distance until we came to some low buildings—Van Heule Farm.

These were some of the concrete pillboxes of which we had heard. In front of them were six dead Germans and a disembowelled mule. Then I saw Colonel Hanson and Hoskins standing against the wall signalling to Ewing, who ran across to them. When he returned he led us off the road to the right, on to the churned stretch of shell-holes, and gave the signal for artillery formation. I led my platoon off to the right and we continued to move steadily across that muddy waste until I realized that we were walking into a curtain of fire. We were right on top of the German barrage when glancing round I saw Ewing give the signal to halt.

I repeated the signal to my men, and we all dived into shell-holes right on the fringe of the shell-torn zone. With my head just over the edge of my shell-hole I lay blinking into the shrieking, crashing hail of death 30 yards in front. We were too close to fear anything except a direct hit and fascinated I stared at that terrible curtain through which we soon must pass. One gun was firing regularly onto a spot only a few yards in front of me and as I watched the bursts I became aware of Private Bishop in the shell-hole in front with a thick red stream running down his back. I shouted to him, 'Are you hurt, Bishop?' Turning round he said, 'No, Sir' in surprise. So I leaped across the edge of the hole and found that the stream proceeded from a shrapnel wound in a carton of jam in his haversack.

We were laughing about this when a runner tumbled in on us—for now machine gun bullets were sweeping over us— and told me that Ewing wanted me to send a patrol to find Border House which, when located, I was to occupy. I sent Corporal Wood on this job, and having watched him disappear into the barrage, I sat down to await his return. It only seemed a few minutes before he returned, saying he had found it, but one man had been killed.

Dully I hoisted myself out of the mud and gave the signal to advance, which was answered by every man rising and stepping unhesitatingly into the barrage. The effect was so striking that I felt no more that awful dread of the shellfire, but followed them calmly into the crashing, spitting hell until we were surrounded by bursting shells and singing fragments, while above us a stream of bullets added their whining to the general pandemonium. The men were wonderful! And it was astounding that although no one ran or ducked, whilst many were blown over by shells bursting at our very feet no one was touched until we were through the thickest part of the barrage and making for the little ridge in front.

Then I saw fellows drop lifeless while others began to stagger and limp; the fragments were getting us and in front was a belt of wire. At this moment I felt my feet sink and though I struggled to get on, I was dragged down to the waist in sticky clay. The others passed on, not noticing my plight until by yelling and firing my revolver into the air I attracted the attention of Sergeant Gunn, who returned and dragged me out. I caught up the troops who were passing through a gap in the wire, and I was following Corporal Breeze when a shell burst at his feet. As I was blown backwards I saw him thrown into the air to land at my feet, a crumpled heap of torn flesh.

Sick with horror I scrambled over him and stumbled down

into the cutting, which was the Steenbeck Stream. Crouched
in here we found the Irish Rifles, and we lined up with them.
There was a padre who gave me a cheery grin and further
along was a major smoking a pipe as he sat on the bank with
his back to the enemy. I climbed out of the stream and
saluted him, noticing out of the corner of my eye that a tank
was ditched in the cutting. I sat down beside him and told
him who we were, and then from the heap of flesh that had
been Breeze, I saw the stump of an arm raised an inch or two.
Others saw it too and before I needed to tell them, the
stretcher-bearers were on their way to him. Very gently they
brought him in to where I was sitting. He was terribly
mutilated, both his feet had gone and one arm, his legs and
trunk were torn to ribbons and his face was dreadful. But he
was conscious and as I bent over him I saw in his remaining
eye a gleam of mingled recognition and terror. His feeble
hand clutched my equipment, and then the light faded from
his eye. The shells continued to pour but we gave poor
Breezy a burial in a shell-hole and the padre read a hurried
prayer.

The major told me that he was CO of that battalion of Irish
Rifles and that they were not advancing any further. He also
told me to move my men further away so that we should not
be confused. So I took my platoon off to the left and lined the
bank, standing in mud up to the knees. We had now entirely
lost touch with the rest of the Company, so I sent Dunham
back through the barrage to try and find Ewing, to report our
position and ask for instructions. I told him to take another
man with him, but a few minutes later saw him running back
alone with great black shrapnel crashing over his head.

The ground sloped up so sharply in front that I could only
see for about 30 yards. Behind us was nothing but the shell-
swept waste of mud and filth. So I called to Corporal
Benjamin to come and talk to me. He had just made some
reference to poor Breeze, when there was a clang and he
staggered back, his helmet flying off into the stream. A bullet
had gone through it without touching him and his comical

look of amazement and indignation as he retrieved it made me shriek with laughter.

Dunham returned to tell me that 14 platoon was on our left and that we were to stand fast. So I told my fellows to make themselves at home in the mud and crawled myself from hole to hole until I came to Jimmy Harding with the remains of his platoon. We spread out our troops to meet and we sat between them wondering at the attack. We had neither of us seen a live Boche, and we had no idea how far the waves had advanced or what the situation was. Still, what really mattered was that it was well past noon and we were hungry, so we got out our rations and had a meal. The shelling now fell away until it was negligible, and before long Jimmy was cracking jokes for me to laugh at.

At about 3 p.m. we saw two figures walking back behind us, and recognizing Radcliffe we hailed him and ran across. His right wrist had been shattered by a sniper's bullet and he was very upset for it was a rotten sort of blighty for a Doctor of Music to get. With him was Sergeant Bell who had got a bullet in the arm from the same sniper. It was with real regret that we gripped their left hands and said goodbye—we knew for ever. We felt that this was the beginning of the break-up and we rejoined our troops in deep dejection.

Half an hour later Ewing arrived, breathless from dodging the energetic snipers, and told me that I was to take command of the Company as he was going to HQ as adjutant in place of Hoskins, who had been hit. He also told me that Anstey had a very bad wound in the back and was pretty serious. My instructions were to move the Company at dusk straight over to the left, form up behind the Gloucesters and after dark to push forward and deal with any machine guns in front.

Owing to the murk of battle and the misty rain, we were able to move at 6 o'clock, so stumbling and dodging round the shell-holes we followed our guide over half a mile of mud and water in front of what had been St Julien. The snipers were very busy as we crossed, but the light was so bad that the shots sang over our heads and no one was hit.

By the time we had formed up behind the Gloucesters, it was quite dark, so I immediately sent out four small patrols to locate the enemy line. In a very few minutes machine guns opened out and sprayed bullets over our line. The patrols all returned and reported that the ground in front was a morass of mud and water, and before they had gone a hundred yards the Boche had heard them floundering about, and had opened fire. I believed them but to satisfy myself I took a couple of men and went out towards a spot where I had judged a gun to be. In five minutes we were stumbling into deep holes full of water, and the noise we made dragging our bodies through the mud caused flares to shoot up all along his line and the ground was swept by traversing guns. By the light of one flare I thought I saw a low pillbox with figures standing before it, but I was not sure. In any case it was obvious that to attempt a night attack would be madness, so I took my patrol back. On the way we stumbled into a large swamp and waded about in water for some time before striking our positions.

I found the CO waiting for me and I sat down in the mud beside him feeling dead beat and horribly ill. What he was saying I had no idea, for I must have fainted or gone to sleep. After what seemed a long time I heard a voice saying unintelligible things, and I was just able to mutter, 'I'm awfully sorry, Sir, but I haven't the least idea what you're saying.' He shook me violently and said 'Now, Vaughan, pull yourself together.' Whereupon I was alert in a moment and he repeated his instructions. I was to form up my platoons in depth to the right of where we were then sitting. The Gloucesters were going out before dawn and the following night I was to spread out to the left and form a line joining the Ox and Bucks. Then he left me and I sat for a while staring into the darkness, realizing that we were in a hell of a place.

It was a very different attack from what I had imagined we would experience: terror and death coming from far away seemed much more ghastly than a hail of fire from people whom we could see and with whom we could come to grips.

And now we were in an unknown district and must await through the long night the uncertainties of the dawn. We might be in an open position in full view of the enemy; we might have to attack again or be subjected to a counter-attack; or—most terrible of all—we might be on their barrage line, from which we had no chance of escape. I sat for a long time thinking of these things and then realized that I was staring at four still forms that seemed familiar. I called out to Sergeant Swingler, asking who they were. He came over and murmuring 'I think they're ours, Sir,' he gingerly felt in the pocket of one for his pay-book. Whereupon the body leaped up with a curse, arousing the others who were merely taking advantage of my reverie to snatch a rest. So I laughed and called the Company together to lead them to the new position.

Chalk and I went in front, moving slowly towards Winnipeg; in a few moments a salvo of high-velocity shells kept us flattened out in the mud as they crashed amongst us. As we pushed on again we discerned dimly, through the rain and darkness, a derelict tank. 'What about that for an HQ, Sir?' said Chalk. I assented and when I had positioned the troops in front with Jimmy Harding among them, I led my staff of runners, signallers and pigeon carriers back to that spot. As we approached it, however, we were met by a filthy, overpowering stench and found that a shell had burst underneath it and it had burnt out. The charred bodies of the crew were inside or half out of the open door. So I sought the healthier atmosphere of a large crater 30 yards away and gathered my staff in neighbouring shell-holes.

I was very tired but had to stagger out at once to see that the line was unbroken and I had a rotten time dodging shells. Feeling half dead I was on my way back when I heard a voice yelling 'Stretcher-bearers'. It was Sergeant Swingler with a chunk of shrapnel in his shoulder.

August 17 It was dawn when I dropped into my shell-hole where Dunham had shaped a great armchair for me in mud. I stared vacantly at the large mound behind me like a four-foot-high tortoise until I became aware that I was staring into the face of a dead Tommy, upside down. At the same moment I heard voices behind and peering over the edge saw Ewing and Samuel dashing towards me. As it was now quite light I thought that some matter of gravest importance must have brought them across the open—and I was right. The angels had brought me a bottle of whisky! They stayed for a few minutes' rest, then started to go back. They had not gone ten yards before a couple of shots rang out. Then started a series of spurts and dives as they dodged the snipers whose bullets followed them all the way. I had to laugh at the sight of fat Sammy leaping and capering until they were lost to sight in dead ground.

Although I was tired to death, I could not sleep, so removing my tin hat and ruffling my hair I stood up and looked over the front of my hole. There was just a dreary waste of mud and water, no relic of civilization, only shell-holes and faint mounds behind the German lines. And everywhere were bodies, English and German, in all attitudes and stages of decomposition. No sign was anywhere of a living man or a gun. The morning was clear and bright and everything now was deadly quiet. Sinking back into my mud chair I looked into the face of the body behind me. He had a diamond-shaped hole in his forehead through which a little pouch of brains was hanging, and his eyes were hanging down; he was very horrible but I soon got used to him. Then I heard a faint buzz far above and saw five Boche planes heading over our lines; I fell to watching them and saw a great battle when they were met by some of ours. I was quite sorry when, two of the planes having come down in flames, the combat ceased, the planes flying away to leave the world empty again.

The hours dragged slowly by and still I sat staring into the cloudless sky; my pigeon men slept all day and I was too weary to raise my voice to converse with Dunham in his hole some yards away. I had nothing to eat and in a kind of coma I remained motionless, longing for night. At about 3 p.m. I heard the German guns open and dragging myself up I saw a line of bursting shrapnel far away to the left. As salvo after salvo poured over, I got my glasses onto the spot and saw that they were pounding their own line. Soon a line of figures appeared running back out of the shelled zone; immediately our machine guns opened and mowed them down. I felt terribly sorry for them, for they looked very new and untried, and I was so tired and weary myself.

There was no more excitement after that, save for a few shells which fell near, but did not worry me. At last, to my unspeakable relief, night fell, allowing me to stumble forward to the troops. I wandered round talking to them and had just heard a comical complaint from Corporals Wood and Kent that they had been forced to spend their day in company with a much decayed German, when I heard voices back at my HQ. Returning I found Braham, who had brought up the rations. Then the CO came up and I sent off a party to assist Braham.

The CO seemed very strange; he was quiet and sometimes incoherent. He told me he was a bit worried about the line, for he had just met a Boche who had walked through between us and the Irish on our right. The CO had sent his runner back with the prisoner. At this point a shell fell beside us and flung us down into the mud. From then on they pounded around us as we crouched in my hole talking. He told me that he wanted me to pace out the exact distance from my front post to the remains of the second hedge in front of St Julien, and let him know before morning. Then he rose to go, declining to take one of my runners with him. As he crawled out he said, 'We've just had a shell in HQ.' I asked who was hurt, and he replied 'I think everyone has got it except Ewing.'

As he stumbled away, I saw him bowled over three times by shells before he was lost in the darkness, while another one got me. I was very windy about pacing out the required distance, but follwing his example I started off alone. Pacing along the shattered road in the darkness, I felt terribly lonely and horrified lest the heavy shelling should catch me and leave me there to rot—just another body. But I found the hedge and returned safely to reward myself with a long swig of whisky.

Next I thought I had better get into touch with the Ox and Bucks on my left, so once more in great trepidation I set off through the mud towards their HQ, which I knew was at Hillock Farm on the road to Triangle Farm. After stumbling blindly over and into holes full of water, fearing the whole time that I would lose myself, I was delighted to hear a voice challenge me. It was a company HQ of the Gloucester from whom I obtained a guide to Hillock Farm pillbox. As we left, the OC said, 'You'll have to be jolly careful, it's as hot as hell there.'

My guide did not like his job very much and said, 'When we come to the road, Sir, I'll show you the pillbox, and then, if you don't mind, I'll slip back. You see, the entrance faces Jerry and he's got a machine gun trained on it and as soon as he hears you he opens out. You have to be quick to nip across or he's bound to get you. There's lots of tins lying about, Sir,' he added cheerfully, 'so he's bound to hear you.'

When we could dimly distinguish the shape of a building before us, we halted, and I thanked him in a whisper. Allowing him time to get clear I drew a long breath and dashed across the road, leaping over tins and equipment, wire-rolls, bombs and corpses, and in through the narrow opening, to flatten against the wall as a stream of bullets crackled against the concrete.

When the firing had ceased, I passed through the three blanket curtains into the inner room. It was dimly lighted by candles and crowded with officers and signallers; the air was thick with tobacco smoke. The Colonel was deep in conference with two captains and I saluted, then stood leaning against the door. 'Don't stand there, man!' he said. 'You'll be shot to hell.' So I added my dripping form to the congestion opposite him. After he had ignored me for some time, I realized that as I was in private's uniform he had taken me for one of his runners, so I went over and told him who I was and my errand.

He apologized and gave me a drink, adding that he was too busy to talk to me himself but that one of the captains would be leaving in a moment and would tell me all about their dispositions. When we went out together, we stood for a minute in the outer room to grow accustomed to the darkness. We found that it was raining heavily. It was useless to run when going out, as there was no cover. So inch by inch, bending double, avoiding the glistening tins, we trod over the gruesome corpses, prepared to drop flat into the filthy mess at the first shot. We made no noise, however, and were soon hurrying down the road to St Julien. Shells dropped continually upon the road, and from time to time a burst of machine-gun fire would sweep past us.

After about 400 yards we came to a group of low pillboxes, into the last of which the captain led me, saying it was his HQ. It was a small concrete blockhouse and almost completely filled by a huge cylindrical tank. What it was I do not know, but this building was referred to as the Boilerhouse. A light was burning at the far end, and squeezing along the wall we found two officers smoking and staring at each other in gloomy silence. One rose to give the OC a seat, then sidled off along the other side of the tank. The OC had to make out some reports, so he asked the second fellow to mark their positions on my map. We moved along with a second candle to the machine-gun position and had just spread out the map, when the OC said, 'Where's Vaughan?' I turned round, surprised that he should know my name, but the fellow who had first risen replied 'Down the end—windy as blazes.'

The skipper then stood up and addressed someone standing in the shadows. 'Look here, Vaughan, why the hell aren't you out on the line? You are over an hour late.' My namesake muttered something about fixing his equipment and commenced to fumble with it as the captain sat down again. As I drank a spot of their whisky he had a second shot at getting the reluctant subaltern out of the pillbox, and when I left he was giving him a final warning before putting him under arrest.

Standing outside the Boilerhouse I felt that I could almost understand Vaughan's panic. With the rain pouring upon me I gazed round into the darkness and thought that now I must stumble through the mud, where the shells were still falling irregularly, to my wet shell-hole, where the corpse was awaiting me, where bodies were scattered about for me to tread on, where there was no shelter from the rain and cold and shells and stenches—nothing but fear, discomfort and tension. And thinking of these things I could see what an effort it must be to leave a warm, dry, safe pillbox to plunge into the open. I thanked heaven that my HQ was out in the open.

Then I stumbled back to my shell-holes, finding a definite guide on the way in the form of a short length of the light railway that is marked on the map. Dunham was quite alarmed at my absence, for like a fool I had omitted to tell anyone where I was going. I remained in the hole for half an hour, eating the rain-soaked bread and sandbaggy cheese and drinking some cold tea out of a petrol can. Then I lit a cigarette under my oilsheet and had a peg of whisky, after which I set off to find Jimmy Harding.

August 18 Poor old Rajah! He was absolutely whacked. All his spirit had gone and he sat at the bottom of his shell-hole staring dully up at me and hardly speaking. The feeble jokes which I cracked apparently made him feel sick, so I left him and went round the line talking to the troops. But everywhere was the same dullness and depression and my heart sank more and more.

At 2 a.m. I took 14 and 15 platoons out to the left of No 13, spreading them out until we were in touch with the Ox and Bucks. Then once more I returned to my HQ. There were two messages awaiting me, but as the runner had said that they were not important, I put them in my pocket to read at dawn and sat on the top of my shell-hole watching the distant flash of guns and the burst of shells around me. Only once did a Very light go up from Jerry's line and the excitement of it gave me quite a thrill!

At last the sky grew faintly light, and I, who a little while ago had prayed for night, now thanked God for the day. Dunham suddenly became frisky and pranced about on top looking at corpses, the ruined tank and other interesting sights. Suddenly he appeared from behind the mound which overhung our hole, carrying a shell crate. 'I say, Sir, there's lots of these behind here.' But I was too occupied with my thoughts to pay much attention to him, and I just stared into the lightening distance until it became too dangerous, when I slid down into my seat and opened the two messages.

'Our heavy artillery will register this afternoon at 3.20 p.m. on WINNIPEG, 3.30 on SPOT FARM, 3.40 on SPRING-FIELD, 3.50 on VONTIRPITZ FARM, and 4 p.m. on GENOA FARM.'

Well, thought I, that will be something to break the monotony, anyway. And I read the other.

'You will be relieved tonight by "C" Company 1/6th Warwicks. On relief proceed to Bridge 2A.'

'Hooray!' I shouted, which brought an enquiry floating across from Dunham. 'You go to sleep,' I said, for I could not call out the news for fear of Boche listening posts. I felt very cheery then; the sun was bright, the sky clear, and there were no shells falling anywhere along the front. I didn't feel so tired now and thought I would try to pick out the points on which the guns were going to register. So with my glasses I searched the ground in front. I immediately picked out Winnipeg, Springfield and Triangle Farms, but failed to spot the remainder. So I decided to pinpoint my position on the map by taking compass bearings onto the three known points.

I had just got these readings when there was a whizz and a bang as a shell crashed a few yards away. Down I ducked as another and another came. Salvo after salvo burst about us and as I grovelled in the mud one hit the edge of the hole and half buried me, another hit the mound and kindly buried my dead companion—all but his feet. Then there was silence and I was left to wonder why they should have chosen *my* paltry little patch for their unpleasantness. I was not long wondering. I sang out to Dunham and the others to see if anyone was hit, and finding they were all right I marked out my bearings on my map. The three lines met pat on the tiny red triangle which signified 'German ammunition dump'. So that explained the shell crates that Dunham had found and the concentrated strafe.

Thus employed the time passed quite pleasantly and at 11.30 I took a breakfast of cold meat (with sandbag whiskers), bread and cheese and more whisky-tea. I had had no sleep since the 15th but even now I dared not close my eyes. I just stared into the sky, trying not to think; this effort, however, was far too strenuous and I was forced to divert my mind by climbing up again to look around. With my glasses I slowly traversed the landscape, dwelling chiefly upon the ridge in front—the famous Langemarck Ridge. The enemy lines have always a charm for me—mysterious and fascinating—to wonder what life and activity exist there, how they are affected by our actions, whether they are as frightened as we, and as despairing.

Despite my searching, I could discover nothing of interest; the ridge, churned into a broad brown mudheap, showed no sign of life; there were no pillboxes on the slope and the horizon was so ragged that it was impossible to locate the various points. There only remained a few tree stumps and a few broken posts to show where gunpits had been. Then I lowered my glasses and fell to examining the foreground.

The outstanding characteristic of this area was, of course, death. And this seemed to be brought home to me, not so much by the numerous corpses, as by the stranded and battered tanks. The nearest one was that which we had visited when we arrived here, and I shuddered to see it standing gaunt and grim, its base distorted by a shell and a horrid black corpse half-tumbled out of the open door, whilst around it lay the black charred shapes that had been the crew. Close by was another tank which had churned deeper and deeper into the mud until its top was level with the ground; others were ditched with noses or sterns pointing into the air. The majority were stranded where they had broken down or been hit by shells, at all angles on the uneven ground—here a caterpillar belt blown away, there a great gaping hole in the side—all with the appearance of dead, abandoned giants.

Then with gruesome fascination I concentrated on the bodies—tried to read the shoulder plates or recognize the battalion markings. The causes of death were mostly all too obvious, for death at Ypres is a fierce, distorting death—death from a direct hit or from a huge fragment. The mud which drags us down and breaks up our attacks has the one merciful effect of deadening the blasts of shells and localizing their death-dealing power.

Bodies there were in German uniform, mostly old and black, but many English killed in the last attacks with black, clotted blood still upon them. These are the most terrifying—if they can be terrifying now. There were no peaceful postures, except a few amongst the Boche; the remainder had stayed as they had fallen, sprawled headlong into shell-holes, contorted with their struggles, or twisted with explosions. There was one which upset me. He was lying with the top of his head towards me; caught in the remnant of wire entanglement his two fists were raised clutching a strand. The backs of his hands looked white and slim, his hair fluffy and dusty like a miller's. I don't know why I didn't like him, but he seemed somehow much more gruesome than the uglier bodies and I turned suddenly sick and was forced to sink down into my seat.

I felt thoroughly tired now, but when I closed my eyes my mind was filled with a dreadful numbness and sense of loss which I dare not attempt to define. I could only sit and stare into the blue sky, now dotted with aeroplanes and archie-puffs, until my watch had crept round to 3.10, when I climbed up with my notebook to observe the registration of our heavies. Promptly at 3.20 I heard the boom of a gun behind me and then the moan of a shell growing louder and louder until with a gurgle like a giant's bath it crashed down close beside the target. As it burst another was on the way, and there followed a succession of bursts on or near the Winnipeg crossroads. I had watched six or seven shots when there was a crash close to me and iron and mud went flying over my head.

Jerry was at it again and once more I sought the bottom of the hole as he continued to plaster me. He was not so close as he had been in the morning, but he kept me down so long that our registration was finished before I was able to resume my position on top. For a while after the firing had stopped I stood staring into the distance. All was perfectly quiet and still, the aeroplanes had gone and the archies had stopped; I was alone—quite alone in the world. There was no other life. Why couldn't I get up and walk back in the bright sunshine to Berles? To Berles where we had been so happy, or to Péronne? Why was the sun so bright on the torn brown earth? I must just get up and dawdle back to Poperinghe—it was cheerful there; Raddy and I would dine at La Poupée and tease Ginger—and then I collapsed in my mud chair and burst into tears.

I was going out in a few hours, back to the old happy life—but not the same. Raddy had gone and I would never see him again, Hammond was gone and Jimmy I knew was finished. I was a company commander now, but of what company? Not of the one which had lived so merrily in Péronne and Berles, nor the one that two short days ago had marched singing up from the canal bank. It would be a company of saddened men with some of their best NCOs gone and all of their officers except myself. It seemed the ruin and decay of the life in which I had revelled and with my face against the wet mud I lay choking and gurgling, and longed for the hateful sun to go and take away the memories of similar bright days now lost for ever.

My agony was respected, for at 5 o'clock the sky was overcast, and a heavy drizzle turned the landscape back to the sullen drabness that was more congruous. The twilight followed swiftly and by 7 p.m. I could walk about on top. No one else got out and alone I walked round behind the mound and stood looking back through the mist to the ruins of St Julien. Here, although there were no houses left, it was easy to see that there had been a village, for there was a slight mound of ruins with one or two German pillboxes and a number of shattered trees.

When it was dark enough I passed forward from shell-hole to shell-hole arranging for the relief. If the troops were glad to hear the news, they showed no signs of it; everybody wore that mask of tiredness and complete indifference which I knew was drawn across my soul. But I tried to be easy and natural and at last I found a spark of humanity still glowing in the soul of Bobby Wood. He actually sprang up with energy and stood beside me with rifle slung, looking across at Jerry's line. We talked and even laughed a little as we walked over to the left to warn the Ox and Bucks that we were being relieved. As we returned, the German guns opened and sprinkled 4.2s liberally along our line. 'Always the same,' said Bobby. 'Rain and shells just as the relief is due!' 'But it makes it all the better when you get out, doesn't it?' I replied. 'If you *do* get out,' he said gloomily, and we continued to dodge the shells in silence.

It was rather a strain waiting for that relief, for the darkness was intense and the rain and shelling heavy, but at last I heard the welcome sound of splashing and stumbling, the rattling of rifles and equipment and Stook, my runner, led the party up to my HQ. The officer in charge was Spencer who had made himself so objectionable in our dugout at Biaches. He was as windy as a rabbit; he could hardly speak for trembling and as soon as he reached the hole he jumped down and told his sergeant major to carry on. I sent my platoon reliefs forward and told Chalk to lead my HQ staff back to the canal as soon as he was ready. Then I jumped in beside Spencer and told him all the cheerful news. 'No bombs, no ammunition, no wire in front, no trenches to clean and no Germans. Nothing to do but sit here and eat, drink and be merry for tomorrow you may be relieved.' I hadn't the heart to tell the poor devil what he was in for, for already he was jumping, cowering and grunting for every shell burst, though not one was nearer than 50 yards.

When all the troops had dribbled back and the platoon commanders had reported relief complete, I told Jimmy Harding to march the Company back to Bridge 2A. Now all the Company had gone except me and a runner—Hancocks— I felt immensely relieved. I was a Cook's tourist and could go back when I liked. So I stood on the top and said to Spencer, 'Well, what about a trip round the line?' He remained at the bottom of the hole, and replied, 'All right, you push off and I can find my own way round.' I guessed that if he did not come out now he never would, so I determined to see him round before I left and replied 'Oh, but I shouldn't feel justified in reporting relief complete, if I hadn't shown you round. I suppose you want your sergeant major to come round too? Sergeant major! We're just going round the line.' So the little blighter had to come out and we started off, Hancocks with us.

The shelling actually became much warmer as we walked along the line. Once, while we were halted, I noticed that Hancocks was shaking visibly and I was surprised, for he is a very brave lad. However, I led them pitilessly on until we reached the left post where my lads had joined several holes so as to make a rough kind of trench. Although it was already crowded with troops, Spencer and his sergeant major jumped in and crouched down.

Then Jerry suddenly speeded up and shell after shell whizzed through the darkness to burst with blinding flashes around us. I felt terrified but elated, and continued to sit on top making conversation while Hancocks leaned against me shaking. I was getting worried about him and kept giving him prods with my fist. Then suddenly there was an extra loud whizz and a smack as a dud slid into the mud almost under Hancocks. Spencer gave a hollow groan and Hancocks gave a loud shout of laughter, lying back with tears rolling down his face. I gave him a push, for I thought he had got shell shock, but when I realized that he was really tickled, I started to laugh too for the situation was really funny.

The sight of Spencer—bent almost double with his head pressed into the earth, looking at me and answering me upside down, his great bespectacled face white with fear and streaked with mud, his incoherent babblings, his starts and grunts at every shell burst—made us forget the danger. So Hancocks and I sat on the wet mud in the midst of the rain and shells and darkness of Ypres and laughed ourselves into hysterics.

After a while I realized that it *was* hysterics—that it was a temporary madness that had kept me dawdling in the shell-fire, a disinclination to return to the reality of a new life out of the line. That my nerves had been giving way under the strain until I was reduced to the childishness of laughing at another man's fear. But now the valve was opened and much sobered I rose and bade Spencer good luck as I set out for home. Our path took us by the ruined tank, and without consciously willing it, I paused for a fraction of time only on the spot where Chalk had said 'What about that for an HQ, Sir?' It was a sneering gesture to Jerry who had failed in his many attempts to blot us out of that spot. Then at 12.30 a.m. we left the St Julien crossroads and set off down the road up which we had marched on the 16th—how many years ago that seemed!

August 19 Sunday. At Vanhuele Farm we met Samuel who was standing in the rain waiting for the companies to report 'Relief Complete'. I wanted to talk to him but was so dazed that I could find nothing to say, so on we went through the heavy shelling to Admiral's Crossroads, on down the Buffs Road and the trench-board track to the canal bank. The shelling now ceased and along the towing path were a large number of wounded men. I was talking to some of them as I rested, when a voice called out 'Is that you Vaughan?', and there was dear old Ewing waiting to lead me back. I was jolly glad to see him but still unable to talk, and he only made the remark that we were in tents at Reigersburg Château, then we walked on in silence. It was so peaceful here, that when at Salvation Corner a large shell burst in the road, I gave a jump that even Spencer might have envied, and Ewing drew his eyebrows together and ducked his head in the old way I remembered so well.

I couldn't follow our direction very well, but after a while we emerged from a railway track on to a main road which we crossed to find ourselves in a field of tents. From the far end came the glow of the cookers to which I made my way. I returned to Blackie Neale the rifle which I had borrowed for the show and was directed to my tent. Harding was asleep in his valise, and I sat down on the floor and cut my puttees off with a knife. I had shed my sodden clothes and rubbed down with a towel when Martin came in with my supper. He, like all the others, was rather uneasy and made no reference to the attack. I got into pyjamas and ate my stew lying in bed. It was wonderful to have a hot meal and I was grateful for it after my four days of nibbling at filth.

The tent flaps were laced over, the rain had ceased, the guns were silent and Jimmy Harding lay motionless. I ate slowly and dully, staring at my candle. I took my Palgrave from the valise head; it opened at 'Barbara' and I read quite coldly and critically until I came to the lines

> In vain, in vain, in vain,
> You will never come again.
> There droops upon the dreary hills a mournful fringe
>   of rain

then with a great gulp I knocked my candle out and buried my face in my valise. Sleep mercifully claimed me before my thoughts could carry me further and after my four days of strain I slept for eight hours—and at noon I was awake and sitting up with Jimmy eating sausage and bacon with the sun streaming in through the wide opened tent flaps.

'It's all wrong,' said Jimmy whimsically.

'What is?' said I, with a mouthful of toast.

'That coughing Lizzie out there.'

I regarded him questioningly and he assumed his shocked expression. 'Is it possible that you were so debased as to indulge in Aunty's Ruin last night? For my part I didn't sleep a wink all night,' said he blandly. 'Ugh! There she goes again, the spiteful cat!' and I spilt my tea as a terrific roar shook the earth.

'What on earth is it?' I asked.

'Oh, merely a 12-inch gun that has been firing all the morning.' And walking to the tent door I saw the smoking barrel of a naval gun towering over the hedge 30 yards away. I could hardly imagine myself having slept through a number of explosions like that, but Jimmy assured me that I had.

'Incidentally,' he added, 'it's not going to be too healthy for us here when Jerry starts trying to find her.' I agreed. We then dressed and went out into the camp in clean, comfortable clothes with shining belts and buttons. We were in one of many camps of Reigersburg, about 500 yards out of Ypres. Troops were astir everywhere, busily cleaning their clothes and rifles, and as we walked among them we found that they were considerably more cheerful—as we were. We sadly missed Radcliffe and Ewing and as we did not seek the company of other officers we became very lonely. Therefore we retired to bed early and had a long night's rest.

August 20 My next few days were very busy. I had casualty returns to render, deficiencies to replace, reorganization to carry out and—worst of all—letters to write to the relatives of fellows who had been killed. In my leisure time I would go for a stroll with Jimmy or Pepper, or lie smoking to watch Jerry trying to hit the road junction.

August 21 Once Jimmy and I walked up to Ypres, but

were turned back by a military policeman because we had not
got gas-masks with us. We know that another attack is to take
place shortly, but have not learnt any details about it. I have
been warned, however, that I will be in command of 'C'
Company, which is rather a blow for me. Smallwood has
gone for good, Ewing is coming back to 'D' and Mortimore
taking over as adjutant.

August 22   For some reason we had to shift our tents across
into the next field today—probably because we were so close
to the big gun. As it happened our move was most untimely,
for Jerry immediately commenced to shell our new position.
Pepper and the doctor—Carroll—amused me mightily by
feigning abject terror and fighting to stand behind a tiny
sapling about five inches across, whence they leered at the
reeking shell-holes while chunks of iron sang about them.
Pepper is awfully good fun nowadays: he is commanding 'A'
Company and is jester-in-chief to the Battalion.

Scales of 'B' Company went up the line today to reconnoitre for the next attack. He had bad luck, for a shell fell very
close, killing two sergeants who were with him, and pepper-
ing him with small bits of shrapnel. He was not seriously
hurt. Ewing and I are going up tomorrow.

During the night I was awakened by half a dozen tremendous crashes, apparently close to our tent. There were no yells
and I was too tired to get up, but the next morning we found
that the shells had all fallen within a hundred yards of us.

August 23   I got sudden windup this morning, for no
reason whatever; they were not shelling but I was frightened
that they *might,* so I went over to a neighbouring field where
there were a lot of tanks which provided a certain amount of
cover. While I was there I talked to a tank officer who gave
me a ride in one of the brutes. I didn't enjoy it in the least; it
was horribly stuffy and full of fumes. The movement on the
level ground was most unpleasant and I should hate to travel
in one over shell-holes.

Ewing and I started off on our reconnaisance at 2.30 p.m., passing up the railway track, where a big naval gun is now mounted on a truck, to Salvation Corner, thence by Buffs Road to Cheddar Villa. We did not learn much as it was a road that we had already twice traversed, but I suppose the taste of shelling and danger on the way up did us a certain amount of good.

I went to bed at 10 p.m. and at about midnight was awakened by an unusual sound. Far in the distance was the clanging of a gas gong—a warning that was taken up and came nearer and nearer until our own gong was struck. I woke Harding and went out of the tent to find the air faintly charged with a sweet scent of peppery butterscotch. I put on my gas-mask and went round the tents to find the men wearing theirs and playing at being lions and bears. Ewing, who had his tent flaps laced, did not smell the gas, so took no notice of the warning. He was not affected and the gas had dispersed in under half an hour.

August 24   I received details for the attack this afternoon. It is to be a tremendous push. Our battalion is to be the second wave of an attack over our late sector with our right boundary on the cemetery, our left on Springfield. The 7th Warwicks attacks first and captures the enemy front line, from Winnipeg to Triangle Farm, then we go through and capture the top of Langemarck Ridge from Arbre to Genoa Farm. Then the 4th Berks will take the final objective along the line of Von Tirpitz and Hubner farms.

In our attack, 'A', 'B' and 'D' Companies will be the leading wave and I will bring up 'C' Company in support. On the night of the 26th, the whole of the leading battalion will form up in the area which I had been holding, and I have been detailed to take 'C' Company up tomorrow and work each night on improving the shell-holes to receive them. All the work we carry out is to be camouflaged before dawn so that the enemy will not know that preparations are afoot.

August 25 Having dressed in my Tommy's uniform and made personal preparations for the attack, I led 'C' Company out at dusk to bridge 2A which we crossed at 8 p.m. We had a very nerve-racking journey, for Jerry was shelling the track and as the men were carrying shovels and the track was badly battered I had to walk very slowly. Buffs Road was a pandemonium of shelling, with bodies of men and horses everywhere; the misty rain kept the reek of shells and decay hanging about the ground. I had only one officer in the Company—a quiet fellow named Wood. We had several casualties along this stretch.

At Admiral's Crossroads there was nothing but a churned area of shell-holes where limbers and tanks were shattered and abandoned. The battery of 60-pounders which Ewing and I had visited two days earlier had been blown up and now there remained only the yawning holes, with burst guns, twisted ironwork and bodies. It was in sickly terror that I led the Company off to the left towards St Julien.

Through an avenue of shell-bursts we reached the 'village' and striking across the mud to the left came to the concrete blockhouse which was to be our shelter. It was a very long pillbox in which a corridor opened into about eight baby-elephant cubicles. The 5th Warwicks were holding the line, and Major Bloomer and his staff had one of these cubicles; the next one was filled with German flares and Very lights; the next I took for Wood and myself. Into the remainder I crammed three platoons. Then I led the remaining platoon forward across the Steenbeck to the Boilerhouse, where they were to stay until called upon during the advance.

Then I went back and reported myself to Major Bloomer. He was a ripping fellow, so chummy and utterly unruffled that it was difficult to believe that he had been sitting under Ypres conditions for four days. I sent Sergeant Woodright with a couple of other fellows on to the road to intercept the limbers bringing camouflage, and then I went out into the open to look round. This was a foolish move, for as I gazed into the inky darkness, rain pouring off my tin hat, shells crashing on to the road and screaming overhead to the batteries, with the filthy stench of bodies fouling the air, an absolute panic seized me. There was nothing but death and terror, and the fitful flicker of guns and bright flashes of bursting shells filled the night with maddening menace.

I found myself staggering from hole to hole towards the Boilerhouse. As I dragged myself through the mud of the Steenbeck, I saw dimly the figure of a corpse which terrified me. I could just see the outline with a startlingly white chest on to which the rain beat, and a horror seized me of being hit and falling across it. I simply hurled myself away from it, and reached the Boilerhouse in a fever heat. There, in comparative safety, I calmed down. A couple of candles were burning and I smoked a cigarette as I explained to the men the scheme of attack and the digging job we had to carry out. When I left them I was too terrified of the white corpse to go straight back, but chose the shell-swept road. In St Julien I found Sergeant Woodwright and one of his companions, gibbering like monkeys. They had been blown up and shell-shocked. I sent them back to the aid post and returning to the pillbox I despatched another party to await the camouflage.

I had just settled down in my cubicle with Wood when shells began to fall about us; the fourth one hit the wall outside our door with a mighty crash. Our candle went out and chips of concrete flew across the room. Then there came a strange spitting and crackling and the darkness flared into horrid red and green flame. We dashed out into the corridor and followed the escaping troops, for the dump of pyro-technics in the next room had caught fire. For 20 minutes we cowered from the shelling amongst the dead bodies in lee of the pillbox, before we could return to our rooms. Even then the woodwork was blazing and the place was filled with pungent fumes.

Wood, who had appeared to me all along to be very windy, was now absolutely helpless; he could not walk or even talk but lay shuddering on a wire bed. I gave him whacking doses of rum until he went to sleep. Then I went in to Major

Bloomer and taught him how to play patience at a franc a card. We played until 2 a.m., when he paid me 30 francs. I told him to keep it and play it off after the attack, but he replied grimly that it would be better to settle up then. At 2 a.m. I had some food from my small supply.

August 26 Sunday. The limber did not arrive at all, so no preparations were made for the incoming troops; I did not get any sleep. It rained heavily all night and when I went out at dawn I found the shell-holes filled to the brims with water. The ground about the blockhouse was a most ghastly sight. Dozens of English and German bodies were strewn about the entrances and dotted between us and the Boilerhouse. Wire, broken ironwork, timber and equipment were littered all over the mud. Jerry stopped shelling as the dull day broke and I returned to my room to sleep. As I lay down a runner brought me a message to say that the limbers had been hit by shells and that the camouflage would be sent up at dusk.

I slept fairly well throughout the day and at dusk was much more cheerful. The nearness of the attack was rather appalling, but the necessity for a certain amount of intelligence tended to suppress my fear. The 7th Warwicks moved in at 9 p.m. and took over the line, so Bloomer left me in full possession of the pillbox. At 10.30 p.m. our battalion rolled up and was led off to their forming-up position near some old gunpits. There was still no sign of the camouflage, and in any case the heavy rain had turned the ground into a huge swamp upon which it would have been impossible to do any work. There was a terrific congestion of traffic on the road, including tanks, shell-waggons, cookers and limbers. From midnight on our machine guns kept up a constant fire to drown the noise of the tanks crawling up into position.

August 27 In the rations came a gift from General Fanshawe which consisted of a special meat and vegetable meal in a self-heating tin called 'Auto bouillant'. They were remarkably good and the troops blessed Fanny for a hot meal. There were also a lot of cold cooked rabbits in the rations! I said to Dunham jokingly. 'You hang on to my rabbit, I'm going to eat that on Langemarck Ridge.'

Just after midnight I made my way over to the Boilerhouse where Pepper now had his HQ. He was in fairly cheerful mood but ridiculed the idea of attempting the attack. The rain had stopped for the time being, but the ground was utterly impassable being covered with water for 30 yards at a stretch in some parts, and everywhere shell-holes full of water. He showed me the final orders which detailed zero hour for 1.55 p.m.—a midday attack! My instructions were that at zero minus 10 (i.e. 1.45) I was to move my troops forward to the line of the Steenbeck. Then as the barrage opened Wood was to rush forward with three platoons to the gunpits while I reported to Colonel Hanson in the pillbox next to the Boilerhouse.

While we were talking a message arrived from Brigade: 'There is a nice drying wind. The attack will take place. Render any final indents for materials forthwith.'

Pepper read this out to me in a tone which implied 'This is the end of *us!*' Then he scribbled a few words on a message pad and tossed it across saying, 'Shall I send that?' He had indented for '96 pairs Waterwings. Mark III'. I laughed and bade him 'cheerio'. As I went out, I met the CO moving up to his HQ. He stopped for a moment while I explained why I had done no work. Then I said 'It doesn't look very promising for the attack, Sir.' 'No,' he said, seriously, 'but it's too late to put it off now.' Then we parted and I returned to my blockhouse.

Wood was still lying on his bed in a fuddled state with eyes staring out of his head, and as I turned in I thought to myself bitterly, 'What chance have we got of putting up a show tomorrow! My only officer out of action already and me commanding a company in which I don't know a single man and only about two NCOs by sight. Thank God Merrick is a sergeant major I can hang my shirt on!'

At 8 a.m. I woke to find the air quite silent. Not a gun was firing anywhere along the front and bright sunlight was flooding across the mud and water. Dunham had prepared breakfast which I ate with Wood who, although a little brighter, was still singularly lifeless and very nervous. Then at 10 o'clock I went up to HQ to see if there were any new instructions. I took with me an old oilsheet with which to cover that distressing body at Steenbeck. My impression that his chest was white had been erroneous, for he is coal black but had dragged his tunic open to try to staunch his wound, and now a more or less white vest was exposed. I covered him up because I was frightened of his unnerving me when I passed him for the last time at zero hour.

I found the CO and Mortimore sitting in the open on the lee side of their little ruin of a pillbox, and I sat down beside them. They had no further orders to give me, and after we had talked casually about affairs in general for a few minutes, realizing that they would have plenty to occupy their time, I saluted and returned to my HQ. I tried unsuccessfully to get a little life into Wood and then as noon came on I had some more food. As the hands of my watch whirled round I busied myself with totally unnecessary enquiries and admonitions amongst the troops in order to keep my mind free from fear. Then from my wrist in lines of fire flashed 1.45, and feeling icy cold from head to foot I took my troops out and through the ominous silence of the bright midday we advanced in line to the Steenbeck Stream.

My position in the centre of the Company brought me right into my oilsheeted friend; I had grimly appreciated this when an 18-pounder spoke with a hollow, metallic 'Bong'; then came three more deliberate rounds: 'Bong! Bong! Bong!' An instant later, with one mighty crash, every gun spoke, dozens of machine guns burst into action and the barrage was laid. Instantaneously the enemy barrage crashed upon us, and even as I rose, signalling my men to advance, I realized that the Germans must have known of our attack and waited at their guns.

Shells were pouring on to the St Julien–Triangle Road as

we advanced, and through the clouds of smoke and fountains of water I saw ahead the lines of figures struggling forward through the mud. It only took us five minutes to reach the Boilerhouse, but during that time I saw, with a sinking heart, that the lines had wavered, broken, and almost disappeared. Over our heads there poured a ceaseless stream of bullets from 16 machine guns behind, and all around us spat the terrifying crackle of enemy fire.

At the Boilerhouse I sent Wood on to the gunpits with three platoons, while I grouped my HQ staff under shelter of the concrete wall before reporting to the CO. I found him peering round the corner of the pillbox watching the attack and I stood beside him. With a laboured groaning and clanking, four tanks churned past us to the Triangle. I was dazed, and straining my eyes through the murk of the battle I tried to distinguish our fellows, but only here and there was a figure moving. In the foreground I saw some of Wood's men reach the gunpits, but the bullets were cracking past my head, sending chips of concrete flying from the wall; the CO pulled me back under cover and I heard him muttering 'What's happened? What's happened?'

Then, standing on the road in front with drums of ammunition in each hand, I saw Lynch shaking and helpless with fear. I ran out and told him to go forward. 'Oh, I can't, Sir, I can't,' he moaned. 'Don't be a fool,' I said, 'you will be safer in the gunpits than you are here—right in the barrage.' 'Oh, I can't walk,' he cried, and I shook him. 'You know what your duty is,' I told him. 'Are you going to let Rogers and Osborne and the rest go forward while you stay here?'

'No, Sir!' he said, and ran across the road. Before he had gone three yards he fell dead.

Then I returned to the CO and we waited on and on; the shells continued to crash around us, the sky clouded and rain began to fall. Time after time he sent out runners to find out what the position was, but none returned. Two of the tanks were stranded on the road just beyond Hillock Farm, and in front, save for occasional movement near the gunpits, there was no sign of life. The hours crept on; our barrage had lifted from the German line and now was falling on Langemarck Ridge. At last, when sick with the uncertainty and apprehension the CO, Mortimore, Coleridge and I were huddled in the tiny cubicle of HQ, a runner arrived with a report from Taylor that the attack was completely held up: 'casualties very heavy'.

It was then 6.30 p.m. With grey face the CO turned to me saying, 'Go up to the gunpits, Vaughan, and see if you can do anything. Take your instructions from Taylor.' As I saluted, backing out of the low doorway, he added forlornly: 'Good luck.' I called up my HQ staff and told them that we were making for the gunpits, warning them to creep and dodge the whole way. Then I ran across the road and dived into the welter of mud and water, followed by Dunham and—at intervals—by the eight signallers and runners.

Immediately there came the crackle of bullets and mud was spattered about me as I ran, crawled and dived into shell-holes, over bodies, sometimes up to the armpits in water, sometimes crawling on my face along a ridge of slimy mud around some crater. Dunham was close behind me with a sandbag slung over his back. As I neared the gunpits I saw a head rise above a shell-hole, a mouth opened to call something to me, but the tin hat was sent flying and the face fell forward into the mud. Then another head came up and instantly was struck by a bullet. This time the fellow was only grazed and, relieved at receiving a blighty, he jumped out, shaking off a hand that tried to detain him. He ran back a few yards, then I saw him hit in the leg; he fell and started to crawl, but a third bullet got him and he lay still.

I had almost reached the gunpits when I saw Wood looking at me, and actually laughing at my grotesque capers. Exhausted by my efforts, I paused a moment in a shell-hole; in a few seconds I felt myself sinking, and struggle as I might I was sucked down until I was firmly gripped round the waist and still being dragged in. The leg of a corpse was sticking out of the side, and frantically I grabbed it; it wrenched off,

and casting it down I pulled in a couple of rifles and yelled to
the troops in the gunpit to throw me more. Laying them flat I
wriggled over them and dropped, half dead, into the wrecked
gun position.

Here I reported to Taylor and was filled with admiration at
the calm way in which he stood, eyeglass firmly fixed in his
ashen face, while bullets chipped splinters from the beam
beside his head. He told me that the attack had not even
reached the enemy front line, and that it was impossible to
advance across the mud. Then he ordered me to take my
company up the hard road to the Triangle and to attack
Springfield. He gave his instructions in such a matter-of-fact
way that I did not feel alarmed, but commenced forthwith to
collect 'C' Company men from the neighbouring shell-holes.
Of all my HQ staff, only Dunham was left—the others had
been picked off, and were lying with the numerous corpses
that strewed the ground behind us. I sent Dunham all the
way back to the Boilerhouse to lead the platoon from there up
to the stranded tanks.

So many of our men had been killed, and the rest had gone
to ground so well, that Wood and I could only collect a very
few. The noise of the firing made shouting useless. I came
across some of 'C' Company and amongst them MacFarlane
and Sergeant Wilkes. I said to MacFarlane, 'We're going to
try to take Springfield, will you come?'

'No fear!' he replied. 'We've done our job.'

'What about you, Wilkes?'

'No, Sir. I'm staying here.'

Finally Wood and I led 15 men over to the tanks. The fire
was still heavy, but now, in the dusk and heavy rain, the shots
were going wide. As we reached the tanks, however, the
Boche hailed shrapnel upon us and we commenced rapidly to
have casualties. The awful spitting 'coalboxes' terrified the
troops and only by cursing and driving could my wonderful
Sergeant Major Merrick and myself urge them out of the
shelter of the tanks.

Up the road we staggered, shells bursting around us. A

man stopped dead in front of me, and exasperated I cursed him and butted him with my knee. Very gently he said 'I'm blind, Sir,' and turned to show me his eyes and nose torn away by a piece of shell. 'Oh God! I'm sorry, sonny,' I said. 'Keep going on the hard part,' and left him staggering back in his darkness. At the Triangle the shelling was lighter and the rifle fire far above our heads. Around us were numerous dead, and in shell-holes where they had crawled to safety were wounded men. Many others, too weak to move, were lying where they had fallen and they cheered us faintly as we passed: 'Go on boys! Give 'em hell!' Several wounded men of the 8th Worcesters and 7th Warwicks jumped out of their shell-holes and joined us.

A tank had churned its way slowly round behind Spring-field and opened fire; a moment later I looked and nothing remained of it but a crumbled heap of iron; it had been hit by a large shell. It was now almost dark and there was no firing from the enemy; ploughing across the final stretch of mud, I saw grenades bursting around the pillbox and a party of British rushed in from the other side. As we all closed in, the Boche garrison ran out with their hands up; in the confused party I recognized Reynolds of the 7th Battalion, who had been working forward all the afternoon. We sent the 16 prisoners back across the open but they had only gone a hundred yards when a German machine gun mowed them down.

Reynolds and I held a rapid conference and decided that the cemetery and Spot Farm were far too strongly held for us to attack, especially as it was then quite dark; so we formed a line with my party on the left in touch with the Worcesters, who had advanced some 300 yards further than we, and Reynolds formed a flank guard back to the line where our attack had broken. I entered Springfield, which was to be my HQ.

It was a strongly-built pillbox, almost undamaged; the three defence walls were about ten feet thick, each with a machine gun position, while the fourth wall, which faced our new line, had one small doorway—about three feet square. Crawling through this I found the interior in a horrible condition; water in which floated indescribable filth reached our knees; two dead Boche sprawled face downwards and another lay across a wire bed. Everywhere was dirt and rubbish and the stench was nauseating.

On one of the machine gun niches lay an unconscious German officer, wearing two black and white medal ribbons; his left leg was torn away, the bone shattered and only a few shreds of flesh and muscle held it on. A tourniquet had been applied, but had slipped and the blood was pouring out. I commenced at once to readjust this and had just stopped the bleeding when he came round and gazed in bewilderment at my British uniform. He tried to struggle up, but was unable to do so and, reassuring him, I made him comfortable, arranging a pillow out of a Boche pack. He asked me faintly what had happened, and in troops' German I told him 'Drei caput—others Kamerad,' at which he dropped back his head with a pitiful air of resignation. I offered him my waterbottle, but when he smelled the rum he would not touch it, nor would he take whisky from my flask, but when one of my troops gave him water he gulped it greedily.

Then he became restless, twisting and turning so that his leg kept rolling off the platform and dragging from his hip; I took it on to my knees and moved it gently with him until at last he lay quiet. On one of the beds was a German flash lamp and I sent a fellow out to signal to our lines '8th Warwick in Springfield'. Time after time he sent it, but there was no acknowledgement. All was quiet around us now, but the Germans were still shelling the St Julien road. Suddenly I heard a commotion at the doorway and two fellows crawled in dragging a stretcher which they hoisted on to the wire bed in front of me. It was an officer of the 8th Worcester who greeted me cheerily.

'Where are you hit?' I asked.

'In the back near the spine. Could you shift my gas helmet from under me?'

I cut away the satchel and dragged it out; then he asked for a cigarette. Dunham produced one and he put it between his lips; I struck a match and held it across, but the cigarette had fallen on to his chest and he was dead.

I picked up a German automatic from the bed and in examining it, loosed off a shot which hit the concrete near the Boche's head; he gave a great start and turned towards me, smiling faintly when he saw that it was accidental. Then he commenced to struggle to reach his tunic pocket; I felt in it for him and produced three pieces of sugar. Taking them in his trembling hand, he let one fall into the water, gazing regretfully after it; another he handed to me. It was crumbling and saturated with blood so I slipped it into my pocket whilst pretending to eat it. I now produced some bread and meat; he would not have any, but I ate heartily sitting on the wire bed with my feet in the water and my hands covered in mud and blood. Dunham was sitting near me and pointing to the shapeless mass of mud-soaked sandbag I asked, 'What the hell are you carrying in there Dunham?'

'Your rabbit, Sir!' he replied stoutly. 'You said you would eat it on Langemarck Ridge.'

But when he had peeled off the sacking, we decided to consign the filthy contents to the watery grave below.

Now with a shrieking and crashing, shells began to descend upon us from our own guns, while simultaneously German guns began to shell their own lines. In my haversack all this time I had been carrying a treasure which I now produced—a box of 100 Abdulla Egyptians. I had just opened the box when there was a rattle of rifles outside and a voice yelled 'Germans coming over, Sir!' Cigarettes went flying into the water as I hurled myself through the doorway and ran forward into the darkness where my men were firing. I almost ran into a group of Germans and at once shouted 'Ceasefire!' for they were unarmed and were 'doing Kamerad'.

The poor devils were terrified; suspicious of a ruse I stared into the darkness while I motioned them back against the wall with my revolver. They thought I was going to shoot them and one little fellow fell on his knees babbling about his wife and 'Zwei kindern'. Going forward I found that several of the party were dead and another died as I dragged him in. The prisoners clustered round me, bedraggled and heart-broken, telling me of the terrible time they had been having, 'Nichts essen,' 'Nichts trinken,' always shells, shells, shells! They said that all of their company would willingly come over. I could not spare a man to take them back, so I put them into shell-holes with my men who made great fuss of them, sharing their scanty rations with them.

Re-entering the pillbox I found the Boche officer quite talkative. He told me how he had kept his garrison fighting on, and would never have allowed them to surrender. He had seen us advancing and was getting his guns on to us when a shell from the tank behind had come through the doorway, killed two men and blown his leg off. His voice trailed away and he relapsed into a stupor. So I went out again into the open and walked along our line; a few heavies were still pounding about us, but a more terrible sound now reached my ears.

From the darkness on all sides came the groans and wails of wounded men; faint, long, sobbing moans of agony, and despairing shrieks. It was too horribly obvious that dozens of men with serious wounds must have crawled for safety into new shell-holes, and now the water was rising about them and, powerless to move, they were slowly drowning. Horrible visions came to me with those cries—of Woods and Kent, Edge and Taylor, lying maimed out there trusting that their pals would find them, and now dying terribly, alone amongst the dead in the inky darkness. And we could do nothing to help them; Dunham was crying quietly beside me, and all the men were affected by the piteous cries.

How long, I wondered, could this situation last. No message had reached me from HQ and at any moment the Boche might launch a counter-attack to recover Springfield. My pitiful defences would be slaughtered in a few minutes, and behind us, as far as I knew, was no second line, though somewhere in rear was the 4th Berks Battalion in reserve. We had no Very lights and only the ammunition that we carried in our pouches. In desperation I returned to the pillbox and commenced to flash messages back to HQ—knowing all the time that they could not be read through the rain and mist.

Suddenly, at 11.15, there came the squelching sound of many bodies ploughing through the mud behind. Wildly wondering whether the Boche had worked round behind us, I dashed back yelling a challenge; I was answered by Coleridge who had brought up a company of 4th Berks. 'To reinforce us?' I asked.

'No. To relieve you'—and my heart leapt. 'We are going back to Reigersburg.'

He—and the whole of HQ—had not known that we had got Springfield, and he had reached me by spotting my lamp flashing. I told Wood to carry out the relief of the line and march the troops back to Reigersburg Château. Then I handed over to the company commander—a calm, brave fellow who, after sitting under the barrage at the back all day, had now to take over this precarious position for four or five days, with a much depleted company. When we had walked round the line, I picked up Coleridge, and the one runner whom I had told to wait, and started back.

The cries of the wounded had much diminished now, and as we staggered down the road, the reason was only too apparent, for the water was right over the tops of the shell-holes. From survivors there still came faint cries and loud curses. When we reached the line where the attack had broken we were surrounded by the men who earlier had cheered us on. Now they lay groaning and blaspheming, and often we stopped to drag them up on to the ridges of earth. We lied to them all that the stretcher-bearers were coming, and most resigned themselves to a further agony of waiting. Some cursed us for leaving them, and one poor fellow clutched my leg, and screaming 'Leave me, would you? You Bastard!' he dragged me down into the mud. His legs were shattered and when Coleridge pulled his arms apart, he rolled towards his rifle, swearing he would shoot us. We took his rifle away and then continued to drag fellows out as we slowly proceeded towards HQ. Our runner was dead beat and we had to carry him the last part of the way.

I hardly recognized the Boilerhouse, for it had been hit by shell after shell and at its entrance was a long mound of bodies. Crowds of Berks had run there for cover and had been wiped out by shrapnel. I had to climb over them to enter HQ, and as I did so, a hand stretched out and clung to my equipment. Horrified I dragged a living man from amongst the corpses. The shallow passageways and ruined cubicles were filled with wounded, amongst whom the medical staff were at work.

I crawled into the HQ cubicle where Colonel Hanson and Mortimore were sitting; the CO looked years older. My face was a mask of mud and I had to tell them who I was, and that we had got Springfield. As I talked to them, my eyes were fixed above Mortimore's head on a huge block of concrete which at every shell burst moved half an inch inwards. It was only a matter of time before the pillbox would collapse. I asked the CO if there was anything I could do there, but wearily he told me that there was nothing except that I should report the situation to the Brigadier at Cheddar Villa. Mortimore also asked me to have some stretcher bearers sent up from Brigade.

Then I went out and walked with Coleridge down the shell-swept road to St Julien, where, at the crossroads, a regular hail of shells was keeping most of the traffic out of the mud. But we were past caring, and walked through them unscathed. Before we reached Cheddar Villa our runner was killed and we dragged him out into a hole.

Brigade HQ was an elaborate concrete blockhouse with many rooms; I found Beart (the Brigadier Major) and Walker (Intelligence Officer) interrogating a German major. Beart greeted me cheerily and told me to go through to the Brigadier, so raising the blanket of an inner door I entered a small room lit by numerous candles. At a table covered by a clean cloth and bearing the remains of a meal sat Sladden, our Brigadier, and Watts, General commanding 145 Brigade. Sladden peered up at me, asking 'Who's that?' 'Vaughan of the Eighth, Sir,' I replied, and he cordially bade me sit down while he poured me a whisky. He was very bucked to learn that we had come from Springfield and he asked me numerous questions about the intensity and accuracy of the barrage and the present dispositions of the enemy.

When I went out I asked Beart to send up stretcher-bearers, which he promised to do, remarking that he had already sent up eight parties which had all been knocked out. We left the building just as the Boche major was being taken out by two Tommies. He was very sulky because they were hanging on to his arms, and when they jollied him, he made no reply. I called out some remarks to him and he took no notice until one of his escort said ''Ere! that's an orficer be'ind.' Whereupon he halted and, by an authoritative look, made his escort involuntarily release him; then he walked beside me.

August 28 With ironical politeness I apologized in French for the condition of the roads and he replied in all seriousness that we had made a greater mess of theirs. Thinking he might be interested, I told him that Springfield had fallen, and he immediately asked me what had happened to the officer. He was very distressed when I told him for, he said, they had been at school together and also served together in the army. Close to Irish Farm he was taken off to the prisoner of war cage, while we continued on to Reigersburg. Not one word did we speak of the attack, and in the camp we separated in silence. I found that I was alone in my tent, which I entered soaked in mud and blood from head to foot. It was brightly lighted by candles and Martin had laid out my valise and pyjamas. As I dragged off my clothes he entered and filled my canvas bath with hot water.

Doggedly driving all thoughts out of my head I bathed, crawled into bed and ate a large plateful of stew. Then I laid my utterly vacuous head upon the pillow and slept.

At about 9 a.m. I dragged myself wearily out to take a muster parade on which my worst fears were realized. Standing near the cookers were four small groups of bedraggled, unshaven men from whom the quartermaster sergeants were gathering information concerning any of their pals they had seen killed or wounded. It was a terrible list. Poor old Pepper had gone—hit in the back by a chunk of shell; twice buried as he lay dying in a hole, his dead body blown up and lost after Willis had carried it back to Vanheule Farm. Ewing hit by machine gun bullets had lain beside him for a while and taken messages for his girl at home.

Chalk, our little treasure, had been seen to fall riddled with bullets; then he too had been hit by a shell. Sergeant Wheeldon, DCM and bar, MM and bar, was killed and Foster. Also Corporals Harrison, Oldham, Mucklow and the imperturbable McKay. My black sheep—Dawson and Taylor—had died together, and out of our happy little band of 90 men, only 15 remained.

I thanked God that Harding was safe, but he had not been in the show; he had been transferred some days ago to the School of Musketry. The only officers who are left are Berry, Bridge, Coleridge, Samuel and MacFarlane, in addition to the CO and Mortimore.

So this was the end of 'D' Company. Feeling sick and lonely I returned to my tent to write out my casualty report; but instead I sat on the floor and drank whisky after whisky as I gazed into a black and empty future.